Frank

An International Journal of

Contemporary Writing & Art

Number 16/17   *double issue*

Editor/Publisher: David Applefield
Managing Editor: Joe Marshall
Sense of Place Editors: Carol Moldaw and Arthur Sze
Design/Production: Christiane Charlot

•

Frank, founded in 1983 in Boston, is published by **Frank Association** in Paris and distributed internationally. **Frank** attempts to promote diversely creative and original work that demonstrates excellence, innovation, vision, and engagement. The Editors look favorably on work that responds artistically to social, political, and global issues, as well as texts and images that reveal original and passionate perspectives on the world, its cultures, traditions, and languages. Work that conveys a sense of necessity and implores readers to pay attention is what belongs on **Frank**'s pages. Unsolicited manuscripts of previously unpublished and original work of all kinds are welcome accompanied by International Reply Coupons or the equivalent amount of postage in check or money order in US $ or FF.

•

Subscriptions (four issues): $38 US / 225 FF. Institutions: $76 US / 450 FF.
Back issues available at $10 US / 60 FF.
Visit our Web Site: http://www.frankonline.org

•

Frank is distributed by Midpoint Trade (New York, NY), Small Press Distribution (Berkeley, CA), Ubiquity Distribution (Brooklyn, NY), Mosaic Press (Oakville, ON, Canada), Calder Publications (London, UK).

•

Send all other orders, submissions, and queries to:
Frank Association
32, rue Edouard Vaillant   Tel: (33) (1) 48 59 66 58
93100 Montreuil / France   Fax: (33) (1) 48 59 66 68
email: frank@paris-anglo.com

•

Dépot légal: 2è trimestre 1998   ISSN: 0738-8299   ISBN: 2-913053-00-9
Directeur de la publication: David Applefield
Frank, under license from the Editor, is an activity of the French not-for-profit organization **Frank Association** (*Loi de 1 juillet 1901, but non-lucratif*).

•

Frank wishes to thank Yale University Press for permission to publish Ellen Hinsey's "The Art of Measuring Light" and Wildwood House/London, which published an earlier version of Michael Zwerin's "A Case For The Balkanization of Practically Everyone."
The Editor offers a special thanks to Gary Shapiro, the Harvard Club of NYC, and the National Arts Club for their valuable help in promoting this issue of **Frank**. The Editor publicly thanks Julia, Alexandre, Anna, and Ernesto for their patience and support. And to Marit, *takk*.

•

Cover photograph: DA, "Whitewash," Bogota, Colombia.

WILLIAM KLEIN - *Paris May 1968* - *photograph*

contents

&fiction AMERICA

EDMUND WHITE
"Yankee apologist"

photo: SABINE MILLE

B orn in Cincinnati in 1940, shuttled between tiny hotel rooms and a palatial mansion (following the chaotic divorce of his parents), educated at the University of Michigan where he studied Chinese, Edmund White ultimately chose in 1983 the quaint island of Ile Saint Louis in Paris as his home.

Continuing a *va et vient* existence, White enjoys the status of best-selling author in Europe while teaching periodically at Ivy League schools in the United States. Although fabulously accomplished, he tends to occupy the ambiguous position of gay, niche-market writer in America. Despite his achievements, Edmund White is oddly and undeservingly obscure.

He speaks impeccable French, has lived in Rome, is published in numerous languages and seems equally at ease anywhere. He is a calm and self-deprecating man with a clear passion for effacing borders and social mores. Elegant in his manners and soft-spoken, White is nonetheless forceful and provocative when it comes to his principles. He was a participant in the Stonewall uprising in New York City in 1969, a momentous event in the movement for homosexual rights in the United States. One of his editors, David Bergman, aptly called him an "odd combination of innocence and worldliness, prolonged naiveté and enforced sophistication."

Author of a dozen books of diverse genres and disparate styles; novels, a major biography (*Genet*, for which he won the National Book Critics Circle Award in 1993), *The Joys of Gay Sex*, and scores of articles on everything from AIDS (he's HIV positive himself) to the hidden treasures of Paris, Edmund White has won a Guggenheim Fellowship and the American Academy and Institute of Arts and Letters Award. The elegance and movement of his prose and his unique talent for capturing the particularity of the banal, may best be observed in lines like the following from his first novel, *Forgetting Elena*: "Low swells of water heave and sink and travel, like knuckles gliding under a blanket."

For Edmund White, success isn't fitting in — for a long time his writing was pigeon-holed for its primarily gay and erotic content — it's about following an internal voice and creating works with an impetus to reexamine marginal modes of thinking. He writes at his own pace and from within his own personal joy and pain. He brings out books when they are ready and not before, moving onto the next one when the time and place seem right.

An exemplary American in Europe, a cultivated European in America, Edmund White shares his ideas with **Frank** readers on living, writing and publishing across cultural and gender-sensitive borders.

Books by Edmund White include: *Forgetting Elena* (Random House, 1973), *The Joy of Gay Sex* (with Charles Silverstein)(1977), *Nocturnes for the King of Naples* (1978), *States of Desire: Travels in Gay America* (1980), *A Boy's Own Story* (NAL/Dutton, 1982), *Caracole* (Vintage, 1985), *The Beautiful Room is Empty* (Vintage, 1988), *The Darker Proof* (with Adam Mars-Jones)(NAL/Dutton, 1988), *Genet* (Vintage, 1993), *The Burning Library* (Alfred J. Knopf, 1994), *Skinned Alive* (Alfred J. Knopf, 1995), *Our Paris* (with Hubert Sorin)(Alfred J. Knopf, 1995), *The Farewell Symphony* (Alfred J. Knopf, 1997). In France he is published by PLON (*Ecorché vif* and *Edmund White: la bibliothèque qui brûle*).

RALPH PETTY, 1998 - watercolor & ink drawing

Frank: *As an American writer living in Paris, you remarked in an interview with Tony Leuzzi that you "always look at American culture the way a foreigner might." Now teaching in Princeton, New Jersey, can you cite some examples of how contemporary America seems strange or disturbing? What is different about your students' or colleagues' perception of the world and approach to literature?*

EW: In my first two weeks of teaching this term I received in class a story in which a 38-year-old man begins to have sex with an 18-year-old girl, the daughter of his hosts. He breaks off the act and runs into the ocean and commits suicide. I said, "Did I miss something? Did he rape her or what?" "Oh, no," the kids replied, "she was urging him on." "Then why did he kill himself?" "Because," the student author said, "he was guilty of intergenerational sex." Suddenly, I understood why the release of the new filmed version of *Lolita* in the States has proved such a problem.

In my other class we read a story about a 23-year-old man who teaches skiing to a younger woman, a beginner. He's attracted to her because she "walks like a virgin," whatever that means. Just as he's making some real headway with her, some snowboarders come bounding over the hill, land on his back, break his spine and turn him into a quadriplegic for life. No one in the class thought this punishment was excessive. After all, as they said, he was "slime."

"... like knuckles gliding under a blanket"

I found these attitudes nearly incomprehensible. When I asked the guys in the room if they didn't all have such thoughts from time to time (or face it fellows, like constantly), they all chuckled with recognition, but a second later they'd stiffened and their noses had turned another shade bluer. I've always disliked it when the French speak too readily of American "puritanism," since, strictly speaking, the real enemy to American happiness and progress is not Puritanism, with its tragic view of predestination and its progressive social policies, but rather hysterical evangelism, with its red-neck bigotry, its we're-saved-and-you're-damned certainties, but I feel that at least a hypocritical sort of sexual-Puritanism-by-convention is now more thoroughly dominant in American life than ever before, even if it exists side-by-side with erotic TV channels in which totally naked people finger their private parts.

I suppose the two stories point to two other American trends: a horror of mixing lovers from different generations that Toqueville first noticed and that Mrs. Trollope also commented on in *Domestic Manners of the Americans*. The other trend is a strong, Old Testament taste for retribution that co-exists with a readily-admitted but quickly-forgotten sense that we're all "slime," if you really face it. I can't imagine my students approving of Felix Krull or Lafcadio or Benvenuto Cellini or any of the great scoundrels in the history of literature. Nor does comedy, which is nearly always about the difference between morals and manners, exist for them. Their stories aren't funny, since they refuse to look at hypocrisy. And the word "morality," for them, refers only to sexual conduct, never to ethical behavior. Of course, in all this I'm being typically "European," drawing broad conclusions from the slimmest possible evidence.

Frank: *Woody Allen said in the recent documentary* Wild Man Blues *that when he's in New York he wants*

to be in Paris, and when in Paris he longs to be home. Do you feel European in the United States and American in France?

 EW: After living in France for four or five years I noticed that in my thoughts I started to refer to Americans as "them." I felt — as I feel now — that I could predict the reaction of someone French to a given situation far easier than the reaction of a "fellow" American. Perhaps it's just because I've lived almost constantly in France since 1983, and I read *Le Monde*, watch French talk shows on television and hash everything out with my French friends. Or perhaps, as I sometimes think, it's that American culture, especially American "folkways," change more rapidly than they do in France. The breathless transformations in the United States make it seem elusive, incomprehensible.

Since I've been back this time, several things have shocked me. First of all, the brouhaha surrounding President Bill Clinton's sex life. Although people here pay lip-service to the idea that what may be reprehensible about Clinton's behavior is his alleged urging of Monica Lewinsky to commit perjury, it seems obvious that what fascinates everyone is ... his sex life. In France *la loi de l'atteinte de la vie privée* would probably mean that the presidential sex shenanigans would not be discussed at all. My European friends all shrug and think the tempest is definitely taking place in a teapot — who cares about another *petite histoire de cul*? What they seem to criticize most is Clinton's choice of partners, women who seem incapable of "discretion," which is surely one of the greatest virtues in France.

Perhaps a hierarchical country such as France places a higher value than America does on loyalty to the clan. When the question of former French president François Mitterand's "natural" daughter Mazarine came up, people in Paris yawned and said, "But everyone already knew all that." Of course everyone is *le Tout-Paris*, two thousand people. If the French are blasé, unflappable and a bit melancholy, Americans are excitable, even hysterical.

Which goes even deeper to a more fundamental difference. The French seem to have taken seriously Michel Foucault's warning not to make too much of sex. He taught that in this post-Christian age we've retained the idea of the "confession" that leads to the "secret" that contains our "essence," but it's no longer a sin that we can expiate but rather the ineradicable and unvarying truth about our sexual nature, which dictates the rest of our behavior — which is, in fact, our destiny. France, with its universalist ideas of the abstract individual, has always resisted this overemphasis

on sexual behavior or sexual orientation; no wonder feminism and gay liberation have never gotten off the ground in France, or rather were quickly taken up and dropped as disposable and dateable "fashions" in the 1970s. In America, the land of lobbies, special interest groups, identity politics, gender studies, queer studies and third-generation feminism, sexual behavior is still regarded as key.

To be sure, the polls show that the majority of Americans are waiting for more evidence before they pass judgment on their president, and most say they're not even interested in his sex life, but the high ratings of TV shows that deal with the scandal suggest otherwise.

Frank: *Concerning your most recent novel,* The Farewell Symphony, *the latest installment in* The White Pages, *the critical reaction in America seems to be severe? Does the eroticism in this work (and prior work) make it difficult to have a readership outside of certain more liberated pockets of the world? Or do the cultural differences of readers account for the varying critical responses?*

 EW: I understand a bit better now the bumpy reception *The Farewell Symphony* received in the United States. After the book garnered rave reviews in the top six newspapers in England, made several writers' lists of favorite books of the year, and even appeared briefly on the English best-seller list, I suppose I thought the reaction in the United States would be a pushover. In fact, the American reviews were either lukewarm or ferociously hostile. The novel portrays a first-person narrator as he lives through the seventies and survives the AIDS-era of the eighties, although he loses most of his friends and even his French lover to disease. True, the book could not be franker nor more obsessional about gay sex, but it's also about many other things, including a writer's struggle to survive, get published and perfect his art, about a gay man's self-hatred, his inability to keep a lover but his compensatory gift for friendship, and so on. These themes were all properly weighed and registered in England (except by the neo-reactionary Germaine Greer, who loathes homosexuals because they do not "procreate" and because one of them, David Plante, once attacked her in print). In the United States, however, most straight reviewers couldn't even seem to grasp the salient features of the book, as though the heterosexual/homosexual gulf is so great that gay culture and gay history make no sense at all to straights. Many of the gay reviewers, following the lead of the activist-demagogue Larry Kramer, denounced the book for being irres-ponsibly "sex-positive" at a time

when "gay leaders" should be preaching nothing but safe sex.

To me all the fracas seemed very wide of the mark. It ignored that the main action of the book takes place in the 1970s, well before AIDS, and that to ignore the promiscuity of the epoch would have been untruthful. But there is little interest in the truth or in history; Americans prefer polemics and controversy, and the past is only supposed to be a moralistic restaging of current ideals. But, as I started out saying, history changes so quickly in the United States that often just two decades later it is next to impossible to recreate the ideals of that earlier period. For instance, African American gays now consider Robert Mapplethorpe's erotic photos of Black models to be dehumanizing and fetishist, forgetting that in the 1970s Mapplethorpe was a revolutionary appreciated most of all by Black gays themselves. I would have no problem with Black gay critics today denouncing erotic photos of African Americans taken by a white man now, but the ahistorical *ex posteriori* criticism of Mapplethorpe seems just wrong-headed.

Frank: *In attempting to integrate oneself into a second cultural tradition, one's original or native tradition undergoes an unavoidable modification, a reinterpretation that can be distancing. Do "expats"* *always end up living on some created "third continent"? How has straddling two cultures affected you as a writer?*

EW: There's always the danger of *mauvaise foi* about living for long years "abroad." One ends up neither integrated in the new country nor at home in the old. I have always felt like an outsider, perhaps because I came out in the repressive 1950s in the Midwest; living as an expat simply gave me an "objective correlative" for this innate feeling. But perhaps my detachment from both countries allows me to be even more self-centered and less engagé than previously, when I was an American in America.

For a writer, living international-ly promotes double vision. I can see the eccentricities of my compatriots as easily as the foibles of my "host country nationals," as they say in the Peace Corps. When I have had too large a dose of French "elegance" and "discretion," the Texan in me wants to let out a rebel yell. When I've been overexposed to American Oprah-style "avowals" and high-pitched, inhaled-helium voices, I long for *le non-dit* and a purely ceremonial Parisian evening. I once said that, "Fiction is finding which issues obsess you," and I'd say that my "dual nationality" (figurative, not literal) dramatizes the split observable in my writing between

decorum and urgent emotion, between the long-shot of comedy and the close-up of tragedy, between a continental respect for the intellect, tradition and culture and an American esteem for spontaneity, self-invention, originality. If my writing has any virtue it's that it is lively through a constant change of tone, high to low, demotic to hieratic, and my double nationality dramatizes that heterogeneity.

Frank: *How do you explain the philosophical differences in the way European and American governments view the role of art and culture in society? What do you see as the consequences of these opposing postures?*

EW: Just as I accept that the French subsidies for the arts are useful and necessary (especially given that France does not have a tradition of private, individual patrons), nevertheless I also recognize that America has produced more important art in every domain in the last two decades than has France. France has great readers and few gifted writers at this moment; America has brilliant writers (Don DeLillo, Thomas Pynchon, Russell Banks, John Updike, Philip Roth, to name just five) but few competent readers.

There lies all the difference between an old, burnished society that knows how to treasure artistic accomplishment wherever it occurs and a brash, materialistic but highly energetic society that produces geniuses but doesn't know how to care for them or feed them.

Of course at the moment America is a hotbed of creativity in the novel for a few simple reasons. The writers I've mentioned were all nourished by the utopian, communitarian ideals of the 1960s, to which most of them remain faithful. If not, they at least still believe that the novel should be accountable to the society as a whole. America is now the single mega-power in the world, which means that its writers feel peculiarly enfranchised — even obliged to write big, summing up novels that reflect the *Zeitgeist*. At the same time, most Americans, including the writers, feel the country, though powerful, has lost its direction — again a strong reason for novelists to attempt to sum things up, weigh options, test waters.

In France the rupture between the privileged and the disinherited is more glaring than ever. The heartless American model of capitalism has been rejected by a strong French trade movement, but France can't afford to pay the price for maintaining its entire social package (including swelling unemployment benefits). Germany, its major partner, is only slightly better off, but is sinking quickly. Simultaneously, France is aware that

as a generator of high (or pop) culture, it has lost ground to what it calls "the Anglo-Saxon" world. Too many of the leading French writers belong to an elite in which writing at least one novel is perceived as a social, if not an artistic *rite de passage*. Only in periods of social chaos in France can real talent (writers such as Genet, Céline, Sartre) rise to the top; in periods such as our own everyone who is published has some *piston*, unfortunately no guarantee of ability.

To me France seems more humane if less hopeful than the United States, more cultured if less creative. France is also much more open to other civilizations than is the US; just compare the percentage of books in each country that are translations (minuscule in the US, nearly a third of all book production in France). France is certainly more tuned to developments in the Muslim world than is the United States; since the next century will almost certainly be dominated by the Arab countries, France is in a stronger position than America.

I remind myself of Stendhal's unflattering description of Byron's behavior in Italy. Stendhal wrote that Byron wanted all the nobles to treat him as a poet, and all the poets as an aristocrat. In France I'm a Yankee apologist and in the United States, *plus francais que moi tu meurs*.

photo: DAVID APPLEFIELD - *"Ira Cohen and Lips"* . *Paris. 1998.*

Frank Selections: Stories, poems, creative non-fiction, images, documents, recipes, lost histories, winning speeches, old wills and new testaments, erotic epistolaries, hate mail, archives, editorials, revolutionary thoughts, and other collected expressions of frank writing.

The New Presence, The Prague Journal of Central European Affairs

ROBERT MENASSE

The Story Is Short and Eternal

A Project

The child has many names.

Manoel Dias Soeiro — a respectable Portuguese name. Manoel, like the Portuguese king who persecuted the Jews in a particularly cruel way and forced them to be baptized. The most beloved male first name among the country's old Christian families. To officially christen a child of secret Jewish ancestry with this name was an almost too-clear sign of assimilation, and perhaps also an attempt to exorcise danger in the name of danger. At the same time, an old Jewish name was hidden in or behind this pseudonym, the actual name, the one that was really meant: Not Immanuel, from which Manoel was derived, but which immediately achieved its complete emancipation as an independent Christian name, but rather — Samuel, a name from the Old Testament, the last judge of Israel, the visionary and prophet. Spoken so softly, so quickly that someone who happened to overhear it, or even often the child himself, might imagine that he had heard only Moel, a hastily pronounced Manoel.

The child has many names, not only that of the annihilation and the hoped for deliverance. In the caresses of his parents and when playing with other children, they melt into Mané, an ambiguous name, since, in colloquial Portuguese, Mané means something like "little fool," "naive person" — to which child does this not apply? But can a child be naive beneath the double burden of his public and his secret name?

The child has many names. In Mané also echoes the name that this child will receive later, in Amsterdam, in freedom, when the cursed Marranes can discard their pseudonyms and replace them with names that are openly Jewish: Manasseh or Menasse.

Under this name he will finally become famous, as a writer and intellectual, as a rabbi and diplomat.

But however good the public sound of this name was to become as the name of a free and successful man, a name that need mean nothing more than that which its bearer could represent — in his innermost being, Manoel, Samuel and Mané would resound eternally as an echo of a time long past but also as an echo of the reputaion he had achieved. Manoel, the assimilated; Samuel, the visionary; Mané, the naive.

The story is short, the rabbi wrote: We believe we have taken a stick in a relay race and that we can carry it to the goal. In reality we go in a circle, and often go back to take up this stick again, which was already lost. We want things that have been, things that seem to be over, to be meaningless; we want to consider the sound that continues to roar somewhere to be a fading echo. In reality we run screaming to the place where people have screamed.

In a treatise about the various possibilities for examining a man's life, the rabbi introduced an autobiographical passage. Although he later removed it from the main body of the text, it has remained intact. This autobiographical text begins with the words: The child has many names. An event is narrated that must have taken place during the escape from the Iberian peninsula, before the arrival in Amsterdam. The escape was successful, but they had not yet arrived at their destination. There is no mention of where the following event took place. Only this: There was a large, silent lake, and night was falling. The family settled down by the shore. The rabbi wrote that he was still a child at the beginning of this experience, but that he was a man when it was over. A few minutes lay in between, perhaps a quarter of an hour, but in any case a moment of eternity. His father prayed. When his last words faded away, the child thought he could hear an echo. But how could it have been? How could there be an echo here, in front of this plain of water, blank as a mirror? Maybe it existed only in his head, or maybe it was a wonder of nature. The child told his parents about it. He was immediately excited, and was eager to try it himself: Would his words — what words? — or only a scream return, clearly recognizable to the others as an echo?

Manoel

Samuel

Moel

Mané

Manasseh

Menasse

He screamed. Shyly at first, like a croak, then, after taking a few deep breaths, as loud as he could. There was no doubt; the scream returned. The initial joy at having produced an echo gave way to fear, and then panic: Why didn't this echo stop? The scream seemed to resound continually from the horizon and over the lake — why didn't it stop? — the sound remained, continuing on and on, how long had it already been going on and how much longer would it continue? The echo remained and was audible even now — for how long? Minutes? In any case, he felt it had lasted much longer than his first scream.

Had he released a scream into the world that now belonged to the landscape and the lake and no longer to him? He could not bear it any longer, the sound beat in waves against his heart, duller every time, but without fading; the child threw up his arms, pressed the palms of his hands against his ears, but this only made the scream louder and darker. Why did the scream no longer belong to him? Had it ever belonged to him? Where did it come from? Why didn't it stop? From time to time it seemed to be fading, but this was only so that it could rise up again even more powerfully. Now there was nothing more to see. Had night fallen in the meantime or had he closed his eyes from fear? Now there was nothing but endless listening. He would never scream again; no man should ever scream again — if only this echo would stop. He struck his ears with his hands, as though he could knock the echo out of his head, when suddenly he felt a hard pressure at his mouth, a hand that had been pressed against his mouth. It was his father's hand, and he realized that it was not that the echo had not stopped but rather that he had never stopped screaming. He had been screaming the whole time, on and on, convulsively, throwing himself around; for a short time he continued screaming through his father's hand, but then he finally understood and fell silent. The darkness had been beaten back, the black material of his mother's dress, who sat up, her face as white as a distant moon. Now he and his father lay in each other's arms, crying. What had his father heard? His own, unheard screams in the torture chambers of the Inquisition? But it was the son who had produced the eternal echo.

Borders in Europe have been falling constantly.

The rabbi observed that, although his parents had still called him Mané immediately before this event, they never did afterward. From then on he was called Menasse; after all the other names, he finally had the one that he was to keep. But, as the rabbi says at the end of this description, perhaps this is only how it appears in his memory.

Rabbi Menasse ben Israel lived over three hundred fifty years ago. And yet the scream of which he spoke can be heard by everyone who is alive today.

Borders in Europe have been falling constantly. But this has not always made Europe larger, not always. Or, more precisely: the migrations of peoples that followed such events were almost never a sign of greater freedom and mobility. When, for example, the border fell between Spain and Portugal, Europe became incredibly small. At that time it was as large as the city of Amsterdam. The wave of refugees had a fixed idea: this Europe. What they expected there was a more or less liberal system of government. What they brought with them was a singular, deeply European experience. The more brutally people behave, the greater is their need for "propriety," and also, to some extent, for the rule of law. Every cross-examination in the torture chambers of the Inquisition was transcribed, and the victim was given a copy of the transcription. The idea of the state founded on the rule of law, the rabbi wrote in Amsterdam, originated in the dungeons, but was immediately doubled there — as the longing of the victim and the legitimacy of the perpetrator. And if this thought does not seem unfamiliar, this is because it is part of our reflections on the Nazi period.

That is why the history of Europe is so complicated: because everyone who wanted and wants to "determine" what Europe is always *runs back screaming to the place where people have screamed.*

Europe also became smaller in 1938, with the fall of the border between Germany and Austria, and soon it was no larger than England and Switzerland. In the time of Rabbi Menasse ben Israel, Jews were not allowed to live in England. The rabbi traveled to London in order to negotiate with Oliver Cromwell about the re-admission of Jews into England. Abstractly, in terms of legal history, the right of my family to flee to England from the Nazi terror goes back to the diplomatic mission of this rabbi, who had to flee from Portugal to Holland when he was a child. Portugal and Holland or Austria and England and on and on — today Europe is the *one* name in which many names echo and resound.

With regard to the trauma of his family, the Inquisition, the rabbi wrote: *What was once real remains eternally possible.* This sentence appears again in Theodor W. Adorno's reflections on Auschwitz. Not as a quotation; and what is a sentence that is not a quotation but is the same word for word with something that has already been expressed? It is an echo, and eternal echo, and whoever does not hear this echo does not have his senses about him.

It is simultaneously the echo of a single scream for freedom, for the freedom from fear, for self-determination and inalienable rights, and this scream is eternal because it is screamed again and again, eternally.

A.J.

To My Dear Enemy

Adapted from the French by David Applefield

RAYA SORKINE - *drawing*

They have spoken to you of me
as a monster with two heads,
six arms, three legs,
nourished by the blood of children.
So early, you have been taught to hate,
and the single goal of destroying,
to preserve what's yours,
you have gained.
On our common plains,
you have sowed my being,
and, only in finding me dead,
laid out at your feet,
can you discover our resemblance.
Don't ever let this instant arrive;
hesitate no longer;
push open my door and enter.
My house is an open space;
sit yourself down at my table
and together we'll learn.

CAPTAIN JACQUES-YVES COUSTEAU

The Management of Risks

When words have lost their original meaning, when simultaneous political decisions are often contradictory, when information becomes universal but unreliable, citizens lose their bearings, become temporarily intoxicated, AND may wake up to violent protests. The public must be associated as an adult, responsible partner in all difficult decisions, such as the acceptance of certain risks. All human enterprises may fail. Airplanes fall. Gas tanks explode. Nuclear plants themselves have proven not to be safe against mechanical or human failures. It may even be possible that with the sixty kilograms of enriched uranium missing in the official world inventories, unidentified terrorists or an irresponsible national leader may use the ultimate atomic weapon. In the meantime, red and green mud are dumped into the sea; ships founder with their loads of arsenic, nerve gases, or defoliant; black tides multiply. Scientific and technical progress have successfully fought sickness, increased the average life span, improved comfort, and have inevitably generated some risks. But among these risks, we must decide to refuse those that have irreversible consequences and to minimize the others. It is urgent to introduce, in international politics, a new concept: the management of risks. This management of risks necessarily includes the evaluation of the consequences of possible accidents, not only in the short term, but also in the long term and even very long term. Indeed, as long as human beings keep procreating, they implicitly express their desire to see our species survive and develop harmoniously.

When the Harvard Business School opened (1906), it was cheered as a miracle. Since that event, the word "management" has been in vogue. Everything has been reduced to a question of management or of administration. Schools of administration or of management have proliferated. They are mainly involved in short-term management, which accommodates businesses quite well. Each company, each city, each region, each nation continues to grow, with increased efficiency, each in its own interests. Everything is managed, but no one is yet seriously addressing the future. The rising generation, armed with a global consciousness and advanced technology, can and must begin to undertake the management of the future of our species.

Suppose that, beginning tomorrow, the leaders of the entire world, magically converted to *Ecotechnie*, were to take the necessary steps to reduce inequalities, to control consumption and waste, to reduce population progressively, and to develop renewable energy ... we could then reasonably hope to organize the future of our species so that the planet might be astronomically habitable, in other words for about four billion years.

That is the goal we must put forward: to do nothing that might compromise the duration of our species' possible future — four billion years.

Of course it is not just a matter of assuring food, housing and security for an uncontrollably growing humanity, but also to assure the harmonious development of its consciousness as well as its science; of its own culture as much as of agri-, aqua-, sylvi-, bovi-, ovi-, or aviculture; of artistic, literary and musical creation as much as of technical inventions. These difficult problems are being studied, but today the balance sheet is very worrisome.

Living resources are either abusively exploited, as in the sea, or massacred without restraint: already nearly one million species of plants, insects and animals have been exterminated! That is eight percent of all known species. Many have disappeared even before being studied ... before learning how humanity might benefit from them!

Today popular awareness of ecological problems has sometimes exercised a healthy pressure on responsible authorities, and certain animals have thus been saved. The best example is that of elephant seals, and recently whales have won a tentative moratorium. It is, nevertheless, necessary to emphasize that the same does not hold true for small human ethnic groups that have no chance of survival. Those, for example, whom Darwin himself in Tierra del Fuego compared to beasts more than humans. There are no more of them, hunted by settlers with rifles. Elsewhere, the Qawashqars in Chile, reduced to working in mines, have been completely eliminated. And when humanitarian considerations stop massacres, there is still cultural genocide, often perpetrated by school systems, which interrupt the transmission of traditions.

I could go on with the litany of absurdities, more or less criminal, that endanger the integrity of our magnificent planet, and consequently the tomorrows of future generations. But it is essential to unmask the great cause of our troubles: overpopulation.

Within my lifetime — in just 84 years — the world population has more than tripled, going from 1.7 billion in 1910 to 5.6 billion today. Whatever we do now, in the year 2030, the population will reach 10 billion people, and if no Draconian measures are taken, it may reach the absurd figure of 16 billion human beings. Every six months, the equivalent of France (50 million) is added. Every ten years, a new China is born in the poorest regions of Earth. Let us be realistic: it matters little whether population stabilizes at 18, 16, 14, or even 12 billion, these figures are all unacceptable. Even if we manage to feed this human tidal wave, it would be impossible to provide decent living conditions for such a multitude. "Enough to survive on" — that is not what we should bequeath to our children and grandchildren. We must guarantee for them the joy of living and dignity.

FOUR BILLION YEARS"

The tragedy is that technocrats believe that the public is not able to understand problems, that we have to be talked down to like ignorant children, that the technicians are the only ones who know what to do. It is not true. They don't know what they are doing.

An improtant problem is to get rid of the arrogance of technocrats. We want to know the truth when an accident occurs. We want all people to have the right to decide on what risks they will or will not take, to protect the quality of life for future generations. The most serious problems, such as pollution, desertification, depletion of the ozone layer, warming up of the planet, transportation of dangerous materials by sea or by air, or elimination of living species, the threats that menace our planet and our future are all caused by *population explosion*. The fact that this momentous danger is never mentioned by any kind of leaders, is a demonstration of how serious the confusion is.

Today, everybody agrees that Power — political, economic or industrial power — is only justified if it serves the people. And the people, finally emerging from ignorance, but drowned by a flood of incoherent information, are struggling in an ocean of confusion. They need clarification, they need to know the facts, even bad news; they have been lied to so often that they do no trust their leaders, their representatives, nor the media. And the relationship between science and media is at least as confused. These two communities do not speak the same language, and a few specialized interpreters are not sufficiant to reassure the public. The new responsibility of scientists is to help change such a dangerous lack of faith, to dissipate confusion of the minds, to restore confidence in our destiny and individual pride in every human being.

Scientists of the past such as Aristotle, Newton and even Darwin, were much more familiar than their modern counterparts with non-scientific disciplines such as philosophy and ethics. The absence of separation between church and state, or between God and the natural wonders of the world, kept science within the domain of philosophy and ethics, that is to say within the concept of a moral view of the world.

As Western civilization has developed, with its vast acquisition of information, the overwhelming amount of knowledge has caused a compartmentation of information, thus separating science from other disciplines. This is a tragedy because it destroys the necessary connections between the very roots of science and humanism.

Isolated from ethics, morality and humanities, many scientists have become proud of their "objectivity." In what some call their "ivory tower," scientists

"WHO IS RESPONSI

have pursued "truth" but such isolation from reality has created logical absurdities. The *value-free* scientific interpretations can become *valueless*. This separation has enabled some technologies to spring from science which should never have been developed. Actually, the entire military-industrial system is contrary to any world view which values human life and the dignity of the individual.

The production of highly toxic materials and their release into the
environment is another of many logical absurdities. Ignorant politicians and
technocrats, who have no understanding at all of the application of science in
meeting the needs of humanity, have promoted or allowed policies that destroy
the vitality of living systems. In some cases the living systems are humans.
In other cases they are ecosystems which provide a habitable environment
for humans.

How have such policies developed? Who is responsible? As always the
answers are complex, but one thing is sure: scientists have not done a good job
of informing the public or policy makers of what science is, of what it is not,
and of the moral implications of science.

The world can no longer survive without the help and total commitment
of us all. Isolationism is unacceptable. Scientists themselves are absolutely
vital to translate highly technical issues to all those who will elect or choose
decision-makers. The public needs help. Citizens of the world must understand
the consequences of, and the alternatives for, every course of action. But mere
factual knowledge is insufficient by itself. There are moral and ethical issues
which cannot be ignored. There is a growing consensus among scientists that
science alone is flawed. We must find a way to integrate science with the
humanities.

B L E ? ”

a few biographical notes

Letters from Henry Miller

The following unpublished letters come from the archives of the celebrated literary agency Hoffman and Hoffman, who represented Henry Miller in Paris. The letters belong to the Fond Hoffman and are part of the Archive collection of IMEC (Institut Mémoires de L'Édition Contemporaine), Paris.

2/4/56 – from New York City

Dear Dr. Hoffman –

Just got your last about your success with Hachette's claim. Good news! In a few days I shall send you (2) typescripts which would make a short book – title: "Quiet Days in Clichy." The mss. turned up in a strange way, upon the death of a Chicago book-seller. I imagine that Girodias would be the only one to publish them, in English and in French. By the way, is he going to republish <u>Plexus</u> in English? And did you ever get an apology from publisher of "Black Spring" for using H. J. Miller as my name? (Just found another copy in N.Y.) Will also write you shortly about publication of my Paris Journals – 3 Vols. Wrote you months ago about this, but you were then on a trip.

I buried my mother some few days ago. Now I am trying to find the right person to take care of my sister – a very diffi-cult job. So I may be here another two weeks. It has all been a terrible ordeal. Now I know for certain what a Paradise Big Sur is.

Will write again shortly. Address me to Big Sur as usual.

My best to you – and to M⁻ᵉ Delage.

Henry Miller

P.S. I may forward the mss. to you under another name. Contains much that is censorable – but ~~they~~ they are riotously funny, I think. Written perhaps 15 years ago.

Henry Miller--Big Sur, California--Biographical data

Born Dec. 26, 1891, N. Y. City; parents also born in N. Y. ;
   grandparents on both sides born in Germany.
Married four times; present marriage is with Eve Byrd Mc Clure
   of Berkeley, California, since Dec. 1953.
Two children by former marriage: Tony,/tMxxx seven years old,
   Valentine, 10 years old. By first marriage a daughter, Barbara, 36 years old.
Education: through High School and one month at college. Xxxxxdx
   No other training of any kind.
Work: Held many, many jobs until I began to write. First was
   with Atlas Portland Cement Co. N. Y., at age of 17. Last and
   most important job was with Western Union Telegraph Co. N. Y.,
   from 1920 to 1924, as personnel manager. Vowed never to work
   for any one again, but took a job for several months, when in
   Paris, with Chicago-Tribune (newspaper), as proof-reader.
   Writings: After 10 years of struggle my first book to be
   published (wrote three unpublished before) came out in Paris,
   in 1934: Tropic of Cancer. A complete bibliography of my works ,
   including foreign editions, may be found in the Appendix to
   "My Friend Henry Miller" by Alfred Perles, published by Neville
   Spearman, London, 1956 (January).
   Have never belonged to any organization whatsoever.
   Nearest of kin is a sister, Laurettĵa Anna Miller who lives
   in Brooklyn. Am in New York at present, owing to my mother's
   imminent death.
   Will terminate a new book on returning to Big Sur, which
   New Directions, N. Y. will bring out this winter: "Big Sur
   and the Oranges of Hieronymus Bosch", dealing with my eleven
   years at Big Sur. The underlying theme is Paradise, what it
   is, what it means, the problems it raises. Terrestrial Paradise,
   bien entendu. Inspired by Bosch's triptych, The Millenium,
   as interpreted by the German author Wilhelm (?) Franger: "The
   Millenium of Hieronymus Bosch".

   H.M.   3/14/62

28

Dear Dr. Hoffman —   from N. Y. City
                                        3/14/56
    Here are a few biographical notes, for
your files. Sent copy to Guilde du Livre.
There is more data at close of "The Cos-
mological Eye", I think. Written in 1939-40.
    MacGregor is writing you about the
Rowohlt p.b. all OK, I understand. But
don't know what you mean in reference
to "Via Dieppe — Newhaven" piece.
    From a friend in Tokyo who knows Tanaka
I understand Shincho-cha are bringing out
Capricorn this year, in Japanese. Nothing
further on Plexus, Vol. I. (English) from Tanaka,
I suppose? The Italian publisher, Long-
anesi, wrote Plexus would soon be out.
Rowohlt writes that Plexus is a success
there — looks for a 2nd edition before year
is out. Any word from Girodias on
a 2nd edition in English from Paris?
    As you see from enclosed notes, I hope
to finish "Big Sur" book in a very few
weeks on returning. Expect to cut here
and there, add a new chapter, and keep
the length down to 500 — 550 pages, so
as to permit publication in one volume.
    The Signet people will bring the
moré and chapter out — title uncertain
yet — as a pocket book this June!
They expect it to do well.
        Nothing new here — waiting momen-
tarily to hear mother has passed away.
Am in a veritable trap. And my
sister — her future — is almost an
insoluble problem, thus far, at least.
    My astrologer (friend) in Hollywood
promises great things this year —
as regards books and rewards therefrom.
            All the best! Henry Miller

CLAUDE "THE BARMAN" DECOBERT

Hemingway's Gun

Translated from the French by David Applefield

In 1947 when I was 16 I started working at the Ritz turning the revolving door of the hotel. Soon there was an opening and I became a bellboy and then finally I was promoted to the bar where I remained for forty years.

Mr. Hemingway was a regular guest of the hotel between his journeys around Europe and Africa and his hunting and fishing trips. He'd stay for a week or two, sometimes three weeks at a time, and used to come into the bar regularly, mostly to be alone. Although it has been said that he drank heavily, he never drank a lot in the bar and we never saw him drunk. Everyone thinks of him as a big and brash man, but with me he was always friendly, even tender. He'd have a glass of champagne or two, or something like that. He didn't have a favorite drink or a favorite spot in the bar. He'd just come in to be alone.

photo: MARY HEMINGWAY

We talked a lot and he'd tell me about his hunting and travels and when I had a chance I'd often visit his room. We always spoke French; my English was functional but not more. Good evening, sir. What can I serve you? That sort of thing. Mr. Hemingway spoke French well and having spent a lot of time in the streets and cafés of Paris he mastered Parisian French with all the *argot* of the day. His was more a popular French than an elegant or schooled French. But in any case, he spoke well and had a good vocabulary. Once I went up to his room to talk. There he kept twelve rifles for the different types of hunting that he did, different guns with different gages depending on what he was shooting and where. That day he asked me, "Claude, if you could have one of these which one would you pick?" I looked at the long row of guns with a bit of confusion. I didn't have much use for any of them but I reflected and said if I had to pick one I'd take the *canardière*, a long rifle used specially for shooting wild ducks.

He replied, "Good choice, Claude. Next time I'm in Paris I'll take you shooting." This worried me in that I wasn't at all an accomplished marksman. So on my day off I went out to a skeet shooting range at St. Léger le Boissière to practice. Finally, I wasn't too bad.

When Mr. Hemingway checked out of the hotel he first came into the bar.

"Claude, I have a little gift for you."

"*Ah bon*," I replied, noting that he was carrying a brown rifle case.

"This is for you." It was the *canardière*. "But, Claude," he slowed down as to warn me, "there are conditions."

"Oui, Monsieur Hemingway." I listened attentively, excited that Mr. Ernest Hemingway was giving me one of his prize rifles, me, just a boy who worked in the bar at the Ritz.

He looked me straight in the eyes and spoke with great seriousness.

"This is a symbol for your life. This is a symbol of the battles you'll face in life." And he looked down at the gun case. "Because as you grow older you're going to have to fight for your life. All the time." He looked down at the gun. "Claude, never give it away or sell it. You should save it and preserve it as something precious. Each time you have a problem, a worry, anything difficult that needs to be resolved, you'll have to do battle. And this gun will be the symbol of your personal war."

"Petit poisson comestible pour hors D'oeuvre"

I listened carefully. That's why I remember that moment as if it just happened. Those were his words. My eyes glided between the hand that grasped the brown case and his eyes that were fixed on me. He then continued. "You'll go out into the world. You'll have experiences and lots of challenges. And it's certain, you won't always win at everything. You have to be prepared to lose sometimes, but even when you lose what's important is that you've defended yourself. You must always fight back. Never let yourself be beaten without putting up a good fight. It's the fight that matters. Every battle is a test, and the next one you'll know why you lost the last. The next time you won't make the same mistake. And you'll win."

He looked me straight in the eyes. It was a powerful moment. He was completely sincere. I was caught in his gaze. He handed me the *canardière* and turned and I watched him leave. He waved over his shoulder without looking. I slid the gun behind the bar onto the shelf where I kept a little notebook for guests' autographs. I understood exactly what he was saying. It made sense. In life you can't let yourself be taken advantage of. That was his lesson to me when I was 16.

Years later when *The Old Man and the Sea* came out in French I bought a copy of it to have him sign it for me.

photos: DAVID APPLEFIELD

For Marechal de Logis Claude Decobert from his old friend and fellow hunter Ernest Hemingway 12/9/56 Fait à Paris Lu et approuvé. EH

As I read it I realized that that was the book Mr. Hemingway had been writing
at the time he gave me the gun. And I made the connection. Mr. Hemingway
was a man who was always doing battle. He battled against himself, it was
obvious.

A few months later when back in Paris, Mr. Hemingway came into the bar
and said, "Okay let's go have that gun fitted for you." I brought the gun in
the next day and we drove over to the famous gunsmith Chalo — it still exists
today — near the Gare de Lyon to have the *canardière* fitted to my size.
It was a double-barrel Browning 12, made in Belgium, and the cross had to be
shortened; it was too long for my shoulder. And we had to lighten up the
pressure on the trigger. Each hunter has his own touch. Mr. Hemingway's
trigger was rather stiff. To shoot his gun you really had to squeeze hard.

Another time Mr. Hemingway was in Paris he took me to the shooting range
in Issy le Moulineaux, where today there is the Heliport of Paris, to shoot
pigeons. Mr. Hemingway loved shooting pigeons. He used to buy a dozen
birds, and as pigeon shooting was done then, rip their tails off and stuff them
into a small wooden box, which was then balanced mechanically by a wire and
pulley. Then we'd take our positions with our guns and the wire would be
pulled and the box would open. The poor little creatures would flap out in a
flurry, but without their tails they couldn't fly straight; they couldn't keep to one
direction and they would flutter into the sky in a frantic crazy way, and we'd
shoot them. It was supposed to be like that to give the hunter a handicap.
It was good practice. Looking back now, it seems barbaric.
    We ended up going there often, maybe five or six times together.
    I remember once we stopped at the Hotel George V to pick up
Mr. Hemingway's friend, Gary Cooper, and the three of us, Mr. Hemingway,
Gary Cooper, and myself went to shoot more pigeons. But that was only once,
and Mr. Cooper wasn't all that much fun. He kept to himself and didn't say
too much.

When he died in 1961, I wasn't at all suprised. I knew why he ended up the
way he did, by removing himself from life. I remember hearing the news on the
radio while I was driving in Normandy. I wasn't surprised that he'd taken his
life. After his second plane crash in Kenya his arm and his side had been badly
injured and he couldn't write. This destroyed him. He wasn't the same man.
He could no longer fight. He'd come into the bar and we'd talk, but it wasn't
the same. The last two years of his life there was no more fight. And when the
fight was over there was no more life. I remember the last time he came in

to say goodbye. There was nothing at all left. He said he had no more creative ideas in him. I understood by looking at him. I knew his time was over. I knew that he was very sick. He had became a common man and he didn't want to be a common man.

Today, Mr. Hemingway's gun sits quietly on a top shelf in my house in a little town about an hour east of Paris. I rarely take it down. But I think about it. And I'll never give it up.

JOHN CALDER

The Three-Headed Hydra

*from **The Garden of Eros**, a tour of post World War II literary Paris and contemproary culture*

Janet Flanner, the American journalist who for many years, from the thirties onward, covered literary and expatriate Paris for American magazines, wrote in her introduction to one of the most important literary histories of the pre-war period:

> In the evolution of literature the book publisher had undeniably been the second main essential. Yet individually he had been rarely famed as the necessary major element connected with the appearance of a new great book nor even much thanked by his readers. He has been literature's common carrier, like a donkey, with the authors and occasionally their weight of genius loaded on his back. (Hugh Ford, *Published in Paris*, 1975).

She was thinking of Sylvia Beach and of those other literary publishers whose names have been linked with a writer or a few writers to whom they gave attention and devotion well beyond the usual professional relationship, based on a mutual interest in making money from books. In thinking of the Hydra, the many-headed monster, whose heads were chopped off by Hercules only to have them grow back again, I see an analogy of that literature which rises time and again through, and in spite of, opposition, disapproval, censorship, fundamentalist ideology and the incomprehension of the plain reader (the last sentence of the "Proclamation" issued by the writers associated with *transition*, the most important of the English-language pre-war Parisian magazines, ended: "the plain reader be damned.").

It is the writing, damned or at first dismissed, that usually emerges as the significant literature of its time, and like the Hydra can be defined as "a thing hard to extirpate." Such literature may be cut back at first, but it will be kept alive by its devotees, often by other writers and friends, as happened with the Joyces and Kafkas of their day, until the academics and the pundits are able to declare the writer a genius and his works as classics. Personally I see the Hydra as having three heads, the writer, the publisher and the bookseller. But others can be imagined, such as the literary agent, the librarian, the teacher, the proselytizing admirer. But only a few of the potential geniuses ever emerge into the light of day. I have seen enough real talent in manuscript to know that there are probably as many genuinely original unpublished writers as there were flowers blooming unseen in Gray's country churchyard, but there are never enough publishers willing or able to lose money on them; only a few are lucky. It is the publisher who takes the prime risk on a new author and often he does not stay in business very long, but credit must also go to the genuine booksellers of taste (Sylvia Beach was both) who read a writer, recommend and sell him, sometimes having to face prosecution for the privilege of doing so.

The role of the bookseller as a purveyor of culture is often underestimated in literary history. Long before public libraries of any kind existed, booksellers not only sold books but produced them, often by subscription from their customers. For the two centuries before the twentieth, and more recently on a more specialized level — because so many books are published, and very few could be called in any way literary — the role of the bookseller in recognizing unusual talent, in helping it, either through publication or more commonly in stocking and promoting an author where others would not, has been crucial. A town with a good bookseller will often produce young people with intellectual curiosity and interests, whose minds he helps, often unwittingly, to develop and

only the exceptional school-teacher is as important in this respect as the
exceptional bookseller: if he is dedicated to his trade he becomes a centre of
culture, and lucky is the small town or even village that has such an establish-
ment. It is usually, although not necessarily, small and dusty with some new
books and many old ones, where it is the author on the shelf that counts, not
the edition or even necessarily its condition, although the true book-lover does
enjoy handling a well-made book with good type, paper that will last, and a
handsome binding. Sylvia Beach's Shakespeare and Company in Paris and
Frances Stelloff's Gotham Book Mart in New York were two of the most famous
of such individualist book shops that have become part of literary history, but
they had their counterparts in London, Chicago, Berlin, Prague, Stockholm and
Milan before the watershed of Hitler, the greatest destroyer of culture in
centuries, brought the arts to a halt in Europe. The good bookseller does not
just supply his customers, he also leads them.

If the exceptional bookseller is the tertiary member of a literary partnership,
then what can be said of the publisher? I, the author, am one myself, and I have
followed in the tradition of those who have given their names to their imprint,
have published for interest and pleasure rather than for profit, and have resisted
the temptation to sell out for a pile of money at times when such offers were
available. My career has been a curved arc that started in the early fifties,
reached its highest point in the sixties, and then began a slow descent into the
nineties. I have been a player in the literature of the postwar period and my
literary success, as well as my lack of business sense, can be judged by my
having published more Nobel Prize winners than any other publisher in Britain
during that time, while making no money doing it, but this means little to the
public: historically, the publisher remains almost anonymous, less known to
those who buy books than the bookseller who meets such readers, and is consequently recommended by one customer to another. Only a few publishers have
had their names linked to an author, and even then usually only for his early
years, such as Kurt Wolff to Kafka and Fasquelle to Proust. The identification
of Sylvia Beach with Joyce lies in her unique reputation as a bookseller who
became an amateur publisher, a person who met writers, encouraged, admired
and flattered them, and thereby became a "celebrity" as far as the public was
concerned. My own identification, and it will not last too long, has been with

Samuel Beckett, in my view one of the four great writers of the twentieth century, along with the previously mentioned Proust, Kafka and Joyce: to a lesser extent I am known for presenting in English the work of the "absurdist" playwrights and the school of fiction we know as the *nouveau roman*.

Coming on my father's side from a line of Scottish crofters, who in the nineteenth century became successful brewers and whisky distillers, and on my mother's from French-Canadian *habitants*, of whom my maternal grandfather ended as a banker, I had no formal background in any literary field and taught myself by reading. The only quality that I inherited from my tough ancestors was a certain stubbornness. From the beginning I wanted to acquire the learning that none of them had the time or inclination to develop, and from childhood I wanted to write, and to read endlessly, being frustrated, like Henry Miller in his youth, at the difficulty of getting books. But I never really had much personal ambition for fame as against scope, wanting to get things done, and I have a natural reticence, which means that I have never objected to being Janet Flanner's "common carrier," a back-room person out of the lime-light.

Mine has been a literary life, partly among the expatriates of Paris in the decades that followed those of Sylvia Beach, James Joyce, Ernest Hemingway, Kay Boyle, Caresse and Harry Crosby, Eugène and Maria Jolas, Gertrude Stein and her circle, George Antheil and Paul Bowles (a composer before he was a writer), Man Ray and the surrealists, Bryher and Robert McAlmon, Scott Fitzgerald, T.S. Eliot, Ezra Pound, Ford Maddox Ford and all the other names we associate with the twenties and thirties; some of them, like Henry Miller, bridge the pre-war and post-war worlds. The connection between what one does in life and the way in which one lives is the principal justification for biography and literary history; it is difficult, if not impossible, for a public figure, even a writer, to keep many secrets from biographers and the interested readers of the future; he is perhaps wise not to hide too much or he will be misunderstood, misinterpreted and have many fallacies tied to his name by future generations. Biographers have to imagine or invent their "facts" to fill the holes. Even the most reclusive of writers cannot afford to be too secretive.

Paris of the fifties and sixties has attracted nostalgia and interest in a later age of scarcity and decline. It was a time of growth and excitement lived under the threat of nuclear war, that encouraged those who were young to live intensely and fast, because extinction, even the end of the world, seemed always near. That age of positive thinking under threat later turned into a general pessimism about what was to come, which from the perspective of the nineties holds an infinite number of unknown futures. As the century draws to a close we are all more cynical, aware of the presence of conspiracy, much of it criminal, in the shaping of present and future events, which was not a part of the awareness of earlier generations. We have come to take corruption and criminality for granted. No one is above suspicion any more, or is believed to represent what they pretend; there is not much surprise when an apparently clean tycoon or politician is unmasked. Electors vote for what they perceive as the lesser evil, not for what they really want, because no one will offer them that. Democracy has become a sham in every country where there are too many conflicting interests or ethnic minorities in collision. The re-emergence of tribalism in every society makes a mockery of democracy, which depends for its existence and proper working on a knowledgeable, educated, aware and politically-active electorate being given clear choices. Choices today are never clear, and this has led to an estrangement of the intellectual community, those who live by their talents as artists, teachers or media people, from the general population of those who simply want a good life, permanent employment and peace. Control still lies with an oligarchy which, although insecure, is indifferent to the well-being of the majority. In the troubled times to come the arts will always continue to exist, because the artist will always find a way to express himself, even if he has no audience, but culture — the shared climate of imaginative and thought-provoking activity that can only exist where life is otherwise apparently secure — is in ever-greater danger. Few politicians give culture more than lip-service and in the United States it is usually too dangerous even to mention. George Bush, when he was president, could not admit to a liking for classical music, while in France any politician who did not have at least a veneer of culture could never be elected. The French want to be led by those with good minds and good educations, Americans too often by the lowest common denominator, those who affect to be most like themselves. Although the arrival of younger politicians like Bill Clinton and Al Gore had lead one to hope that perhaps that might change. Alas, not! The British vote to support whatever will most hurt the class-image of the class they hate most. There are different cultures in Britain and they tend to clash, cancelling each other out. The British seem to like living with dissatisfaction.

The relationship between art and culture is often confused. One can exist without the other. Culture is a climate in which one lives: it includes our working as well as our leisure lives, our attitudes, prejudices, pleasures and obligations: the arts are a part of it, but usually only in so far as they are accepted, and have become anodyne and generalized, appealing almost invisibly, like *muzak*. Minority cultures often invade the larger ones because they are "discovered" and can enrich an art scene that has faded, whereas a culture seen as too foreign, irrelevant or imperialistic can be totally rejected by a community, country or a continent. Beethoven and Shakespeare have no place in African culture, nor do most of their modern equivalents, but Peter Brook and John Cage would not be so alien there. On the other hand African art, and some writers like Wole Soyinka and Chinua Achebe, have marginally invaded western culture. A general culture, as distinct from a high culture, is what is accepted at a given time, but it disintegrates under great stress, usually brought about by war, famine, earthquake or economic collapse. Art, on the other hand, a principle component of high culture, is constantly created, but may not survive even a minor upset because it is fragile by nature: both the artist and his art can disappear because of malice or accident. The wars of the sixteenth century in Italy saw the destruction of all but a handful of the works of Leonardo da Vinci, and of many other masters of the high culture of the high renaissance. Much poetry was written in the trenches during the first world war, but only a handful of it has survived, poetry having been the natural means of artistic expression for the young officer class of Britain at the time, and most of it died in battle. One can only speculate on the art destroyed by the Nazis who killed so many artists. But new art has always continued to be created, although only a small part of it becomes part of a majority culture. What can be said is that there is a culture of philistinism that stifles creativity — not its creation as much as its reception — and a culture of art, that by definition is necessary to a good society, one in which it is pleasant and stimulating to live. Unfortunately, when such a good society exists, and it is usually the result of special circumstances like the aftermath of a war and much individual and group effort, it tends to be destabilised by undemocratic forces, by power-lust and cupidity. Those who live in fortunate times quickly become complacent and make too little effort to defend what they have come to take for granted.

Individualist publishers are not necessarily literary, but it is the literary, and to a great extent the political publishers — often they are the same — who change the world a little. I have admired many before my own time, although some, like Victor Gollancz, the product of an earlier age and morality, disapproved of me: my publishing did not conform to the Fabian ethic he espoused. I am aware of myself as sometimes being a loose cannon, and have always been considered eccentric by colleagues. My campaigns against censorship, and the campaigns of others, have sometimes had the effect of opening doors to the random exploitation of sex and the cheapening of it, which I regret: sex should always have a mystery and sense of wonder and excitement, not possible in the plastic age of Madonna, but we have still not lost the censors: they have shifted their ground, always finding new ways to control how we think, what we do, what we buy, which way we vote. Sex has become matter of fact and freely discussed, which is healthy enough; what is not healthy is the way it is exploited for gain, for the most cynical of reasons. Maurice Girodias, Barney Rosset and I, mavericks of the fifties and sixties, and others who have followed us after 1970, liberated sex to remove guilt and make it natural and enjoyable as it has always been for an uninhibited minority, and we did so by allowing authors to describe it honestly and poetically, as well as erotically. What counted for us all was the adventure; the financial gain, where there was one, was a fortuitous by-product.

Adventure is what my own career has been about. The "Lost Generation" that preceded us was in part deadly serious (Sylvia Beach *et al.*), partly romantically mad (Harry Crosby), and partly opening the doors to eclectic experiment (Eugène Jolas). This refers to the pre-war Paris scene, although similar things were happening in Germany, Britain and elsewhere. What followed, after the years of war, was an age of enjoyment, one we are unlikely to see again, perhaps ever, in a world of growing population and shrinking amenity, with general culture and education (in the best sense) declining as specialization makes it harder to find, among those under forty, individuals who are fully rounded, with a taste for knowledge outside their particular field of activity. My colleagues and I believed passionately in justice, in achieving a better society, a freer and more stimulating life, and not just for ourselves. All of us, in our individual and eccentric ways, made personal sacrifices to bring what we thought we had ourselves to others.

Most lives end in tragedy and every life ends somehow. We are often the authors of our own tragedies, led by a Will-o-the-wisp or a *Ferner Klang*, an elusive sound we feel compelled to follow, as in Shreker's too little-known expressionist opera. It sometimes seems to me that life is like a mist in which we wander, half lost, half thinking we know the path ahead, in a landscape where our lives cross and recross at random the lives of others, where ambitions become distorted, hopes blunted, and a malignant puppet-master pulls the strings. I have already mentioned Beckett as the writer with whom, as a publisher, I have been most associated. He has been much more than a friend and an author I helped to establish: I have found in his writing, which is still part of my everyday consciousness after the man and our friendship are gone, great comfort and ever-greater aesthetic enjoyment. Beckett's parables satisfactorily and convincingly describe our existence, which can never be objectively explained. In one of his most powerful metaphorical novels *How It Is*, he sees all mankind crawling or swimming through a sea of mud, trying desperately to stay on the surface, while the pull drags us downward; some get a temporary relief as they crawl over others, or give some respite to others as they are pushed down by those who crawl over them. This grim parable offers no hope, but there is still comfort in recognizing our real world in it. Beckett's is cathartic art, depicting real horror, but he enables us to live with it because it is art on the highest poetic level; the excitement of his work enables the thinking individual to escape in his mind the daily torture of living and facing reality. That brings me to my other motivation as a publisher and an activist in the world of the arts, and occasionally of politics (I have stood for office, but being outspoken, have never been elected): I have tried to spread an awareness of the art that creates awareness, the presence of which, whether as creation or appreciation, separates mankind from the other species with which we share the planet, and without which, to quote Nietzsche, "Life is a desert."

ALEXANDER TROCCHI

merlin editorials

"MERLIN is for any innovation in creative writing which renders creative writing more expressive."

"MERLIN will hit at all clots of rigid categories in criticism and life, and at all that is unintelligently partisan."

Although the Paris-based journal Merlin *remains lesser known than its contemporaries (*The Paris Review, *for example) and its lifespan was short (1952-56), its contribution to modern literary history is extraordinary.* Merlin's *quality has been lauded by Jean-Paul Sartre, Albert Camus, Stephen Spender, Bertrand Russell and Sir Herbert Read, among others. Read wrote at the time, " ... in its pages one can find the best experimental work in the arts that is being done on both sides of the Atlantic." The driving force behind this remarkable journal, as leader, editor, fund raiser, counselor and writer, was Alexander Trocchi. After receiving the Kemsley Travelling Scholarship (£400) and a degree in philosophy from Glasgow University, Trocchi embarked for Paris in 1950. He described himself in those early days as, "a long-haired ill-clad creature, unshaven, an anonymous member of the army of foreign shufflers who walk Paris streets." Trocchi wouldn't be anoymous for long.*

Merlin was born from a meeting in the Hotel Lutétia with Jane Lougee, the daughter of an American banker. Despite Jane's contribution (a monthly allowance and fruitcake care packages from home), finding sufficient support for a new literary journal was difficult.

Merlin *would later be housed in a tiny apartment at 8, rue du Sabot. Collaborators included Christopher Logue, Richard Seaver, Austryn Wainhouse, and Maurice Girodias.*

Nearly half a century later Alexander Trocchi's vision gains a new poignancy. A number of today's literary giants, in many cases unknown in the early 1950s, were published and encouraged by him. The tables of contents from issues of Merlin *read like a canon of modern literature: Samuel Beckett, Henry Miller, Paul Éluard, Jean Genet, Jean-Paul Sartre, Eugène Ionesco, Arthur Adamov, Robert Creely, William Samson, Pablo Neruda, Italo Svevo, W.S. Graham, Nazim Hikmet, P.W. Bowles and others. Here follows two of Trocchi's editorials from early* Merlin *issues.*

JM

Number Four, Spring-Summer 1953

MERLIN is an expatriot magazine. While we wish to translate and to publish foreign writing, it was part of our original intention to be a clearing house for that Anglo-American writing which for one reason or another and in one sense or another is expatriot. That term must be understood broadly; so understood, the tradition of that writing is an important one. It did not, as popular journalism sometimes implies, begin and end with Scott Fitzgerald. It is as old as Xenephon. The cock-sparrow provincialism of temperament implicit in many of the contributions to the recent symposium in the *Partisan Review* — Norman Mailer's was an honourable exception — was a disquieting symptom of a national culture neither old nor young enough to be quite honest with itself.

Expatriot writing is not necessarily wild, indeed, it has often been more classical than the home product. Nevertheless, the rebel is often a very young man, and if he cannot get published at home he is naturally enough tempted to identify himself with the professional abroad; but the truth is that his so-called "experimentation" is often a mask for his incompetence. Experimental writing — it is an imprecise term — is not an easy way out for a man who has nothing to say. It is questionable whether further experimentation has any meaning in the present-day context. Consolidation is necessary. The great experimenters of the first half of the century are by no means generally accepted, far less digested; that being so, it is not only a question of whether it is advisable to "proceed farther" but of whether it is possible. The word "originality" is a dangerous one; it is often the instrument of a fool's own suicide. Below the level of competent writing no one is going to look for originality.

Number Five, Autumn 1953

It is seldom useful to distinguish between *what* is said and *how* it is said, for the expressive element in language is part of the content. If there is something vitally new to be communicated, the texture of the language through which it comes into being will reflect on the objective level the originality of the subjective attitude. Words, combinations of them, will be used in a new way. Stock phrases, imprecise as they are, will be used only for specific technical (e.g. satirical) reasons. Otherwise, not at all.

Thus, our first glance at any piece of writing will be at its texture, at the vitality and above all at the precision of the language, especially where the syntax is most unconventional. Only after having satisfied ourselves that it is texturally of interest, will we deem it worthwhile to consider plot, structure, form, what you will. That, basically, is the distinction between serious and popular writing. Both may have plot, structure, or form; the latter is devoid of interest from the point of view of texture.

If the expressive element in language is indeed part of the content, then there is no "new way of saying old things." The so-called "old things" are impregnated even in conception by the individual quality of the mind; they are transformed in the process of original expression. The serious writer has always been concerned primarily with texture, with the manipulation of language itself, and his aim has always been *to say new things*.

A recent English critic writing on "the novel" was forced by the stricture of his definitions to the conclusion that Joyce, Lawrence, and Virginia Woolf amongst others, were inferior novelists. He admitted (of the latter two) that they were nevertheless, "great artists." If that is so, his peculiar subject, "the novel," is of little interest, and he would be well-advised to leave the "the novel" alone and to concern himself with "the writings" of significant writers.

In twentieth century prose, the two pioneers of "charging language with meaning" were James Joyce and Gertrude Stein. We would do well to consider them. In a literary climate in which we are exhorted to remember that "novelists ought to write novels" — where accent, that is, is laid upon plot — we might point out that the imperative is redundant, that novelists, we suppose, and by definition, do, although serious writers, we feel, may not.

IRA COHEN

A Letter to No One

for Nadine Ganase

A letter to no one
about crossing borders,
about time and impermanence
Would you wear my shoes?
Could I throttle time?
A man wearing a baseball cap
carries a woman's breast
in his overnight bag
We step over the cracks,
dream of teleportation,
try to get to the other side
of What
It's mindboggling to see
the blind man led by a dog
I'm with you in spirit
I've transcended light
Where you live it's daytime
My life is bounded by night
If you can't see my mirrors
I can't see you
We're crossing another border
Why is every one asleep?
It's better to just drive
through it
Meet you in the middle,
neither here nor there,
but in that mythical place
called everywhere.

IRA COHEN

French Kiss

for G.O.

"This sad, this proud exile,
is it possible that it is a trap?"
                                        Verlaine

We went together to the gardens
of Luxembourg
talking about Zanzibar
I drank a glass of yellow fog
while you went swimming
with two blind men
who kept bumping into you
you were weightless in the water
trying to remember the words
of an old song
"Deshabillez-moi, mais pas trop vite,
Deshabillez-moi, mais pas tout suite..."
You sang as the blind men
followed in your wake
I sewed my sleeve back on,
hoped to discover the color of autumn
in your mouth
when an earthquake in South America
woke me up and I saw how everyone
was sitting alone waiting for winter
Come now before it is too late
already the light is swimming in the air —
A smile from you is a risk worth taking
Let tonight be its own remembrance
Sex is a habit of light.
Do not expect it to happen again.

IRA COHEN - *Charles Henri Ford*

IRA COHEN
Allen Ginsberg "Bandaged Poet Series" - Amsterdam 1979
William Burroughs & Jim Carroll - New York mid-70s

D. H. LAWRENCE/ALDOUS HUXLEY

Postcards From Bandol to New Mexico

French bibliophile Yves Morice, whose mother, A. Morice-Kerné, translated Lawrence into French, has spent many years tracking the life and works of Lawrence and his contemporaries. The following, recently-discovered postcards from Lawrence and Huxley, were contributed by Morice.

Postcard from Aldous Huxley to Madame Douillet in Bandol in the Var in France while visiting "Madame Lawrence" in San Cristobal, New Mexico in July 1937. Note the Indian ponies from the Kiowa Ranch on the front.

*O*ne of the first important writers in the English language to be spiritually attracted to New Mexico, D.H. Lawrence wrote in the summer of 1922 in a letter to Catherine Carswell (**The Savage Pilgrimage**, Secker, 1932) about his connectedness to the place.

"*Taos, in its way, is rather thrilling. We have got a very pretty adobe house, with furniture made in the village, and Mexican and Navajo rugs, and some lovely pots. It stands just on the edge of the Indian reservation: a brook behind, with trees: in front, the so-called desert, rather like a moor but covered with whitish-grey sage brush, flowering yellow now: some 5 miles away the mountains rise ...*

We have a pretty busy time, too. I have already learnt to ride one of these Indian ponies, with a Mexican saddle. Like it so much. We gallop off to the pueblo or up to one of the can[y]ons. Frieda is learning too. Last night the young Indians came down to dance in the studio, with two drums: and we all joined in. It is fun: and queer ...

Perhaps it is necessary for me to try these places, perhaps it is my destiny to know the world. It only excites the outside of me. The inside it leaves more isolated and stoic than ever. That's how it is ...

It is all inwardly a hard stone and nothingness. Only the desert has a fascination — to ride alone — in the sun in the forever unpossessed country — away from man. That is a great temptation, because one rather hates mankind nowadays. But "pazienza, sempre pazienza!"

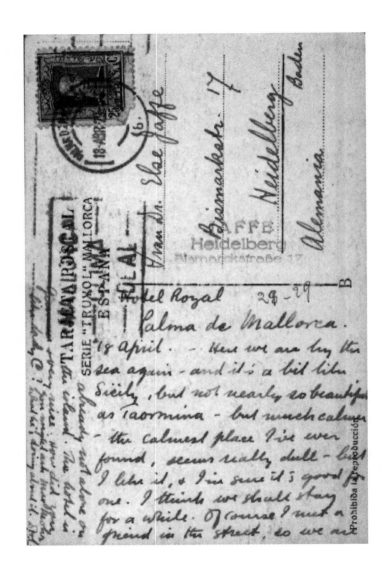

Frau Dr. Else Jaffe
Bismarckstr. 17
Heidelberg
Baden
Alemania

JAFFE
Heidelberg
Bismarckstraße 17

Hotel Royal   28-29   B
Palma de Mallorca.
18 April. — Here we are by the
sea again — and it's a bit like
Sicily, but not nearly so beautiful
as Taormina — but much calmer
— the calmest place I've ever
found, seems really dull — but
I like it, & I'm sure it's good for
one. I think we should stay
for a while. Of course I met a
friend in the street, so we are

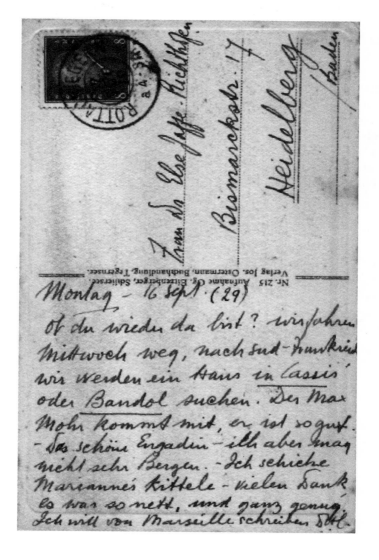

Two Postcards from D.H. Lawrence to Frau Dr. Else Jaffe-Richthofen, Frieda's sister in Heidelberg, in April and September 1929 from Mallorca and the Black Forest, respectively. In the first one, Lawrence refers to his not yet published manuscript **Lady Chatterly's Lover.** *In the second one, note Lawrence's perfect German.*

C. MULROONEY

quisqueya (after So-Shu)

hard it is to work
under the juvenile Muzak
me Noriega you Army
oh yes fuck me fleurette
when eggs fry in Nome
on the sidewalks
this bird will warble blatherskite
he fosters a very Aubrey Beardsley
sort of consternation douche
oh what a very chilly shower
you have become at length
HOLLYWOOD
Santa Monica —
even the ChristianScientists
have gone domestic Postmodern
"a bird, a bee, and a butt
-erfly" and then he awoke

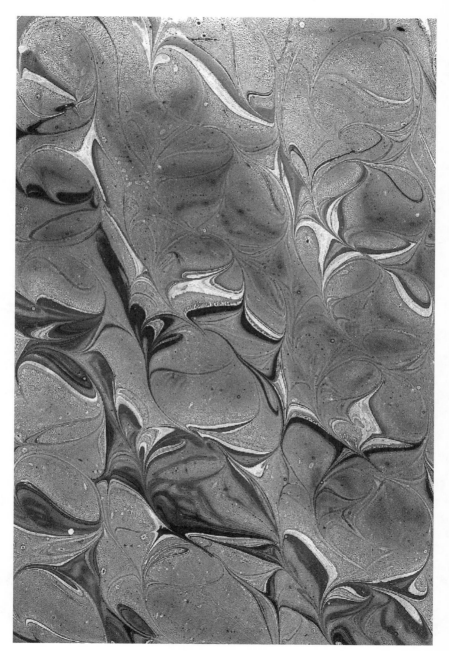

CHRISTIANE CHARLOT - *Marbleized paper - 1998*

Zia Sun Symbol

The Zia Sun symbol, New Mexico's insignia, and the central image on the state flag, originated with the Indians of the Zia Pueblo long before the arrival of Europeans. The symbol reflects the Zia belief in teaching the basic harmony of all things in the universe.

To the Zia Indian, the sacred number is embodied in the earth with its four main directions — in the year, with its four seasons; in the day, with sunrise, noon, evening and night; in life, with its four divisions — childhood, youth, adulthood and old age.

Four is the sacred number of the Zia, and the figure is composed of a circle from which four points radiate. These points, made of four straight lines of varying length, personify the number most often used by the giver of all good gifts.

Each person has four sacred obligations: a strong body, a clear mind, a pure spirit, and a devotion to the welfare of his/her people. Everything is bound together in a circle of life and love, without beginning, without end.

Adapted from the New Mexico, Enchantment USA Website

ERIC MICHAELS - *sketch*

sense of
place

NEW MEXICO,

SITUATED IN THE SOUTHWESTERN UNITED STATES, has a population of nearly two million people and a projected population growth of 55%, one of the highest in the United States. It is bordered by Colorado, Oklahoma, Texas, Utah, Arizona and Mexico. It includes a remarkable diversity of landscape and both indigenous and transplanted culture. The state hosts many extraordinary places, premier among them is Chaco Canyon, dating back to 900 A.D. There is both great continuity and rich diversity among the Pueblo, Navajo, and Apache populations here. Santa Fe, the capital, was formally founded by the Spanish in 1610. Like some kind of permanent existential reminder, New Mexico also houses Trinity Site at the northern end of White Sands, the location of the first atomic blast. Today, Santa Fe is a remarkable and oftentimes tense mixture of Native, Hispanic, and Anglo cultures.

It is a pleasure to present in this issue of **Frank** a selection of poetry, fiction, and drama by twenty four writers currently living in New Mexico. True to New Mexico's richly mosaic and diverse literary heritage, the concerns and lineages of these writers are widely diverse and resist categorization. There are Native American, Hispanic, Asian, Jewish, and Anglo authors represented, and the range of their writing includes the experimental as well as more traditional work firmly rooted in the region's history and landscape.

New Mexico's modern literary history can be said to start with Alice Corbin Henderson, poet and editor from Chicago. Soon after settling in Santa Fe in 1916 she produced a special issue of *Poetry* featuring Native American chants. Corbin, along with Mabel Dodge Luhan and Mary Austin, created a literary scene which drew other well-known writers to New Mexico. Willa Cather, D.H. Lawrence, and Witter Bynner are among the mid-twentieth century writers whose work was influenced by their time here. In the late 1950s and 1960s, Robert Creeley lived here and became a seminal influence on many of New Mexico's contemporary artists.

Today, there is a vibrant group of writers living throughout New Mexico. There are regular readings in Albuquerque, Las Cruces, and Santa Fe, and a tradition of Poets-in-the-Schools which has brought poets to the state's most rural recesses. The programs in writing at the University of New Mexico in Albuquerque, the College of Santa Fe, the Institute of American Indian Arts, and New Mexico State University in Las Cruces attract writers from all over the country. Jeff Bryan, through La Alameda Press in Albuquerque, publishes books of poetry and fiction by mostly New Mexican authors. *New Mexico Poetry Renaissance*, edited by Sharon Niederman and Miriam Sagan, and published by Red Crane Books in 1994, is a virtual compendium of the state's poets. The literary magazines include *Puerto del Sol*, edited by Kevin McIlvoy and Kathleene West, *Blue Mesa Review*, edited by David Johnson, *Countermeasures*, edited by Greg Glazner and Jon Davis, and *Yefief*. From 1985 to 1990, *Tyuonyi*, a literary magazine published through the Institute of American Indian Arts, and edited by Phillip Foss, published experimental work. Also during the 1980s, Tooth of Time Books, founded by John Brandi, published over twenty individual books of poetry, promoting many emerging Native American and Asian American authors. Initiated by Denise Chavez, the annual Borders Book Festival in Las Cruces brilliantly celebrates multicultural writing. In addition to La Alameda Press, other significant small press publishers in New Mexico include: West End Press in Albuquerque, and the Institute of American Indian Arts Press, Pedernal, and Katydid Books in Santa Fe.

Of great importance as well are the literary bookstores in the state, notably in Taos: Brodsky's, Moby Dickens, and Taos Bookstore; in Santa Fe: Collected Works, Garcia Street Books, Railyard Books, and Old Santa Fe Trail Books; in Albuquerque: Page One, Borders, and Bound To Be Read; and in Mesilla: Bowlin's Mesilla Book Center. Also worthy of note is the small press distributor Desert Moon.

In choosing contributors for this issue of **Frank**, we have attempted to represent as wide a selection of sensibilities as possible. By juxtaposing these diverse voices, it has been our intention to share a sense of place by presenting, through the work of its writers and artists, the vibrant literary and spiritual life in New Mexico.

Carol Moldaw and Arthur Sze

NEW MEXICO

Utah   Colorado

Arizona   NEW MEXICO   Oklahoma
                              •Rio Grande
Navajo Reservation   • Taos   Texas
                    Abiquiu•
          Chaco   •
          Canyon   Los   •
                   Alamos   • Santa Fe
                            Cochiti Pueblo
                            Santo Domingo Pueblo
          •   •   Sandia Pueblo
          Zuni   Acoma   Albuquerque
          Pueblo   Pueblo

                   •Rio Grande

                   •
          Gila Cliff   •   Mescalero Apache
          Dwellings   • Trinity Site: White Sands
                   • Las Cruces
                            Carlsbad •

                            Texas
          Mexico

J IM S AGEL

Blind Curve

L eading the caravan, a pickup labors under a mountainous
load of firewood, its tires wavering in past tense. All I can
do is slow down and notice the stream that straddles the road is
running off with the sunrise — understand that for the "ultimate
in no-frills dining," I will have to pull off at the Lovato Burger
Drive-in. But I don't stop, even though the next sign says, "Jesus
is coming," and three teen angels swing their voluptuous legs in
unison from the tailgate of a Toyota 4 X 4 in the shade of a
mammoth cottonwood. I follow the lurching truck past
escarpments of granite still glowing from the Big Bang; past the
descanso with its five white crosses and plastic roses marking the
spot where Juan — simply "Juan" — left his surname in the
wreckage of his body; past Ducky's Meats specializing in hay,
custom slaughtering and choke cherry jelly; past a bent-backed
couple walking hand in gnarled hand with poles baited for
rainbows. Rounding a blind curve, I realize the truck full of
firewood has vanished with my loneliness.

JIM SAGEL

Lighting Up

Six a.m. at the Wagon Wheel Cafe. Bestubbled wheat farmers with tobacco-stained teeth and Dekalb Seed Corn caps welded to their skulls crouch over meaty hands as if the wind were blowing at their backs. They eat eggs greasy side up and talk cattle through a haze of cigarette smoke.

Bonnie, the waitress, stubs out her own Camel and addresses the cook over the sizzling sausage. Got a new dye job on her hair, did it herself because she wasn't about to go to no hairdresser without no pockets in his pants — says — she don't care if she does look like a blueberry, when you get as old as she is, you can have any color of hair you want.

Methodically making the rounds, she refills all the coffee cups and calls everyone honey while, outside the east window, the sun strikes a match to the yawning clouds.

RENÉE GREGORIO

Gladiola

The hot pink gladiola's beauty
is almost unbearable —
its color like swelled lips,
lips that have kissed too much.
The arc of its stalk curves
as if it's the hand of a dancer,
the uppermost flowers
not yet opened.
Their fragrance, anyway, is slight,
and for all their color, they feel unpainted,
yet generous, like the love of a ten-year-old girl,
before makeup and puberty. I like looking up
at this flower, purchased today at Wild Oats
for exactly $1.59 with the thought of buying
a good deal of beauty at a tiny price.
And, it's true, the slant of the stalk
could set me to dancing — it's Saturday night,
after all, and the buffalo grass is growing,
the laundry's drying on the metal wire
in the backyard, and the moon is only half-full
or half empty, just depending on the tilt
of your thoughts as you dare to look up
into the city sky with its desperate and yearning stars
just dying to show their light.

RENÉE GREGORIO

The Storm That Tames Us

We must do more than look
at the flowers. The gardener's pleasure:
labor and the fruits of labor. The digging
and the careful placing of seeds, the tending, the waiting.
When the green shoot first breaks ground,
it is the sound of birthing we like most.

We've loved over continents and cultures
to bring ourselves here, on the road between this *barrio*
and that neighborhood, loving with a yearning toward
intelligence, a kind of fire of the mind.
Annie Proulx ended *Shipping News* saying perhaps
love is possible without pain and misery. Maybe it is.

I have watched you come at me
like watching clouds gather on the far horizon
toward storm. I have watched the storm of you
gather and have felt it in my breasts
like the wet scent of near-rain in the northeast
air of my beginning, like smelling sage after rain.

Once, I was in the sky all the way to you, asking:
Is this the territory of my dead?
Endless azure and cotton, the roads
snaking far below. There were lights sparkling
across the distant backdrop of a sprawling city.
I come closer to the buildings that house those lights,
just to see the structure there.

Yes, I'm terrified to begin again, as if beginning
holds already the tenuous seeds of loss, made to break us.
Yet the deads' shadows have circled and embraced us.
I ask myself: What was all that's gone before?

Your hands resonate years of lived desire.
I hear the way the leaves are falling.

I have said yes to the question of union.
I've watched you crawl under the colors
of your death-blanket and didn't turn away.
On Xmas, we came through the church door
at Taos Pueblo, from inner dark to the night's dark,
stunning with fire.

I stood in the courtyard looking under the wooden lintel,
through the doorway into more dark, into the white canopy
held over the queen's head, into the wind lifting
the canopy and, beyond, the smoked sky and air
shot the color of pomegranate. The open door,
and again, the white canopy lifting.

We walk the earth with something like intent
circling our days, leave with something more than intent
taking us away. Do we know the seeds of our dying?
You are the vehicle of my return
to this place of silence where objects begin
to live again. Where your eyes save me.

Last summer, at someone else's wedding, I rose up
out of the crowd of single women, as if lifting an arm
to light a torch I could barely reach. I grabbed
that bouquet out of thin mountain air, out of the grip
of another woman, knowing in my blood I am next.
It was a move of pure instinct, born of waiting.

Labor and the fruits of labor.
Days all you get is the digging.
Days all you get is the fruit.
This storm has arrived to tame us.
All these years, the air heavy with it.
Now we get the release. At last we get the release.

MELANIE CESSPOOCH

Black Birds

There is a woman in there
arms wrapped like soft branches
around a steel cross.

She heats the whip
that will slap the bare skin tonight
or maybe she will
squeeze the collar of my t-shirt
and roll me down the concrete stairs
        either way she will be here soon.

There is a woman in there
laughing deep like a man
fingers smoothing the ice beads of a Coors can.

She deconstructs a wire hanger
or pulls loose the belt buckle
and swings when she is up to bat
I know that she is coming
        and she will be here soon.

That woman dreams of babies with teeth
ready to nurse and walk like a man.
She dreams that maybe one day, I too
will be a man and support her crippled back
        and support her crippled back.

She dreams of babies
while I dream of black birds with scales
and devil teeth.

They sit in her closet.

        And you thought
        it was the beatings
        that made me wise.

JOHN BRANDI

Annotations on the Alphabet from a Book in Progress Beginning with "A"

JOHN BRANDI - *collage*

Some learned the alphabet on blackboard, by memory. I learned by color, sitting in a garden, letting each letter assume shape and hue against the sun. Alphabet as solar entity, sound with corresponding tone, each letter a visual, aromatic poem born from nature, asking itself into the flesh. A burst into my eye without the straight lines of the Romans — a tincture, red and round, conducting its own ambrosial emotion. As my life arranged itself with the elixir of Adventure, A became an invisible shape inscribed between every locus on the mandala of my journey: Albuquerque, Agra, Aleknagik, Acongagua, Amed, Ayuthaya, Annapurna, Antofagasta, Ama Dablam. A was no derelict hieroglyph nor reshaped cuneiform, but topography, curve, unavoidable abyss, avalanche, archipelago. A brought constellations into the fingers, wet the tongue with the pomegranate's galaxy, opened the lips with unspoken vowels lodged in the cardiac plexis. A in Krakatoa's quaking, in the heart on Apollinaire's grave, in musical snow banners blowing from Macchapucchare. A in the ritmos, ritual and rhyme of Maharashtra, Pashupatinath, Iztaccihuatl, and Shipaulovi. In the medicinal syllables of Saraswati, Tekakwitha and La Guadalupana. A for creation. A in the womb, asking.

JOHN BRANDI

Tell Me, What Dagger What Thirst?

> *What is meant by happiness? To live every unhappiness.*
> *What is meant by light? To gaze with undimmed eyes*
> *on all darknesses."*
>
> — *Nikos Kazantzakis*

What histories lie hidden
in these veins & wings, these roamers
walking & peddling & circumsizing their young?

What sunrise
through the stink of charm?

What beaker of foam, whose flag
what bloodhounds at the foot of the rainbow?

Where's this kid who comes up to me in a Jakarta alley
with a foetus floating in a bottle for sale
from, what's his life?

What's that guy with no arms tying ribbons
around the sky, singing a song of secret beauty
in the middle of the day all about?

Where's this woman in lowcut red on the bus
whose thigh wets mine in equatorial heat going?

What bruised arms & walnut skin darkened
with rain eats gravel for a living in the noon ditch
while milk leaks from her left breast?

Who? This Laxmi this Fatma this Rangda
of mossy stone sewing costumes
for the living?

What secret grip undid the knot?
What loosened atrium brought from egg & seed
these coughing sisters of unwed mothers?

Rain fills the vacuum of nirvana
Sparks blow from the rose in her hair

Saya sudah pernah datang disini!
Saya belum lancar di manis nya di dalam hidup!

I am going to the same place as you
on your anonymous bicycle, as you
in your trick of mystery

The earth is peopled with us
The dogpack derelict in high towers of glass

I think a thought in a mirror
of canceled evidence, let you suck out my eyes
so I can feel my way through oblivion

Saya sudah pernah datang disini—

Whose leg under mine
understands the world is a cataract
over a perfect eye

We are clownfish in a reef
while shepherds of crime
go about their trade

This skin inside yours, this sultan's
pavilion, these sweepers
of dark streets

I hear them as we scream
I hear the fingers at the window
& my voice like sand

What is it we call it
when we finally remember?
What steeple, what canyon

what lifetime, whose cry
broke the waist of the hourglass?

Jalan Jaksa, Jakarta

DENISE CHÁVEZ

A Family of Feet

I always buy shoes too small. Consequently, I have at least four or five pairs of shoes in my closet that really do not fit me. I neglect my feet. I expect too much of them. I try to squeeze them into shoes too small, my body into clothes too tight, my face behind makeup that only I feel I need.

I'd like to have freedom of feet. Just as I'd like to have freedom of makeup. Except with my feet, the freedom is more personal.

I have arches. This in itself acknowledges me as a chosen one. Much is expected of me, my feet. Everyone in our family views flat feet as a curse, an anathema, a symbol of imperfection. My mother viewed flat feet as a curse of God, a stigma. "You're the lucky one," she used to say, "your feet aren't flat, you have an arch. Only you and your father have an arch in this family. The rest of us, me, your sisters, we have flat feet. All my life I wish I had an arch. It's caused me a lot of pain not having an arch. And not only that, your feet are small. The rest of us have huge flat feet. You're lucky. The only thing I gave you was my long second toe, the Rede family toe. It was your grandfather's toe, it's my toe, and now it's your toe."

Having the "Rede toe" I considered an unnatural curse. It was ugly and caused my otherwise perfect foot to feel deformed. While all my friends and cousins had toes that graduated in size from the largest to the smallest, my second toe was longer than the supposed big toe, and not only that, it was hammerheaded with a bulbous tip. Feeling ugly-toed, I tormented my younger sister who was doubly cursed with her big flat Rede-toed feet. I mercilessly made fun of what I considered her hooked Rede toe. It was only years later that I came to understand this condition called "Morton's toe." It seems to cause the Morton-toed person to have a permanent callous radiating downward behind the toe, and not only that, it causes some kind of shifting compensation in the way you walk. I didn't know that then. All I knew was that even though I was among the chosen few to have an arch in a splay-footed family, I was still singled out by the foot god to be Morton-toed. Having Morton's toe as a child was a distressing and awkward thing for me. Whenever I was out in public I hid my feet. Those few times that girlfriends saw my long second toe jutting out of sandals and made comments, I brushed it off, still bristling inside long after. I consoled myself with the idea that I had arches. And having arches, as we know, was a godly thing.

I remember going swimming with my younger sister at my uncle's house in summertime. I taunted her saying she had long banana feet. It was cruel. I made imprints of my perfect arch with pool water on the hot concrete and challenged her to make arches like mine. Twisting her foot sideways and rolling it across the concrete quickly, before it dried in the hundred degree heat, she would try to match my arch, molding her foot to what my mother deemed perfection. She managed to create an artificial arch, and not knowing she had done it purposefully, seeing her footprints on the humid concrete you might think she was arch-blessed. I remember my sister turning this way and that, imprinting her fake arch as best she could before the sun dried out her handiwork. I stood nearby, arrogant, seemingly nonchalant, feeling my arch-gifted feet superior.

I was brought up to believe that my gift was a sign of my eventual success. Of what I was not really sure. All I knew was that somehow I had been called out by fate to have an arch, a sign of great blessing, a sign that I wouldn't have to suffer the fate of my mother, her purple varicose veins bulging, her veins stripped, always throbbing. I just knew her fate would escape me. She was a teacher and I never wanted to be a teacher. I was created for greater things, a life of more comfort, less sorrow. My parents were divorced and I knew I would never divorce. I would never have to wait like my mother did for the child support check that never came, the occasional fifty dollars that would mean so much. I wouldn't have to sit in front of a small wooden desk like my mother did late at night, figuring out what bills to pay, struggling with a ledger that never balanced out. My feet would take me far away from my mother's life, her constant anxieties, her brutal, all too real battles. I wouldn't cry the way she did and no one would make me work her long hours, on the dusty playgrounds with her charges, never any time to rest. Nor would I marry like my older flat-footed sister at sixteen, having four children and a hysterectomy by the age of twenty-two. As for my younger sister, her lesser fate was sealed by her arch-less boat-length feet, she could never amount to much.

Feet dominated my life.

Feet dominated my life. My sister and I were always attendant to my mother's bad legs, sore feet. As the older daughter still at home, I was the one selected to rub my mother's legs when she got cramps in the middle of the night, and to pop her toes to relieve the pressure when her feet hurt. I hated having to pull my mother's long moist toes, especially her Morton's toe. For years I pulled my mother's cramped toes, hating the task, holding my fingers away disdainfully afterward and washing my hands because they'd touched feet. And yet she was always so grateful, saying, "Oh baby, thank you, you don't know, it helps so much." Secretly I didn't mind pulling and popping my mother's toes in place, but I would never have let on. It was another privilege accorded me by my mother. A vote of confidence and trust for the arch-worthy. These massages and toe pulls gave her tired teacher legs some relief. She stood for hours every day and never sat down. She was always on the go and barely gave herself time to rest. She wore a girdle for countless years and at night she removed it warily, like taking off protective armor. She often remarked that she didn't know what she would do without it.

As children we were cared for by various caregivers, *ayudantes*/helpers and *criadas*/maids, women from México who my mother hired to help us out while she was at school. I remember Belsora particularly, a plain-faced, almost homely woman who tended happily to my mother's feet. When Belsora came into our life my mother finally found someone who could tend to her the way my sister and I couldn't. Belsora didn't mind pulling my mother's toes and seemed to delight in massaging her feet, all times of the day or night, with Vicks or Vapo-Rub, when she got cramps in the middle of the night that made her call out in pain, waking up the entire house. I still hear her voice calling out: "*Ay, ay, los calambres*, the cramps, *ay*! Belsora, *ven*, come here! Hit my legs, hit them, I have cramps. Hit them. Harder!"

My mother's shoe size grew through the years. Once at a shoe sale, my mother, younger sister and I ranged the store looking for shoes we thought the others would like. I yelled out across a great expanse of store to my mother's mortified ears, "Are size eleven's too small?" Mother reprimanded me later, and I couldn't understand why. I think my mother started off her adult life as a size eight shoe, later moving to a nine, then a ten, on to an eleven and eventually a twelve. Because of her bad feet and legs she had to change her shoes two and three times a day. When she found a shoe she liked, a shoe that was comfortable and fit her well, she would buy two or three pairs in different colors. Her closet was full of the same shoes. Shoes for a big flat-footed woman whose every step caused pain.

And yet, for all her discomfort, my mother loved feet. Especially other people's feet. Once a shoe store in town had a sale with all their shoes going for five dollars. Several days later, those same shoes came down to a dollar a piece. Mother bought about fifty dollars worth of an assortment of shoes, all sizes and all colors. She laid them out on our large wooden dining room table, so that whoever came over, and our house was always full of family and friends, could pick out a pair of gift shoes in their size. Four forlorn pair of men's white shoes size nine sat on the table for several weeks, only to be happily adopted by the brother of a friend who was in dental school in México.

I remember my mother in her later years talking about her feet wistfully, wondering how much longer she would be able to get around. She stood up unsteadily, getting her "land legs" as she said, lifted her heavy earth-bound feet, and struggled to move around without limping. It was only much later she condescended to use a cane. Elegant as ever, almost majestic, with her carved wooden cane, a family heirloom, she would take a rest, pause gratefully and with a gentle, quiet sigh would say aloud, "Thank you, God, for my feet, whatever they're like. They go all the way to the ground, and that's all that matters. Now you, you're still young, you have good feet, and an arch. You and your father. You were the lucky ones."

ERIC MICHAELS - *sketch*

GENE FRUMPKIN

Certainty Perhaps

Certainly there was
less to dream about
and more
to designate. There
was much to inspire
certainty.
Very quietly
thus to sit on the lanai
and trespass against
the normal quality
of the water mass.
There was an adage
for every
incarnation. To be
related meant
abandoning
the leafing of it.
There were
royal palms that
made trails
in the sky.

GENE FRUMPKIN

Tableau: Three Men and a Woman

Three men look deadeye into the lens
and believe that for this afternoon at least
they are the Furies. They would rise
together in a second, heave over

the woman who already sits at the bar,
drinking nectar as if she were a word
lost from the sentence that gave her
permission to slaughter men with her sisters

near the mental bend of the Amazon.
The Furies enter quietly, two of them
still wearing black sunglasses. The camera
follows them though they are by now

barely visible. Shielding her eyes, the woman
hopes to hide, turns her head toward
the telephone. Two sit at either side,
one in back of her. They seem to dart

in conversation, though who is talking
is not recorded by eye or ear. In time,
they resume their bodies, identify themselves
as executives of the Fire Department

across the street. She sees that beneath
their sudden, calm visibility they are furious.
She brings to light the queen of her sadness,
armed with shield and broadsword, and begins

to hack away. The Furies are three men
sitting, drinking in a booth, two grinning
at the camera, the third a sourpuss. People
come and go, little suspecting the scene.
Less introspective now, the woman braces
for a refusal. She will give her body
only for a world free of foul bedrooms
and drooling horses, of rules laid down

by that old fool Zeus. A myth flares out
in drinking shots, days of it. The lens
recognizes a dangerous level of suicide, a need for
sleep. Three men stagger out. A woman flies.

Linda Durham Contemporary Art, Galisteo, NM

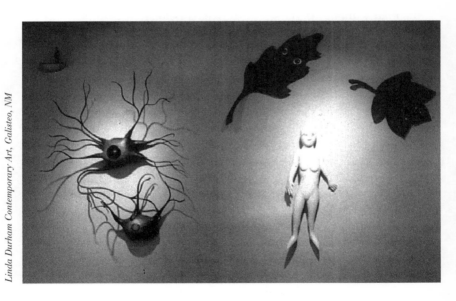

ERIKA WANENMACHER - *Room view of "Spells"* - *1997*

CAROL MOLDAW

The Jewish Cemetery at Penang

In a patch of flattened weeds in front of the graves
where a Kohane's stone-carved fingers part to bless
the remains of Penang's departed congregation,
barefoot Malaysian boys were playing badminton,
a sagging string strung pole to pole their net.
Our Chinese trishaw driver, too old to read
the map without his glasses, with five hairs long
as my five fingers growing from a mole,
waited for us. He'd found the street although
the tourist map was wrong: the name no longer
Yahudi Road, but Zaimal Abidin.

A rusted lock hung open on a chain
slung loosely round the stone and iron gate.
From a tin roofed shanty, a makeshift squat
just inside the walls, a woman watched us
unbuckle the chain and let it hang, the gate
creaking open enough for us to pass.

We walked past the boys, into headstone-high grass.
Lizards scuttled loudly to get away.
It looked decades since they'd been disturbed,
the newest markers twenty-odd years old;
no plastic wreathes; the only pebbles rubble
from the path, unpicked, unpolished, unplaced.
Dozens of graves, from the eighteen-thirties on,
Wolf Horn, Aboody Nahoom, Flora Barooth,
Semali Lazarus, Jacob Ephraim —
who but us had read these names this year?
Who alive could tell me who they were?

Pedaling us away, our spindly driver
had breath to spare, shouting against the traffic
what he'd found out while we were shooting roll

after roll of the cylindrical stone mounds:
there'd been a temple once, the Malaysian woman
had said, but nothing, no cornerstone, was left
of it, nor any living Georgetown Jews.
He himself was fifth generation Malay,
and had no ties to China.

               Later, walking
along the arcaded five-foot ways, stopping
every few steps to gawk — at rows of shutters,
peeling plaster the color of robin's eggs,
cats with open sores, an Indian man
reading a Chinese woman's palm — you point
across the street to a small neighborhood mosque,
its minaret's crescent moon spiked
with crows. They scatter at the muezzin's call,
regather on a red tile temple roof,
where Kuan Yin in her mercy guards her flock
and the air inside is smoky from our prayers.
A can of joss sticks rattle in my hand.
I fan the smoke toward her. What's one less temple
in a city of temples, a city of worship and trade?
What's one less altar? Over on Queen Street, when
the lime rind flares, lit with an oiled wick,
I place it in front of a jet black Hindu goddess
whose bosom heaves for me as I make my rounds.

Sitting here, in a courtyard of our hotel,
on a stone stool, at a stone table, writing
the day's impressions down, I miss my God,
his featureless face imposing itself
among the more expressive others,
whom he himself has banished, but whom
I also love. Remember the beggar this morning,
in front of the Krishna Café, where we ate
using only our right hands, how he grabbed
your wrist in thanks, kissed the back of your hand
and wouldn't let go until I began to tug
at you from the other side. I saw the look
that swept your face and also —

he might have picked your pocket.
Last night, drinking at the E & O, I said
I'd spend all our money on one perfect
ruby, if only I knew where to find it,
how to recognize it, and its true worth.
After I scraped my knee in the monsoon gutter,
I thought of those cats, the open sores on their sides.
One bruise starts before the last one's healed.
To calm myself, I lit a stick of incense,
but now, though far from home, and despite myself,
I find I'm reciting what I know of the *Sh'ma*.

JON DAVIS

Hunger Song

Uncertainty was in the syllables, was tied to each letter like a plastic flag. Like the flags the one-legged surveyor instructed his assistant to tie along the edges of our property. Our property, which existed as a plot, as a map in a file. A file the birds inhabited as random pencil-marks, as coffee stains. A file filled with longing as words are filled with a longing to be things. As the dung beetle larvae are filled with a longing to be language — that afterlife, that surplus value. *Words add to the senses,* but to what do the senses add? Once, in the haze of some over-the-counter remedy, I thought or dreamed or heard the finches' chatter outside my window evolving into a language. Not English exactly, but an imprecise song which said, or seemed to say, *We wake up hungry. We go to sleep hungry. And hunger is what we dream.* Over and over they sang from the juniper by the window. Even past midnight they'd wake from where they'd perched as if filed in a drawer and repeat their two-syllable call: *hun-ger, hun-ger.* And what about me? Hadn't I waded further into the river's chilling waters? Hadn't I sought sustenance in the too-cold dawn, walking the ridgeline underdressed, crawling under wild rose and penstemon to see the yellow bird singing from the low branches of the piñon? Hadn't I hungered to know its name? And hadn't its name called the bird closer? That fluttering shiver, that song distributed all along the sunlight-slick branch, that birdless name, scraps of it clinging to the needles, that name with round black eyes, querulous, calling me into the presence of clouds, slight breeze shearing across my cheek and hair, rough branch pressing my shoulder, rough gravity tugging me earthward, and all of it — bird and birdsong, brush and branch, ridgeline, property, hunger — all of it sliding now (in language) toward the sun.

JON DAVIS

Ma Roulette

> *"fresh leaves, two dark lilac-colored irises*
> *and a mass of orange and sulphur-yellow*
> *marigolds"*
>
> Pierre Bonnard

Not "pleasure," where pleasure expresses
its "evolutionary significance,"
where the tumble of sex
preserves the species, where
the genes cheer
from their orchestra seats.

But first sunlight
on the flowered bedspread.
A lover's handwriting among the unpaid bills.
The "weightlessness of birds."
A dream of prosperity.

Not pleasure as rehearsal for.
Not pleasure as drive.
Not accounts payable, accounts received.

But the journal of moments:
Fingers brushing cheek, nape,
sweeping and gathering.
One finger drawn
behind the ear, along the jaw.
Nerve-ends crackling,
skin waking, shivering.

Not words with their cords dangling.
Not words with their unspecifiable velocities,
their unsteady allegiances.

But lips and tongues and fingers — that actual
assent and lather. Affections gathering
in the air. The air
leaning over them. Behaviors
charging the molecules. Behaviors
swirling among the poplars,
lifting the birds, filling
each absence with meaning.

And form:
The form sunlight assumes
on the wooden sill, the red
stone floor, the plaster wall.
Clouds in a blue vase. Blue
vase in the sky.

Through *la porte ouverte*:
the billowing pleasure of flowers.

DIRK DE BRUYCKER - *Muted Icon*
asphalt, gesso, oil pigments on canvas 1994

JON DAVIS

Bleeding Icons

after the paintings of Dirk DeBruycker

This is the beginning and the end, alpha and omega,
the blotted-out place.

Here where the icons once paraded their sentiments.

Bleeding now because they cannot stop changing.

Bleeding now because they have been canceled.

If *truth: beauty* as *lamb: slaughter.*

Not Morocco.

That, too, blotted-out.

And Belgium.

And Dirk DeBruycker.

And the author of these words.

Canceled.

Now we are figures in paper.

What we intended, gone.

Into filigree, tracery; into splatter and wash.

All the lines uncleated.

Now we mean *So much is lost.*

Now we mean *Can you hear me at all.*

Someone said *What beautiful obliteration.*

Someone said *Help me climb over this barbed cancelation.*

Past these creatures gnawing at absence.

Into the birth canal.

Into the O of orgasm.

Into the crown of thorns.

Into the zero.

Someone said *Why such whimsy in the face of*

Someone said *And all of it canceled.*

Canceled: The body, impaled and lifted above the marketplace.

Canceled: The body sprawled across the spikes.

Canceled: The fruits and vegetables uncrated, the lamb carcasses splayed.

All of it painted in another language.

The absence calling to us in another language.

The absence which has become the darkness.

The darkness where the meanings once slept, tails curled,
heads on their paws.

The bodies stacked and covered with canvas.

The babies who would not last the night without their mothers
(who had died of cholera) lain gently in the back of the truck to die.

In that moment on the screen.

Fifty infants.

Smooth, babyfat hands grasping at nothing.

Hungry, but not afraid of cancellation.

We were eating popcorn when we noticed that the truck bed — in the repetition, in the contrast of rough cloth and smooth faces — was achieving a kind of formal elegance.

Then a darkness canceled all of it.

A canvas flap pulled down for protection.

An artist's brush.

There were six paintings on the wall.

We all wanted to crawl into the one whose center was obliterated.

Whose center was blackness.

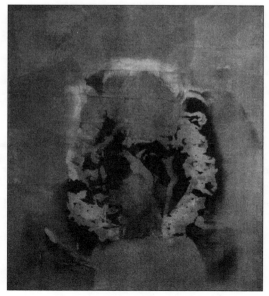

DIRK DE BRUYCKER - *Events of Lust*
asphalt, gesso, oil pigments on canvas 1996

J O A N   L O G G H E

Summer Mysteries

Grasshoppers the size of clocks. Grasshoppers
riding lizards and playing handball.
Grasshoppers the size of mangoes gobbling starlings.

Starlings are shot for robbing the bluebirds'
nest. Starlings are dropping down chimneys
playing violins in the hearths. In the holiest
churchyard a young girl with her grandfather's guns,
popping birds like iridescent popcorn into death's mouth.

Young girls the size of old Oldsmobiles. Young
girls riding horses and playing hopscotch on
the roofs of prisons. Young girls with hair
like sky looms dreaming of their mates who are
red sunsets on feet transplanted from Cuba.

Sunsets the size of spaniels. Sunsets riding
the Jemez mountains and playing harpsichord.
Sunsets with roses in their hair and vacuous
expressions, yearning for another lifetime,
a festival of death and rebirth in their teeth

like Kama Sutras for enhancing the pleasure
of naked moments. Stunning the starlings,
causing them to drop, their bellies full
of grasshoppers, out of the night sky, down
the chimneys of young girls, soot for centuries.

JACK BUTLER

The Truth about the Vampires

Jody Nightwood is a medical doctor turned dream researcher in Santa Fe. She is conducting a study, using herself as one of six subjects. She lives with a couple of cats, Static and Blind Lemon. As the passage opens, she is in the lab, dreaming.

The moon was everywhere. Moonlight on snow.

When the moon was like this, you could become a ghost. You could float, you could pass through walls. You could run to infinity naked. You were a cat let out in the back yard by a sleepy woman. Let out to prowl under the moon while she stumbled back to bed. Worked her head into her dark pillow. Slept again, with her mind full of moonlight. Moonlight on snow.

She looked for her tracks. If she could see the tracks, she could tell who she was. Blind Lemon's tracks were big, like a leopard's. Static's were three-colored, calico. But there were no tracks. The snow was clean. Of course. She was a ghost; she couldn't leave tracks.

To be a ghost was to be naked. She felt her nipples rising. Naked in the snow, you would be cold. And there were cats in the trees. If you had no clothes, they could eat you. Ghost cats, high above, waiting to leap. Hungry, hissing, their voices lost in the wind.

The reason she wasn't cold was the light. What people didn't understand, when the moonlight hit the snow, it changed. When it bounced off the snow, then it was microwaves, so your body stayed warm. Sunlight wouldn't do that, just the full moon.

But people could see you. Nothing but snow and moonlight. Nowhere to go to, nowhere to hide. They could see between your legs, they could see everything.

It was the style this season, she had forgotten. Instead of skin-tight ski-suits, you went naked. Everybody was doing it, so she was ok. What a relief.

You didn't need clothes because the skiing kept you warm. It wasn't radiant heat from the snow. That was nonsense about the microwaves; that was a stupid rumor. Anybody who knew science could tell you better. You were burning calories, you warmed up from the inside.

She had never felt so nimble on her skis. She was naked, and lighter than air. Floating from ski to ski, transparent, her shadow the shadow of traveling smoke. When she hit a jump, she could hang, using her poles to slow her down, like drag-chutes, like wings.

It was Big Tesuque. She had hiked it before, but never skied it. It was crazy to ski Big Tesuque. So many trees to run into. All those edges and ledges and slopes. Crazy to ski Big Tesuque at night, and all alone. But she was fine, she was a feather traveling fast.

The hush of her skis. Shush. Shush. Shush. Falling so fast and free and unafraid.

She knew it was midnight, because the moon was high overhead and full. She was proud of herself for knowing what it meant. She was naked and she couldn't remember how she had gotten here, but she knew how to ski, and she knew it was midnight.

The trees went by, black trees. Flickering by like windows from a train. But they weren't moving, you were. You had to remember that. She wanted the lighted windows, the people in them. She wanted the warm safe rooms with the good people. But the train was pulling out and they were falling behind and she couldn't go back. She sobbed into her pillow.

She ripped across Aspen Vista and launched herself. A herd of Borzoi filling the trail, milling about. She had to jump to miss them. High in the air over the fallaway creek. You saw them jumping on tv, you forgot you didn't know how to do it yourself. Falling through midnight weightless, your stomach spinning with fear. To smash on the rocks of Big Tesuque.

This was why she was a ghost. She had killed herself making this jump. They thought it was suicide. There they are, the searchers, finding her body naked and broken. Lonely,

... she wasn't dead after all.

and so she jumped. It made her angry, the gossip. She would never do that, never, no matter how depressed. It was the dogs, the goddamn dogs. She had had to jump to miss the Borzoi.

She wanted to set them straight, but ghosts can't talk. It made her so mad.

She was looking into her sepulchre, her black marble vault. No, not the sepulchre, but the chapel itself: Thorncrown. There it was, tilted along the slope below, its doors wide open, its smooth floor waiting. She could land, she wasn't dead after all.

She would be able to tell them that it wasn't suicide.

She caught the floor of the chapel just right, an Olympian swooping to tangency.

A massive jerk at her quads. Vision of herself crippled, knees blown out.
Crutches instead of ski-poles. Hobbling along the aisle of the chapel,
stumbling along step by step to her punishment, her funeral. Her coffin up
front, in the darkness.

Do you see your father, Baby, standing in the shadows?

It was Pop, bald round mustache-grinning Pop. Stepping into a spotlight
in front of the casket, his strong arms out to catch her, oh thank God. But his
teeth were long and white. It wasn't a mustache. It was teeth. Long white
teeth. Something was wrong with his eyes. He was young and tall and
beautiful, and she wanted to take him to bed.

The eyes of a cat. Green eyes. Showing his long white fangs. Vampire.

He came toward her. He would eat her now. Her skis were tangled, she
couldn't run. Warm breath on her back, her naked back. He caught her wrists
from behind. They buzzed where he gripped them. His long body against her.
He would penetrate, make her burst into blood. Her wrists buzzed. The skis
were tangled. The slide of his wet bloody body, buzzing with contact. His
hands moving across her skin, delivering arcs of static.

Suddenly it was all clear. They could kill you with electrical shocks,
the vampires. Like eels. It wasn't blood they wanted, it was your electricity.

And nobody knew, nobody in the world knew.

She had to wake up and warn them.

She had to wake up and tell the world the truth.

E.A. MARES

Hydrogen Jukebox Series

Sketches after Charlie "Bird" Parker

1.
Jamming in a chile house

Parker works over "Cherokee"
reaches, stretches out for
that chile house note

and all the Beats
try jamming the words
into off key USA

America of the death penalty
America of the NRA
America of jails stuffed with its own druggies
America of the shunned insane on street corners
America where no one trusts nobody nowhere

no time oh it is a lone note
here where the wind blows
through   down   and up
the alto saxophone

the "Bird's" music wings
fly in that chile house
between 139th and 140th always
on seventh avenue always
and it is December always

and the stone-faced wooden Indian
stares at you, Europa

this too is you, Europa.
You are also an immigrant here.

E.A. MARES

At Concordia Cemetery, El Paso

in memory of Galit

At Concordia Cemetery, El Paso,
near John Wesley Harding's grave
and the Baptist Reverend Reed's,
I think of you. A butterfly

flutters its wings. That small effect
makes an unpredictable wave,
weathers the world and drives a straw
through a tree or sways the sunflower

bending to the pressure of the sun.
You were, you are, that impulse,
a zigzag flight to your own beat
across the stars. The Chinese

on the other side of a dividing wall
sleep beneath their solemn stones.
Gunslinger, preacher, the Chinese
tell their tales to the common loam.

I hear no song in the border sky.
Silence sings where you have been.
I try to remember your voice
and I hear the chorus of the wind.

MEI-MEI BERSSENBRUGGE

Susie, Kiki, Annie

My project with them developed a gentle momentum.

The lovely vulnerability of their situation was engendered
by an unassuming spirit of play and togetherness.

On my way to work, I passed several family members who
had been standing in a group, for some time.

I'm concerned with the intimacy to which each must
concede in the situation.

I ask each one to tell me his or her thoughts, and I try to
remember them all.

My sister had just fixed the motorcycle of her friend Tom,
and now she is waiting for him.

Among them a fox turns to look at me, as if in nature,
but she has drawn it, and it's symbolic.

What can something that looks like one sister encompass,
on a different level if she were not my sister, or if I had no
knowledge of the relation?

In the absence of a loving standard, how can her
appearance be redeemed?

As if a projector in dark were projecting that line of light
under the door.

The energy between the image believed to be real and
the discovery of the strategem that construes it for pure
appearance was continually dispersed along the web
of these interrelationships.

There is, on one hand, a stringent, physical link with
concrete existence, while what goes on inside her is close to
the freedom of my own powers of imagination, so strong as
to appear as deliberate loss of imagination.

As if the fox and its fur were an open structure that runs
empty like a funnel.

One fox enters the world.

It does not appear to be an image.

There's apt to be a relationship in which I am involved,
walking between the two animals asleep in late light, like
blood.

My sister sketches foxes and cats while she waits for Tom.

I'm interested in the realism of the fox, while she sees it
as actually behind the scenes.

The two foxes watch me.

In a sense, my not understanding is shared experience.

Lately I've been interested in failing to make a thing
exciting, equating the physical act of walking from tree
to tree with understanding.

I try to speak to her in a way in which she might take me
seriously and answer back.

I do not ask her to tell me that I've been an inspiration
to her, all these years.

Our situation is an image of her gathering up white toy
horses from beside candles on the reflecting pool.

I stand there for a long time, then take a toy horse out of
my pocket.

I tell her about it as if she were also a lover of toy horses,
but she is not, as I well know.

The way in which I share happiness with her as a matter
of course gives me a sense of guilt, because she does not
feel the happiness.

She isn't what I think she is.

There's a coalescence of the theatrical that inundates, my
story of family life from the past, trying to push an
incident into a space, so it becomes deeper.

I speak more slowly than real speech, at the speed of an
old film.

All the animals in the story, who eventually die, are
comprised of tiny lines scratched into reddish ground, as if
scratched into the dark.

The dark is the gap between the slow-moving images.

For example, the white of an eye is scratched away, but the
pupil is ink left intact.

Slowing speech provides a gap for mental processes to fill
in, memory, anticipation, as when any of the small animals
turn toward you.

Many of whom appear still sleepy, ground squirrel, cat,
fawn.

EMMI WHITEHORSE - *Engulfed by Clouds*
oil, chalk on paper on canvas 1992

PHILLIP FOSS

The Theory of Play

The movement of the stone
is tangential

to those movements
of cloud or

antique
structure of debt

simple act
of transfusion an other's

lungs are inflated
and an aerial soul

is captured
in one's reptilian

memory no more
than one player selective

memory and mutable
history diseased

mind does not
engage that same

reality as those of a blue
heron women

are forbidden
to participate

due to tendency
to abbreviate

violence men
are disallowed

due to inability
to distinguish

the value
of violence-degree no

others shall be
engaged the field

is astronomy
"nothing"

falls a dead beast
is identical

to a living
persona thus foreign

coins are coveted
and raptor wing

feathers are planted
in the floors

of caves appropriation
of Beethoven etc

by impotent
mathematicians

should be appreciated
by those unhearing

mathematics
which determines

the quantity of matter
which accumulates

around the empty
soul

of a geode purpose
of living is to accrete

then shed
energy a cloak

of hummingbird
feathers names

for states
of awareness trivial

ecstasy objectless
anger popular

submersion somnambulant
grammar poetics

of opposition
is degenerative

because it posits
an enemy

(erosion
of indifference)

where there is only
a brief dissipating

shadow or necessity
of creating

incendiary weapons
to prove

history
is ethics

of mutation abstraction is
perceived as a corporal

body this is why people
enjoy killing

an empirical fact similar
to bipolar disorder

is that a collared
lizard always absorbs light.

Speaking with

Yellow Robe

*O*ne of the most accomplished Native American playwrights in the United States today, William S. Yellow Robe Jr., lives and works in Santa Fe, New Mexico where he teaches theater classes at the Institue of American Indian Arts. Influenced by Shakespeare and Eugene O'Neill, Yellow Robe Jr., an Assiniboine (part of the Dakota branch of the Sioux Nation), was born and raised in Montana on one of the last remaining Assiniboine reservations in North America. The only other Assiniboine reservation is Stony Reserve in Canada. Yellow Robe spoke to **Frank** Regional Editor Arthur Sze about his life and work.

Frank: *With more than 30 plays to your credit, tell us how you first got interested in playwriting?*

Yellow Robe Jr.: Well, I started writing when I was very young. I had been a very bad student. In fact, I remember when I was in second grade being picked up by the deputy county sheriff for truancy. I just couldn't stay in school. In sixth grade I finally met a women who was very kind, very gentle. She encouraged me to write. So I wrote my first play in sixth grade.

I think the real turning point in my life, as far as playwriting goes, was when I was in the 11th grade. The Montana Repertory Theater, a professional touring company, came on the reservation and presented Eugene O'Neill's, *A Moon for the Misbegotten*. And it was that production that really turned me around. Also, I had a chance to help tear down the set after. It put a hook in me. And so it was hard to go into other forms. At one point I wanted to be a journalism major. I worked for the tribal newspaper, the *Wotani Wowapie*. I was also a photographer. But these things were so condensed, so structured that there was really no freedom in it. The freedom you have in playwriting is enormous. There are no levels or limits. That's what really appealed to me.

Frank: *In 1974 you left the reservation and entered the Institute of American Indian Arts where you first learned directing from Roland Meinholtz and began your career in theater. Writing plays is one thing, getting them produced is another. What is your opinion of the latter?*

Yellow Robe Jr.: Although most of the plays have aired as either dramatic readings or productions, strangely enough I still haven't had a production of my work on my own home reservation in Montana. In fact, my career didn't take off until I left Montana.

The most difficult thing in being produced, or even in receiving a staged reading, is the economics. It's very hard to have original work produced in this country because of the price tag that goes with it. It's hard to raise ten or thirty thousand dollars to mount a professional production. That's the downfall about being in America. Art takes a beating. There is so little money available for new work. For a Native playwright, where you have a market that is flooded with plays about Native people by non-Natives, it is even more difficult. So you have one obstacle after another, almost interlaced. It's hard. Once you break one you realize you're up against another. I've never complained about it, but when I was teaching at the Institute of American Indian Arts, I always reminded my students if you write a play you're always faced with the question of how you are going to get it produced? That has always been the big question.

Frank: *Are you describing the norm for unknown playwrights in America today or is it particularly difficult for Native writers?*

Yellow Robe Jr.: It is rather grim because the work of Native people is set in the category of what I like to call the "historical plays" or the "magical mystery tour," where you find yourself exploiting your own Native spirituality to get a play produced. It's hard to produce an image of contemporary Native people in contemporary times. People want to see either the angry young Native man or the mystical, magical Native elder or, if you will, almost like the African-American "couch plays" where the only thing that happens is in kitchens. So you are limited as to style, form, and even content for that matter. Even with the theater company I've formed, *Wakiknabe*, the economics have already claimed two of the people that started with me. Maybe I won't end up getting plays produced in this country. But this is an art form that has chosen me. I'm going to reach a point where I can't push any further. I'll hit the wall. And unfortunately it'll be in my own homeland. That's what makes it even more bitter, that this is my homeland and I can't get produced!

The Native person has to face the question: are you exploiting your people and creating propaganda or are you actually telling the truth? There are some things in my work that Native people respond to by saying, "don't air our dirty laundry out to the white people." That misses the point of my work. My point is to address the issues that we face, not to exploit the problems, to provide a vehicle for these problems to be addressed. Also, my feeling is that there comes a time when people have to change. As an artist you are constantly changing. I think Native people have to face that. Unfortunately, in the Native world it's very hard to change because there is such deep repression and alienation from this country that people don't want to address. There are some that want to pull those chains off and can't because they don't have the real means to do it. That's the real tragedy. Art can be the means but even in artistic exploration people are so afraid of stepping out. I've tried to start other Native theater companies and have been involved with Native theater companies across the country. Everybody wants to talk about "the system" and yet they hide within "the system." They use it as a weapon. It's two-fold, two-bladed. They use it as a weapon and at the same time they use it for protection. Just like the blood quantum.

Frank: *Maybe you could explain what the blood quantum is.*

Yellow Robe Jr.: It is an institutionalized system of Native recognition practiced by the U.S. federal government in categorizing Native peoples. It's a pedigree for human beings. Native people tend to say that those who do not make the blood quantum should be excluded but at the same time they complain that it's a form of repression. They use it to protect and they use it to attack. It's really tragic.

Frank: *You're a member of the Assiniboine tribe. Do you also feel American or Native American?*

Yellow Robe Jr.: I feel like an Assiniboine and not an American.

Frank: *Are there Assiniboine traditions that are strong in your life?*

Yellow Robe Jr.: Very few. Colonialism has decimated Native culture. Its effect has been devastating and makes it difficult to learn what has been destroyed. It's like looking at the Mona Lisa after acid has been poured on it: you have to *imagine* what the Mona Lisa might have looked like before the acid burned it.

Frank: *You said earlier that playwriting chose you. I'm interested in exploring that a little bit. You also write poetry and will soon publish a volume called* Pictures of Faith *(Platitudes). What is it about playwriting that poetry or prose cannot do for you? Is it the characters or action on stage or ...?*

Yellow Robe Jr.: Although I tell students all the time that writers must be versatile so as not to develop tunnel vision, for me the theater possesses a sense of touch that's vital and unique. What amazes me is the fact that in playwriting the characters are there almost in a three dimensional state. You can reach an audience emotionally right then and there. You can stimulate them intellectually right there at that presentation. I've not really found that power in poetry or fiction. When you really have the chance to construct your meaning or your message or your love, and present that to an audience, the results can be amazing. The audience is there to experience it with you, with your actors or your director on stage at that given moment. I couldn't find that in other forms of writing. Also, theater is a way of sharing and giving with the Native communities that we play to. It is the best gift we can give.

As far as playwriting choosing me ... I've experimented with lots of forms. I used to play guitar, trombone, cornet and tuba. I've tried oil painting, acrylic, pastels, charcoal, clay. But with playwriting there is an energy that I have not experienced elsewhere. Playwriting starts out very singularly; you're by yourself, but once you get involved with a group of actors and you start a production, you become a community. The spiritual and emotional stress builds. The devastating point is when the production takes off and the play is up, and you've got an audience there ... then it's like coming off a high. A post-production syndrome hits and then you want another one. You set it up ... I find myself taking a break for a week and then I'm right back in it again. It's something like an addiction. And I've had addictions. I know what addictions are and theater is a good one. I don't think I could give it up.

W I L L I A M   S .   Y E L L O W   R O B E   J R .

from The Pendleton Blanket

The Pendleton Blanket *is the struggle of two old friends trying to keep the younger generation of young men around them from destroying themselves. In the following scene, Kenny Tassel, a nephew of Petey First Hand, has stolen a pendleton blanket and has teamed up with his drinking buddy, Joe Hurst, to sell the blanket.*

ACT TWO /SCENE TWO

(KENNY stands outside of the bar. His hair is messed up. His glasses are gone.)

KENNY
"Blue, blue, blue, blue eyes crying in the rain. Blue eyes, don't you make my brown eyes blue, blue ..."

(Takes a deep breath.)

One more time! One more damn time, damn it!

(JOE enters and is carrying a bottle in a brown paper sack. He holds a cigarette.)

Ladies and Gentle-men, Live and in personable!

JOE
What the hell are you screaming about?

KENNY
What? What?

JOE
Damn! We can hear you over the juke box inside. You going nuts on me, or what?

KENNY
No, no, just singing.

JOE
Well shut up!

KENNY
I sing good. Listen-ahem, "Move your sweet lips, a little closer ..."

JOE
To my dick! Now shut up! The bartender will think we're already drunk and call the cops on us.

KENNY
No he won't! No he won't! He's my buddy. Those guys try to take me away — I'll kick some ass. They won't mess with me.

JOE
Will you behave! Christ. You have your drink. Let's go and check out that place.

(Starts to walk away.)

KENNY
What place? Wait, wait up, we can't go Joe.

JOE
Why not?

KENNY
We can't go — my blanket.

JOE
(Laughing.)

You dumb drunken shit! Don't you remember? We sold it! That's how you got your bottle. Christ! Do you think they just gave you that bottle because of your good looks?

KENNY
Yeah. No wait. Wait Joe. We sold it?

JOE
Yeah. We sold it in town. You bought a bottle of whiskey for you and me. And you bought me a pack of cigs. Remember?

KENNY
No, no, when did this happen, hey?

JOE
Christ. Just a little while ago.

KENNY
Who did we sell it to?

JOE
Ant'y Pearl. Your Ant'y Pearl bought it. Now let's go to where you got it in the first place and let's see what else there is.

(Kenny sings.)

Quit trying to sing and let's go.

(Kenny sings.)

Damn. Let's go Kenny.

KENNY
No. I gotta' get that blanket back.

JOE
You promised me you would show me where you got it in the first place. Now let's go. Here, have another drink.

(Hands Kenny the bottle and tries to pick him up.)

If you don't want to go with me Kenny, just tell me. That's all you have to do. Tell me where you got the blanket from.

KENNY
I don't know.

(Joe slaps him.)

JOE
You little lying shit. New tell me where you got the blanket. GODDAMN YOU!

(Kenny slams the bottle across Joe's face and knocks Joe to the ground.)

KENNY
Christ. You don't have to yell — damn. I heard you.

(Looks at Joe.)

Well? Should we book?

(No reply from Joe.)

Hey? You want to go with me and get the blanket back?

(No reply.)

Hey, bro'? Hey!

(No response.)

I guess I can do it myself.

(Starts to walk away and then stops.)

Wait. Who did you say has it? Ant'y Pearl?

(Crosses to Joe and uses his foot and turns Joe over, on Joe's back.)

Heavy bastard. Christ. You're bleeding, hey.

(No response.)

Oh damn. Money.

(Looks at Joe.)

You got any money left?

(Searches Joe's pockets.)

No-damn-wait. Yep! You do.

(Takes out the bills and counts them).

I don't know Joe, this isn't enough. I don't think it is. Maybe I can trade her something. You got anything else.

(Joe's mouth opens and Kenny looks into it.)

Hey! Yeah, that'll do it.

(He reaches into Joe's mouth).

Gold!

(Blackout.)

C H R I S T I N E   H E M P

One Woman's Eclipse

No time to look at that moon
shining in his glass. When she stepped
down the wooden stairs and felt
her way to the car, his voice
mooning from the open window
covering her heart. How could she come
into his orbit again? Beer man, boozy
dancer, knuckles of steel?

She wants to be the earth's shadow.
The ring around her finger grows smaller
and she pushes against the dark.
Who has time for moons tonight when
home is farther away than craters and dust?
When she'd still give every planet
to be broken by his hand?

KEITH WILSON

Still Life

Three old New Mexican men
hunched back on their bootheels
smoke spitstuck brown Durhams
the white circle of paper, black
bull centered upon it, hangs from
each pocket like a badge, a coat
of arms

       — blue smoke curling up
to get lost in sky. Behind them
the rough wind & rain washed adobe
the straw yellow, jagged. In the clear
air the mountains rise up pale blue too.

These old men watch the mountains
not each other, their stiff hats
hard above their eyes, they watch
the changing mountains, grow older.

KEITH WILSON

The Day of the Calf

The dark grasses of the mesa stand hot & stiff
with late summer. The draws fill with cattle
lowing, questioning, pushed along by cowhands
who know too well the work that awaits this drive.

                Ahead, the branding
fires, we squat around them, smoking.
One or two boys, uneasy, wipe their hands
on their Levis, watch the nearing cattle.

The first calf is cut out, runs ahead, is cut
back again by the cowsmart pony, is roped,
deftly thrown: his bellows, heard close
are deafening. His tongue lolls, thick slobbers
about his lips. He's pigtailed now. A man
walks quickly forward, holds horncutters. Snip.
Snip. The two budding horns fly off, jets of blood.

The other man takes his pocket knife, reaches down
slashes the sac, pulls the slippery balls out
cuts them free, the calf's eyes rolling with
shock, twisting in its agony as tar is daubed
heavily into the bloody cavity by the boy.

                The calf, freed, rises
unsteadily, wanders around, yelling deep
in his chest for his mother and the boy wipes
his tarstiff hands on his Levis, moves toward
the next calf which is already down.

KEITH WILSON

The Cactus Wren

sketch, North of Tucson

builds her nest
in the Saguaro trunk.

I see her sharp eye
watching me from within

her green hole. I wonder
how I look to her today?

KEITH WILSON

In a Japanese Garden

— Kyoto, 1953

for Cid Corman

no moon.

our small light
holds the center
of all darkness

even now.

CHERYL YELLOWHAWK

A Letter

I am a satanic ritual abuse survivor. Words cannot describe the horror and terror of satanic ritual abuse, nor do words give justice to the painful, exhausting, frightening, isolating and expensive recovery process of integrating the body, mind and spirit. The abuse occurred in the first five years of my life. In order to survive satanism I split into twenty six different personalities each possessing their own eyesight, voice, hearing, functions, capabilities and flashbacks of mental and physical torture. Somehow I was given the inner strength to survive the first years of my life, to become a multiple and to spend the last twelve years recovering and processing memories through my artwork, and more recently through bodywork. During the recovery process I lost my family, my children, my husband, my career, my home and my community. But I had a responsibility to myself and all of my inner children. And I was determined to integrate and lead a healthy respectful life. I would not allow myself to become a lost number on the street or in an institution. I had spent ten years integrating my mind through art, reading and writing, but in order to fully integrate, I needed to live in a body that could feel and know the difference between pleasure and pain.

Shortly before my mother died in February 1985 I knew that I could no longer function as a cardiac rehab nurse. I gave up my position and took up painting. For twelve years I have produced the artwork which has led me through my wounded past and has brought me into my healthy human condition. The art demonstrates the power of the spirit to know the truth. It is sacred. There are over 250 images that were created by my different personalities. They worked in different media: oil, pastel, ink, magic markers. Art was my lifeline to the soul. The works show a distinct separation into the spirit world in order to process the memories of my body and mind. The chronological progression of images leads one through the personal despair of losing touch with this reality and with the socially acceptable ego which wants to remain looking "ok", that is, producing pretty pictures, but the memories of satanic ritual abuse, sexual abuse, and sexual re-victimization throughout life continued to emerge.

The memories laid somewhat dormant behind the amnesiac barriers of my personalities (except for the relentless nightmares and confusion of pain with sex all of my life) until twelve years ago when my mother died in a car accident. With her death came an onslaught of grief, confusion, depression and the release of subconscious memories and flashbacks. At the time I had held a position of respect as a nurse in our small community. But with the intrusion of memories, triggers and flashbacks during the daylight hours, I had to make the decision to give up my career. I began to recognize that I was losing my short-term memory and I was obsessed with the images flickering through my mind. This was more than processing grief or a mid-life crisis. I was being pulled too far inward. Since I was determined to be productive in my life I retired and took up painting.

With the shock of my mother's death I was thrown into the chaos of my unremembered childhood. It was like a newsreel from Hell, and farther and deeper into depression and confusion I went. But I held onto my one source of strength. Art became my *raison d'être*. I had the desire to create beauty although beauty did not seem to exist between the brush and the canvas. I forced myself to attend art classes until the memories flooded every canvas.

My first images were those of still life, landscape, and people. Harmless subject matter but then my artwork dramatically changed when one of the assignments in a figure drawing class was to draw a self-image without consulting a mirror or a photograph. A strange sensation occurred immediately as I began to draw. I produced an image of myself wearing a Jackie Kennedy hair cut, the way that I had worn my hair in high school in the sixties. I knew something was wrong. I could not imagine why I had depicted myself in that time period since it was then 1985. At that point my paintings moved from the earthly reality of still life and landscape representations to sources of unknown origin. A bridge had been developed

CHERYL YELLOWHAWK
"I Am Human" *pastel 1995*

115

between the conscious and the unconscious parts of my being. An avenue now existed between the past and the present.

My artwork moved through the hands of my inner personalities one after the other. I hid the abuse images and the only works that I accepted as mine were the spiritual images. Then for seven years my adrenaline and anxiety levels raced throughout my being until a part of me could not contain itself any longer. Then that repressed part would pick up a pen, a brush, a crayon, a magic marker or clay and force the doors open into that state of mind which had lived in continual fear and panic. With the outpourings of emotion on the canvas I re-lived the horror which my inner personalities had survived.

In the summer of 1991 I was being psychically pulled across the country. I had packed my van and headed out. I did not know where I was going. I was scared. I lived in the woods until I realized that I needed help. I could not outrun the terror and the turmoil on the inside.

In 1991, having finally sought help, I began to try to understand what I had been painting for seven years. In August I entered a rehabilitation center. My life had gone out of control. And I had become extremely alienated from my self and from my family. The memories I had painted out for seven years had finally begun to seep into some conscious part of me. I could no longer pretend that I was only a spiritual being. My artwork had become only abuse images and the world of the spirit. The spiritual artwork was a place of safety and protection that still resided within me. And it had made me feel special but there was no way to escape from the mounting fear I held every time I picked up a brush or a pen. For a month at the rehab center I had found a safe place to begin piecing together the flashbacks. But my treatment time was up according to the insurance company and so I went home to sign my divorce papers, because I was no longer a "fit wife or mother."

My time and money was limited. I had to figure out how to become functional once more. By Thanksgiving of 1991 after running out of insurance for the rehab center I was alone in my small apartment trying to make sense out of the chaos I inhabited. I lived in a cheap apartment with my art supplies, and there I worked on integrating myself. I had an art therapist who encouraged me to remember and she believed in me even while I was a two-year-old scribbling and coloring in my color books.

CHERYL YELLOWHAWK - "Reborn"
ceramic 1994

The amnesia barriers between the inner selves eroded as they unveiled themselves to me one by one and each released violent memories while my physical body took up the pain and terrors or abduction, drugging, repeated rapes, starvation, enemas, physical and mental torture, being held captive in a cage in a basement, being used in satanic ceremonies, beaten, buried, hung, electric shocked during sex and brain-washed into a type of entity that holds no conscience. During the first five years of my life my mind was shattered and I became a *multiple* of twenty-six personalities and my spirit escaped beyond this earthly realm into a dimension free from man's infliction of power and pain over another human being.

The recovery process from satanic ritual abuse and multiplicity means I had to re-live the mental, spiritual, emotional and physical torture that a *multiple* denies is happening at the time of the abuse. And the mind splits into quivering fragments of neurons that remain encapsulated in time, re-living the torture day and night. And with the recovery process comes the endurance of breaking the programming to return to the cult or to suicide. When the mind feels somewhat whole then the recovery of the physical body is in order. Physiological damage has been incurred by all inner systems of the body, not only the multiplicity of the mind but the nervous system, the endocrines and the immune and musculo-skeletal systems. They also have been damaged. The body and mind had not grown normally or in unison with the natural developmental process. After I realized that I had integrated my mind with art and had re-educated my inner children to read, write and multiply, I sought help for the physical body. That was 1995. For me, this was the last part of the healing process. Vitamins, minerals, good nutrition, massage, shiatsu, homeopathy, osteopathy and chiro-practic have all helped me become healthy once more. Ultimately, I graduated as a massage therapist from the highly respected Scherer Academy of Natural Healing in Santa Fe, New Mexico.

I have overcome a world of insanity, evil, greed, power and viciousness that should not exist on this earth. It is the type of premeditated murder and mind control that exists to destroy love and the ability to determine right from wrong. But I have fought with all of my heart to find my way back to the light of good. "Spiritual Healing: A Shamanic Experience" is a testimony I offer others to be able to share the healing process. I am grateful that I have fully recovered and I have found a world full of life and love from which I paint.

Cheryl Yellowhawk

MIRIAM SAGAN

Pyrocantha

White horse in a field of sunflowers
At dusk, a line of ants crossing back and forth

Between two openings in the earth
Look! Our children point — the finish line!

A red dragonfly lights
On your naked wrist

You hold still, betrothed to something
With this bloodstone

"Your firethorn has berries"
I say, orange fruit against adobe wall

"That's the second time today," you say
"Someone has said firethorn,

Its name is pyrocantha."
We squeeze lime into vodka

The end of summer
Inebriates the edges of the pond

Cottonwoods barely yellow
The children think they see

A burglar's shadow against the wood shed.
By candlelight, slightly stoned

On reminiscence I'll tell you
Pyrocantha is just the Latin

For orange berried
Firethorn.

MIRIAM SAGAN

Esopus Lighthouse

Sand banks along the shore
Hudson, wide and deceptively
Shallow here —
Flats of water hyacinths
Half a dozen white swans
Scattered in a romantic fashion
Mosquitoes bite my ankle
Later today we'll listen
To Bartok's violin duos
Written as student pieces —
Mosquito Song and
Sorrow.

Esopus Lighthouse once lit the river
Marking where depth turned to danger
Less water is the problem here, not
Too much water.
The tower is red and round
Might house Rapunzel
Letting down her long hair
Out of a slit window.
Bartok's other piece
Is Fairy Tale.

What about sorrow?
What piece is missing
From the jigsaw of swan and water
You're dead in the dream
And you're still
Dead when I wake
From trying to explain to you
Why I'm with another man.

At the museum, the stolen
Vermeers haunt me
It's gone, that perfect painting
With its squares of light
There's silence in the music after all
At the end as well as at the start.

MIRIAM SAGAN

Silver Lake

Yesterday, we canoed on Silver Lake
My sister-in-law paddled us out
On water that began to reflect perfectly
Clouds in a sky just turning pink.

The houses came down to their docks
Like old women viewing a famous painting
We unpacked the picnic basket
And ate bluefish pâté and Linzer tortes.

One of the last lines in our notebook
I came across after your death:
I want a canoe and the strength to lift it.
Tonight, past midnight, I sit out on lawn chairs
Hold hands with my lover
Beneath the meteors of the Perseid.

The newspapers announce
There was life on Mars
One-celled animals fossilized in stone
You would have liked that
As you enjoyed evidence of anything
Fabulous in a moving universe.

I saw a falling star skip
Burn twice like a stone skimmed in Silver Lake
You know, I was a little afraid of that canoe
Afraid it would never return to shore
Afraid it would.

MARCIA SOUTHWICK

Portrait of the Live Poet

A collage of lines and images taken from eighteen poems written by members of the Santa Fe Live Poets Society.

1.
You've quit listening to the evening news.
The night's personal revolution begins.
You skirt the raging boulevards,
your breath sucked in. You long
for little things: a sympathetic shiver
in the rose garden or some transparent,
unlocatable fire. What if sanity sends you an invoice?
Your heavy briefcase clunks beside you.
A woman approaches, hands you her business card.
But you must be careful with the ordinary.
Remember how you clung to trees for safety?
You haunt the narrow streets,
as the nightingales sing in the rarified air.
You become a different thing, an exotic hybrid bloom.
And yet the walls are burning. The toaster
is on fire, and the red geranium that blooms in the kitchen
still loves you. You are cruel, senseless in the extreme,
like starlight that falls in lightning bolts.
It is strange to seal letters with wax,
strange to honor your wondrous nostalgia,
and your crisp new writing tablet, strange to see
the urban sprawl, the city lights broadcasting our sameness,
but not so strange to polish your shoes. You are made of more
than dust and rage, or impeccable Italian clothes.

2.
Your black belt in innuendos is getting you nowhere.
You want the sleep of bleached bones, or a simple life:
your old baggy pants hanging low, breakfast and a walk.
You want to fold down the crisp white sheets, and drift again
into tiled courtyards scented by the blossoms of a thousand orange groves.
You'd like to turn inside out and dissolve into a flock of mockingbirds
sitting on a telephone wire. But such things are impossible,
like rescuing a musical note lost from the mouth of a trombone.
So you splash a bit of ink, write a poem or two, give a sympathetic nod
to the passing minutes, and meander into some distant landscape
in which the graying sky lands on everyone's desk by fax.
Every now and then you bring back a relic from your dream-life:
a sunset which symbolizes our differences sinking from view.
Your breath is caught ... by what? Tonight you'll strum your guitar –
much easier than conquering your embarrassing stutter.
It's a matter of words: Gray – the smell of burning. Yellow:
the hands of the clock. Or of lying on your back looking up.
The clouds can't stop you from forgetting your childhood friends.
A distant cousin drops from memory – her large garden,
some birds, a swing, and trees. You've forgotten
the pattern on your shirt. Then you see yourself in the mirror
and know that when you die, it won't break.
Where does time go when it runs out? It hides in your veins,
in your heart as shiny as a tin star.

KATHLEEN WEST

Where There's Smoke

Before he leaves, he lights a cigarette and draws her close, hands spanning her back. Smoke curls over her shoulder, around her side. When they make love, she dies in pleasure, limbs so entwined with his, she cannot tell where one body stops, another begins. She treasures this moment, the clarity of the disarrangement, the endorphins released like red lanterns, gorgeous and promising against black sky. The wind carries them into a single ember, one more glow-in-the-dark reflector. She begins to squirm in this everlasting farewell embrace, the unromantic smell of tar and nicotine, the lingering suspense of the cigarette. Something cringes at the base of her spine. She cannot endure. He finds this erotic.

They snort amphetamines, ground into the counter-top with her chapstick container. She has no knives, no mirror, only a square of heavy-duty aluminum foil for the chapstick-resistant chunk. He holds his lighter beneath the foil; she controls the cut-off plastic straw. As soon as smoke appears, she will inhale. It is safe, he says. In the last five years, she has seen him seven times, a few hours, a week-end, whatever lies between. Their relationship is progressive, a Red Guard flicking belt against thigh, waiting for the requisite passion to flare from hand to buckle and flail leather and metal against skin. It is the first escapade of the latest New Order. The weapons are accessories, the skin tones escharotic and see — how cunningly executed the match of the fabric.

Braunstein/Quay Gallery, San Francisco. Photo: Herbert Lotz

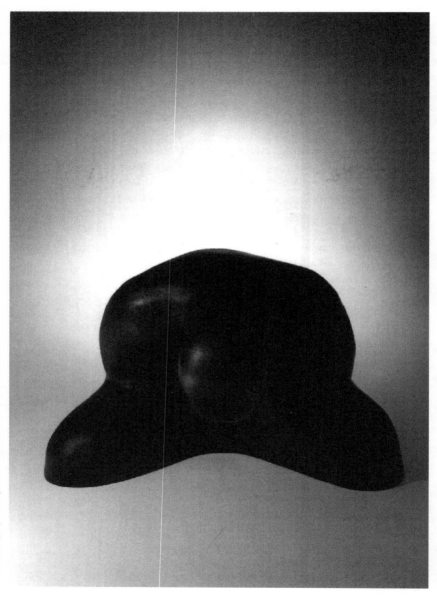

DAVID ANDERSON - *Bowing, Black Robe*
bronze, 1996

Allene Lapides Gallery, Santa Fe. Photo: Herbert Lotz

DAVID ANDERSON - *Higher Alertness (Bowl)*
cast iron, gold leaf, enamel, 1993

SHERWIN BITSUI

Bone Dust

this season
starved my bones
into calcium chalk

tracing my outstretched arms
     reaching limbs
     which pinched cocaine from television snow

every hour smoked its swiveling tail
Frieda Kahlo
stroked my palms

I panted
and asked God
     if he teethed as a child
     or if his fangs bled like mine

he rang
     the black telephone
     after the noon sun

          my arms: drying oars in a canyon stream

calendar crackling within my veins
     when I danced into blue television light
unsung
     looking over Dinetah
with milk film orbs
          through scotch taped trailer windows

paper bag skin
     chopped tongue
          bloodless fingers
          cannot be scraped away by paper metal

     the wind blows bone chalk
     over my body
          drawn running

G R E G   G L A Z N E R

What is Shown

Still it appears almost daily,
not things, and not
of things —
        Allowing the slants
of light at nine, the rippling
of lace panels she arranged
so the bodiless shapes of sewn roses
could drift down
        to the floral sheets,
not the shadow, and not, itself,
the light,
        permitting the whorls
and oils of the floor,
not the pine itself, not grain,
        not echo
of children's voices in the hills,
softened in the evergreens, mourning doves
inside it, in it the cool feel of the hands
in air, letting things arise
        in it, shift
of drought-brilliant pines, chill feel
of breathing,
        suspensions, but not
in things or a succession of things,
not nameable
        as peace, passing, clear
emptiness, veil, all things lighted
from inside,
        source that isn't things
but things of it,
        some trace in the phrase
exceeded some glint
rising drifts of it
in things the words for things
but not of them
        before they're locked down
in their vaults, in discourse
turning the drift to shadows,
        sheer white, roses,
thou gnawed away inside,
        long veil, how changed, fallen
into pleats, gravity, design, cotton thread
sewn shut on the aluminum rod.

GREG GLAZNER

Mr. D's Counterstrophe

Before religious wish could gloss
survival like a wax job, before
the first sub-normal priest could toss
a detailed theory in his bonfire,

at the center of all things were ones
and zeros, an explosion, he said,
slurping coffee, *that cooled down*
as calculus, and multiplied

as fractals, beautiful, he claimed,
as weather, as the CAT-scanned brain.
Of course there seems to be a mind
in there, but it's voltage, sweeping like fame

across the neural circuitry,
just a brief, electric sophistry
that wires cells with celebrity,
just feedback, on and offistry,

he said, and winked, and tapped his Bic
like a little showman's cane. *We*
just seem *to hunger, we just* think
we sing beyond the mindless sea ...

MARTIN EDMUNDS

The Change. The Changeling.

Now, when dusk comes, I know the dark is final,
since, in the dark, I will not find you again.

Your heart was my midnight sun on my midnight sundial,
my compass of love, all of the world I wanted —

seas and stars and woods, rain on the slates,
and on the erotic, delicate foxtails, too,

lifted in wind, or, burning, perhaps, with the season,
found their home in me when I found you.

How my lips loved grazing the flesh of your belly
like a bull in a meadow, seeking, through shine and shade,

that rich patch where the curled grass tasted sweetest,
not needing to eat for plenty, biding my time.

Nights now I am allowed to paw and bellow
loud and long as I want at the horns of the moon.

Days spent raging at the gaping wake of the gleaners,
kicking up mud clods, hungry, warming my feet.

You do not bask on your back like a meadow for me anymore.
The sun has burned out. The world has no rhyme.

LEO ROMERO

from *Crazy in Los Nueces*

Fall! The best time of the year. Even in Los Nueces. It had cooled off greatly. Though "cooled off" might give the wrong impression. What I mean is, it wasn't anywhere near as hot as it had been, so, cooled off. But the nights were definitely cooler. You could see the pecans ripe on the pecan trees around town, and many pecans already littering the ground. There was a gigantic pecan farm on the road to Anthony. I had passed through it those early weeks I was in Los Nueces when Ramon was always inviting me to go with him to Morenito's, that small adobe bar in Anthony.

On the first trip down to Morenito's, I hadn't expected that we'd be driving through a gigantic pecan farm, really a forest. Ramon hadn't thought to mention it; he had driven through it countless times, and he hardly gave it a thought. But to me it conjured images of fairy tales I had read or heard when I was very young, of dark forests where there were trolls under bridges, and little isolated houses where evil old women lived who looked for opportunities to lure small children into their ovens. And wolves that talked and such things. It felt like an enchanted place to me, the way we kept driving, but still the leafy trees seemed endless, spreading far away into a darkness of trunks, and limbs, and deep shadows. Also the way they had been planted so that they were in rows added to the enchanted quality. An unnaturalness in how orderly they were, but for long stretches no sign of people, an eerie leafy darkness and silence. But how beautiful and how unexpected it was, a forest, its dark shadows and shade, and the desert at its border! But when you were in the forest, the desert seemed like it could be hundreds of miles away. And when you drove out of the forest of pecan trees, and there was the desert — the pecan tree forest seemed to me the more astonishing.

It had been the beginning of the summer since I had, last been through there with Ramon. But with Dilia having her car, that was one of the first places I wanted her to see — *I* wanted to see again! But first there was that night, that first night she stayed with me. We sat at the kitchen table and drank our cokes. She placed her hand on the table, and I reached over and touched it. I left my hand on top of hers, and we looked at each other, and then I pulled my chair closer to her, and we kissed, and we stood up and embraced and continued to kiss. And as we kept kissing, our hands making timid explorations, I backed Dilia a few steps and we tumbled onto the bed.

Dilia was extremely passionate with her kissing, and, too, with fondling. This surprised me because when we had kissed in the alley in Burque there had been no passion, no fire, and hardly any fondling. What I remembered about it was that it had been fun, the polite kissing of two strangers trying not to go too far, playing safe, no special attraction, just a little fling. Shortly after tumbling onto the bed we were naked, embracing, and the fall breezes entering through the open windows also embraced and caressed our naked bodies with their satiny coolness. It had started getting cooler as soon as the sun had set. And our nakedness was hidden in the protective darkness of the night. I was thankful that Chopo was out of town for a few days and that he wouldn't be knocking on the door disturbing the wonderful time we were having, savoring each other's lips, caressing bellies and hips; she had pert breasts that I sucked, and I thrilled at the delicate touch of her hand around my enlarged penis and thrilled at the way her fingertips stroked my sensitive balls. We pressed against each other, massaged buttocks and thighs, stroked arms, caressed and kissed necks and shoulders. We explored and kissed and caressed seemingly everywhere. And this went on for a long time until finally I thought, it's time. I parted her legs and tried to enter. But immediately she turned away roughly, her parted legs clamped tight as I fell to her side. She was lying with her back to me, and I was shocked to hear her sobbing.

For a while I didn't know what to say. I was dismayed, angry, but also concerned for Dilia because of her crying. What could possibly have happened, I thought, to ruin such a perfect time?

"Didn't you want to?" I finally said thinking in amazement of the intimacy we shared in bed, thinking of our naked bodies still in the bed, thinking of where our hands and lips had been. She didn't say anything but continued to sob. I stared at the dark ceiling for what seemed to be a long time. Finally I asked,

"What's the matter?"

And Dilia slowly turned her body towards me. In the darkness I could barely make out her features. At least she's stopped crying, I thought.

"You'll have to be patient with me," she whispered. "I've been a nun all these years."

That floored me. What could I say to that. I thought of my limp penis and wondered if it'd ever get hard again in her presence. And I contemplated what she said: that she had been a nun all these years. And that I would have to be patient. We were quiet in bed for a long time, our naked bodies just inches apart, and I kept wondering, what have I gotten myself into?

Arthur Sze

from Apache Plume

Reductions and Enlargements

A Chippewa designer dies from pancreatic cancer
and leaves behind tracing paper, exacto knives,

rubber cement, non-photo blue pencils,
a circular instrument that calculates reductions

and enlargements. A child enters a house and finds
a dead man whose face has been eaten by dogs.

Who is measuring the pull of the moon in a tea cup?
In a thousand years, a man may find barrels

of radioactive waste in a salt bed and be unable
to read the warnings. Sand is accumulating

at the bottom of an hourglass, and almost anything —
scissors, green wind chime, pencil shavings,

eraser smudge, blooming orchid under skylight —
may be a radial point into light. When a carp

flaps its tail and sends ripples across the surface
of a pond, my mind steadies into a glow. Look

at a line that goes into water, watch the wake,
see the string pulse and stretch into curved light.

ARTHUR SZE

Anamnesis

Wind erases our footprints on a transverse dune.
A yellow yolk of sun drops below the horizon

as a white moon rises. Claret cup cactus
blooms in white sand, while soaptree yuccas

move as a dune moves. The mind reduces a pond
to a luminous green speck and enlarges

a flecked *amanita muscaria* cap into a cosmos.
Running my hand along the curve of your waist,

I wonder if knowledge is a form of anamnesis.
When I pour warm water down your spine,

a *boletus barrowsii* releases spores into air.
As a stone drops into a pool and red koi

swim toward the point of impact, we set
a yarrow stalk aside and throw "Duration,"

glimpse a spiral of bats ascending out of a cave;
one by one they flare off into indigo air.

ARTHUR SZE

Starlight

Here skid marks on I-25 mark a head-on collision;

here I folded an origami crane;

here a man writes in grass style: *huan wo he shan*;

here black poplar leaves swayed on the surface of clearest water;

here a downy woodpecker drills high in the elm;

here a dog drags a horse's leg back from the *arroyo*;

here Keene cement burned into my wrist and formed a riparian scar;

here, traveling at night through the Sonoran Desert,
everyone choked when sand swept through the open windows of the
train;

here yellow and red ranunculi unfold under a chandelier;

here in the Jemez Mountains a cluster of *clitocybe dilata*;

here we spot eleven dolphins swimming between kelp beds up the coast;

here we look through binoculars at the blue ion tail of a comet in the
northwest sky;

here pelicans are gliding above a cliff;

here when I pour water down the drain, a black cricket pops up;

here the first thing I saw when I opened my eyes

was a cut peony in a glass;

here is the origin of starlight.

In Chinese huan wo he shan *means "return my rivers and mountains."*

ERIC MICHAELS - *sketch*

Anglophone Writing in Paris Today

British-Canadian publisher John Calder (with manual typewriter)
and **Frank** editor, David Applefield, in Montreuil, on the eastern
edge of Paris, 1998. *Photo: John Minihan*

Updating the Myth

David Applefield

The idea of pulling up stakes and pursuing the life of the writer or artist in Paris never seems to lose its appeal. Since the days of Benjamin Franklin and Thomas Jefferson, Americans have viewed Paris with a cosmic reverence. Although the commercial climate today is less inviting, the popular appeal of Paris has never been greater.

A few staggering statistics are interesting to muse over. Sixty-seven million people visited France last year, making it the most visited country in the world, with Paris, of course, its leading destination. Although numbers are hard to verify, it is fair to estimate that the permanent Anglo-American resident population in the Paris area today — a strange sort of "non-community" which keeps renewing itself — exceeds 200,000. The steady and unrelentless flow of books, guides, memoirs, films, tv segments, and articles (à la Peter Mayle) keeps gushing into circulation each year, glorifying the image of all things French. It influences our fictive imaginations, and reenforces the myth that being in Paris makes you happy or creative. One tends to think that existence in Paris is driven by inspiration and that the City of Light is the capital of love and style. Yet it is, for many, simply the fantasy of being somewhere other than where you were.

There is a constant ebb of English-speakers who come to the French capital to try their hand at living, working and studying, and some who come with the distinct intention of writing or making art. Many leave when their money or patience (or both) run out. Some are bound by the one-year validity date of an open-return plane ticket. A lot don't really know why they've come, however, most are bound by a flirtatious relationship with the unknown.

The appeal originates with the city's undeniable charm, beauty, tradition, and culture. However, it's fair to say that today a disturbingly wide gap exists between the idea and the reality of making the move. The way one feels when visiting a city, and the act of adapting it as yours, are two different beasts. In short, many of the factors that pulled writers and artists from former lives during the twenties, thirties, forties, and fifties — the freedom from moral judgment and censorship, overt racism, Puritanical values on sexuality, crass consumerism, an attractive exchange rate — are barely valid today. While at the same time, a number of the cultural elements that once made Paris so appealing for the creative soul — love and appreciation for aesthetics, passion for dialog, unabashed sensuality, rootedness to history, respect for writers and artists (even penniless ones), cheap and excellent wine, anonymity — are still present. Every time I peel a clementine after a long meal at a Parisian dinner table I feel the delight of living in France. And every time I pass by one of those over-pruned plain trees that line the boulevards, I feel the weight of European civilization closing in on nature, and the soul feels a bit sick. Living in Paris, it's virtually impossible to remain indifferent. You're constantly confronted with the questions of how to live, who you are, what the meaning of things are, and by extension, what and how to write.

The contradictions are blatant and real but hard to sort out. Although the Paris story today is no longer the same as it once might have been, certain nervous strands of commonality continue to run along the cord of the experience. Every so often old stories and living myths — like the bones in Paris's public cemeteries which get unearthed, sorted, and stored anonymously every 300 years in the Catacombs — need a serious facelift, a remake, a re-examination. That's how we feel about the "expat writer in the Paris garret" story. It needs retelling.

In that we are here and **Frank** derives much of its *raison d'être* from the very myth it attempts to debunk, and much of its flow of unsolicited manuscripts come from Paris-based or once-Paris-based writers (or others hoping to take the psychic leap), we decided we'd answer the FAQ "What's really happening these days in the expat community?" Our answer comes in the form of a bold and diverse selection of interviews, texts, poems, translations, drawings and photographs loosely grouped around the heading: Anglophone Writing in Paris Today.

We've avoided the word expatriate in our title because the word has undergone such use and misuse that few of us writing here today can identify with the term. The sense of protest, political statement and spiritual rejection of the homeland is rarely articulated these days. Although there has been a minor resurrection of Philosophers Cafés, where people gather to talk and drink, writers by and large are not homogenized by any single location. Writers in Paris tend to think of themselves as merely people "living in the world." The saying used to go that home was where you tucked your slippers under your bed. Now, one is more apt to say that home is where you turn your computer on or download your email; and when you're from somewhere else, Paris on the whole seems like a pretty good place to be.

In attempting to present English-language writing here, we've tried to minimize the designation "American" despite the clear fact that a substantial majority of the English-language creative writing being done in Paris today is authored by people originating in the United States. We have not made any real attempts to distribute our pages with a geographic fairness. We do have contributors from Canada, Australia, England, and Scotland but we have not tried to be representational and we have not sought to create balance. We use the term "anglophone" because it is applicable, meaning an English-speaking person, especially in a country where two or more languages are spoken. If you live in France and write in English, you're an Anglophone. You'll be hearing and using the word more and more as the role of English, for better or for worse, continues to grow as a global vehicle for sharing all sorts of experience across cultural borders.

The "Anglophone Writing in Paris" dossier includes some 40 contributors. We've done our best to solicit unpublished work from lots of sources. We've advertised, we've turned over rocks, we've combed our slush pile. We've searched our database and called our friends and our friends' friends, and can honestly say that the work found here is a healthy smorgasbord of the creative work originating with today's English-language writers in Paris. As far as we know, there has been no attempt as far-reaching as this present collection.

It goes without saying, however, that any pretention of total comprehensiveness, and any insistance on knowing everything and everyone in a city of ten million, would be wildly foolish. For those who have been overlooked or whose work has not been retained for this issue, we are sorry. Fortunately, there will be future issues.

There are a number of fine writers not represented here for various reasons who merit acknowledgement as part of this literary landscape: Canadian Mavis Gallant, South Africans Breyten Breytenbach and Denis Hirson, Nigerian Wole Soyinka, American sci-fi writer Norman Spinrad, biographer Herbert Lottman, *New Yorker* columnist Adam Gopnik, AP Bureau Chief Mort Rosenblum, *Est-Ouest* editor Georges Ferenczi, Australian poet June Shenfield, *Mediterranean* editor Kenneth Brown, American fiction writers William Wharton, Jerome Charyn, and Ward Just, British publisher Karl Orend, African-American novelist Jake Lamar, Irish poet Harry Clifton, art writer Sandra Kwock-Silve, who organized the American Artists in France retrospective in 1997, and others.

In an attempt to document how the Anglophone writing community in Paris has changed over the years, I asked those who are best positioned to know, the booksellers. Fortunately, Paris has always had a healthy choice of English-language bookstores, many of which offer regular readings, signings and literary events. The Abbey Bookshop, the Australian Bookshop, and of course George Whitman's legendary Shakespeare & Company, all offer events and a broad selection of new and used books. On the Right Bank, there is WH Smith, part of the British chain, and Brentanos, both large and more commercial, but playing a role in serving the needs of the Anglophone reading community. Galignani Bookshop, the oldest English bookstore on the continent, is located in front of the Tuilerie Gardens. Tea and Tattered pages features used books as does the San Francisco Bookroom. Odile Hellier, founder of the Village Voice Bookshop, a leading literary venue over the last ten years, contends that the creative community has shrunk. Why? Primarily because Paris today is too expensive and the laws concerning working in France are so restrictive that the culturally-inclined individual is discouraged. "We all live in a corset. You pay and you survive," she states. "Literary bookshop owners today are becoming dinosaurs. In the 80s, when the exchange rate was highly favorable, reaching eleven francs to the dollar, the expat culture scene was extraordinary." Celebrated Parisian Jim Haynes, who runs the informal Handshake Editions and has hosted over the last 25 years some 70,000 guests at his famous Sunday night soirées, agrees: "The better the exchange rate, the younger and more hip the crowd."

Our issue begins aptly with one of the community's major voices, Edmund White, whom we've featured in our Fiction & America column.

The idea here is not so much to expose a single writer's life and craft but rather to invite a writer to contribute to a larger dialogue between writers and readers on cultural issues relevant to the worlds we are part of. The interview series is designed to create ripples, hopefully waves. A number have been reprinted in collections and anthologies, and serve we're told, as the foci of discussions and arguments in classrooms, park penches, and bedrooms. Each interview works alone, yet collectively they start talking to each other.

Frank, by conviction, has never tried to invalidate one set of literary conventions, styles, standards or aesthetics while heralding or imposing the virtues of another. That's never been our point. The questions for us are more vital than the answers. There are in fact lots of good answers, but culture in general begins to weaken and humans become less interesting when the questions lose their tonicity. So, in essence, at **Frank**, we don't publish merely what we like; we publish what we believe deserves to be read and considered. And more importantly, what helps promote discussion. Maybe that is the greatest attribute of living beyond the boundaries of a former self, you're obliged to look deeper and differently. In Paris it's harder to be complacent.

H A R R Y   M A T H E W S

The Chronogram for 1998

An Exclusive Evolutionary Vortex of World Excursions

NOTE: The rule of the chronogram is that when all letters corresponding to
Roman numerals (c, d, i, l, m, v, and x) are added together, they produce a sum
equivalent to a specific year of the Christian calendar.

*January starts: sun here, stars there. So what joys & fears has the New Year
brought us?*

• In the Irkukst penitentiary ironworks the night shift is finishing its stint,
skirting weighty pig-iron ingots as it regains the prison interior.

• In Pienza, Ernestina is heating tripe *fiorentina* for thirteen.

• In Sing-Sing, wearing surreptitious attire, Phineas, Bishop of Ossining, is
anointing fifteen Fenian ("Fighting Irish") priests in a kiosk of ingenuous piety.

• Bibi is shirring pigeon eggs in Saint Étienne.

• In Brighton, Ignatius is getting high quaffing his fifth straight Irish whisky.

• In Pretoria, gritty Erwin Higginson (age eight), ignoring fatigue & injuries,
is winning his point in a bruising nineteen-eighteen tiebreaker against
Fritz Spitzfinger (age nine) by returning a wristy spinner hip-high & without
hesitation whipping it fair, Spitzfinger then batting it high into the rows
to bring the fifteenth prestigious Witherspoon Tennis Initiation Tourney
to a breath taking finish.

• In Fuji, pursuing a hashish high with Quentin, Kenny is perusing sporting
prints by Hiroshige & Hokusai.

• Arising at eight in Brisbane, Ian, aspiring historian of propitious intuitions,
enjoys the benign aberration that, by getting a grip on his utopian fusion of
Augustinian with Einsteinian reasoning, he is attaining a genuine gnosis.

• In Etrurian Tarquinia, Gigi is eating spaghetti with pepperoni.

• In Austria, zipping past the Inn, ignoring warning signs, Pippo Peruzzi, first-string Ferrari whiz, big winner in Spain & Argentina, is steering his touring bike (pistons & turbine whirring, its stunning furnishings genuine Pinin-Farina) in brisk pursuit of fiery Zizi, his Hungarian skier, itinerant antithesis, antagonist, tigress, priestess, siren, obsession, happiness, wife.

• Bobbie is sitting with Bert in a Parisian bistro, in whose noisy interior untiring opportunists are satisfying pretentious ninnies with inferior white wine.

• Heroin originating in Iquitos is winning first prize with tertiary bargaining arbitrators in Tijuana.

• Bonnie is frying onion rings in Triffin, Ohio.

• In antique Poitiers, Antoinette is refreshing her guests with interpretations of Rossini's quainter offerings, interspersing arias & ariettas with his *"Nizza"* (singer & piano), his *"Raisins"* & *"Noisettes"* (piano), his first *sinfonia* (strings), & his roguish *"Iphigenia"* (bass trio).

• In Tirana, inept Hussein is paying fifty-eight qintars to fortify his Istrian wine with Bosnian raki.

• In the wintry outskirts of Pori, Father Tiki Haakinen — enterprising & itinerant Finnish priest — is repairing hi-fi wiring for a parish benefit.

• In spite of its threat to her ingratiating Gibson waist, Rikki, in Zanzibar, is insisting on heaping & eating piggish portions of spaghetti & fig pie.

• Postponing inopportune issues & putting first things first, Kiwanis, Rotarians, & Shriners are putting their agonizing unity in writing, signing a proposition that reasserts their opposition to atheists, bigotry, euthanasia ("outright assassination"), heroin, pinkos, the Spanish Inquisition, superstition, & unfairness in business arbitration.

• In Antibes, binging on *pastis* is getting Winnie higher than nine kites.

• In Kiruna, in white tie, sipping a Perrier, Fafnir Grieg, high priest of Ibsen initiates, is testing his register & intonation in painstaking preparation for his fiftieth signature interpretation of the protagonist in *Ghosts*.

• In Gorizia, Anita is working up an appetite for *anitra triestina*.

• At Trinity, Robin is boating with his tutor, Isaiah Singe. Isaiah is asking if Robin thinks he is going to finish his thesis (*Affinities with the Orient: Inquiries into spurious interpretations of Hafiz in Ariosto, Ossian & Kropotkin*) within his transitory span of years.

• In Bingen, penurious Winston is spiking his uninspiring Pepsi with Steinhäger.

• Business-wise Erika O'Higgins is sitting in Pittsburgh squinting with attention at the infuriating fine print in an IRS opinion assigning Irish pension benefits she is repatriating. The opinion questions her attestation separating foreign benefits, earnings as insurer in Tangier & those in tertiary proprietary rights in Zaïre; pinpoints gains transpiring through inquiries into unwritten but propitious negotiations in Haiti; & reinstates profits inherent in eight-figure operations she is authorizing in Bisk (Siberia).

• In Bonaire, Georgia, hungry Josiah is weighing into his piping-hot grits & grunts.

• Interiorizing Rienzi in her isba in Gorki, Anastasia thinks of Patti singing in *I Puritani*, of Kipnis in *Boris*, of Kiri Te Kanawa's Rosina in a Göttingen *Figaro*.

• In Ostia, engaging Ethiopian waiters trigger big tips by squirting nips of *grappa* into porringers of out-of-season fruit.

• Batting against the Orizaba Tigres in Irapuato, rookie Juanito Arias first whiffs in eight straight opportunities before hitting a ninth-inning zinger & satisfying the inhabitants' hopes of winning the Zapatista Series.

• Zazie is biting into rabbit thighs in Barbizon.

• Zenia, passionate Aquinist, is pursuing an ingenious hypothesis, assigning the origins of Aquinas's interpretations of Gorgias to an "Osirian" genesis arising in the writings of inquiring Egyptian priests, an origin that the Sophists reinstate, or so Zenia infers in her ingenious synthesis. Questioning the suppositions of post-Aquinist thinkers, Zenia insists on the inferiority of Fourier's "inanities," Wittgenstein's "gibberish," & Austin's "asininities."

• High-intensity spirits inspire high-intensity spirit in noisy Kirin.

• In an uninspiring quarter of Trier, Ohioan Josiah, a boisterous nineteen, is infuriating Swiss Inge, a serious thirty, by persisting in attributing the first apprehension of the Einstein shift to Igor Sikorsky.

• In a *ristorante* in Torino, sheepish Antonio's superstitious hesitation between *arrabiata* spaghetti & risotto with *funghi* both intrigues & irritates patient Giorgina.

• In Ottawa, thirteen Inuit Situationists are signing treaties with the nation's highest authorities guaranteeing that their tribes & regions inherit proprietary herring-fishing rights outright & in perpetuity.

• In Whitby, seagoing Einar, finishing his fifteenth pink gin, insists he is quite fine.

• In Twinsburg (Ohio), when a nitwit intern, threatening to irrigate her intestines with his "own unique quinine infusion," brings out a giant syringe, Queenie, a patient with hepatitis B, her weary inertia shattering at the threat of this aggression, begins reiterating in shrieks of irritation & anguish, "No penetration without representation!"

• Ski-touring in Bennington, Jiri spits out bits of unripe kiwi in a fit of pique.

• Supine in Biarritz, Tristan — unsparing onanist — is perusing Gautier's pornographies, whose swift prurient inspiration stiffens his waning spirits.

• In Rosario (Argentina), fiery Antonio is assuaging his thirst with sweetish Rhine wine.

• Ianthe, in Berkshire, is initiating with requisite ingenuity her inquiry into "Oppositions & affinities in the autobiographies of Gibbon, Twain, & Frank Harris".

• In the Ain, Fifi is eating pike patties.

• In their frigate-repair station in Hawaii, engineer's assistant Rossetti is preparing to assassinate his superior, Ensign Fink, for gratuitous insinuations about his inferior IQ.

• Anisette fizzes are winning the night in Springs, whither Henri is steering Bettina in his antique Hispano-Suiza.

• With gaiety, if without authorization, risking fortuitous gunfire & their reputations, a surreptitious retinue of eight British union bigwigs (no unionists), joining nine attrition-wary IRA-Sinn Fein agitators, is whipping the unpropitious weirs of the Isis in sanguine pursuit of hibernating pike &, out of a forthright repositioning of thesis & antithesis, a synthesis that begins separating negotiating opportunities & the proprietary hesitations, intrigues, obsessions, & sourish passions of the antagonists' institutions & habits. The British suffer their opposites' priggish interruptions & patronizing bias; the Irish are enjoying their outing, with its fortifying surfeit of whiskies, fine wines, & tangerines. These propitiations presage a beginning.

• In Saint-Quentin, Pierre is into his fifth pinkish Pinot Noir.

• Writing *finis* to his reign in the prize ring in Ashanti, Nigeria, "Tiger" Titus (Niger) is forfeiting a bruising fist fight to his Ibo heir, Tobias, thus ratifying his apparent superiority.

• In a quaint inn in Rieti, Kiki & Brigitte sniff quasi-appetizing brain fritters hissing in swine fat.

• Fishing in Touraine, Irwin is unkinking Eugenia's rig & fitting it with spinners. Their skiff sits in a quiet bight where feisty, spiky pike are rising & biting. First strike! It is raining.

• Uriah, Griffin, Jennifer, Tabitha are hitting the Pinot Grigio in a wine bar in Waikiki.

• In Fife, Inigo Higgins finishes writing his iniquitous *Jottings on Kinship Etiquette in Barrie, Rattigan, Braine & Pinter.*

• Gauging his position in the whitening Pakistanian heights, Piotr eats his fiftieth fig out of its tin.

• Its gregarious parties gathering at a transient staging-point, shipping in the Bering Straits, either freight or passenger, is stationary tonight — engines quiet, neither jib nor spinaker astir. As the fortieth ship nears, persistent skiffs begin sprinting through the nippy waters, swapping ostentatious rations & surprising potations & ferrying a rotation of seafaring prostitutes out of Tientsin, Biak, Iquique, Teresina, Kauai, Tenerife, Piraeus, & Hoboken.

• In Whitefriars, Pip infers that he is gaining genuine insights by sharing a firkin of Guinness with Brian.

• In Perugia, unwise Arrigo Panin is preparing a presentation that, straining notions of affinities to their breaking-point, risks irking (or boring) knowing trainees in his Institute for Insight & Orientation by arguing that it is appropriate to attribute Hopkins's inspiration to Whittier, Stein's to Browning.

• Faith is refrigerating nineteen stingers & braising nine satiating portions of bison brisket in Topperish (Washington).

• Hiking in the interior of Shikoku, Kirk is sustaining a tiring Iris with aspirins & interesting attributions of Finnegan's epiphanies.

• Sophie & Étienne, in an Iberian setting, are swigging refreshing pints of sangria *gratis*.

• In Sabine, righteous Sheriff Winthrop Prior, feinting a right, is banging a furious fist into a hirsute rapist's ribs & a punishing thigh into his iniquitous groin.

• Georgianna is nourishing nine aging kittens in Big Sur.

• Benign skies in Arizona. At a prairie spring, Tintin is watering his proprietor's thirty-eight first-string ponies — they're skittish ponies, stirring, neighing, biting, nosing bitten withers. Rising high in his stirrups, reins tight against bit, quirt hanging at his wrist, Tintin spits; sitting, he tips a sparing ration into its Zigzag wrapping. Prairie rabbits thinking: rain. Harriers beating their wings in thin bright air. Tintin thinking: this night's attire — white shirt, string tie — is right for winning his engaging señorita. His pinto whinnies & pisses.

• Sipping saki in Gifu, Roshi is getting quite tipsy.

• Zigzagging in nifty figure eights on a skating rink in frosty Keewatin, Nettie is fantasizing an ingenious haikuisation of Swinburne's "Proserpine."

• In Pistoia, tiny Pierino, stripping a thin bit of appetizing skin off the shining ribs of a spit-roasting pig, bites into it with a grin.

• Within sight of eternity, Keith Asquith, wintering in Antigua, is taking unsparing pains to surprise, spite, & punish his nowise ingratiating Yorkshire heirs — "The shits!"

• In Iowa abstainers are abstaining.

• In Austin, Ira & Justina, a striking pair, registering at first sight no antipathies but intriguing affinities, wishing to kiss, interiorize their inhibitions, banish their hesitations, skip propositions, & kiss, hip against hip. A swift shifting into a pertinent interior to quit their attire: whipping off pigskin trainers, unbuttoning Ira's shirt, stripping off Justina's T-shirt, unzipping her tight-fitting skirt & his khakis, unhooking her brassiere, ripping away panties & briefs, ignoring trinkets, skin to skin ... "Wait," interrupts Justina, insisting, "first this joint," to forthwith initiate brisk intakes & an instantaneous high. Kissing again, Ira's fingertips graze with finesse Justina's hair, ribs, & thighs. Justina seizes his wrists & entwines his waist between jittering tibias. Straining, Ira nips her tits. Thrashing, her nips stiffening, Justina tightens her grip. Gratifying Justina's appetite for kissing with ingenious bites, in his benign yearning Ira using his weight tips her posterior hither, baring Justina's piping fig. Into this engaging shrine Ira insinuates his inspissating thing, an insertion that ingratiates writhing Justina, inquiring in its penetration of her gripping, shifting pith, whose stunning twinges infuse Ira with skittish fire. He begins panting, his sinews stiffen, he hisses, Justina shrieks. It's brief, it's nifty, it's insane. Supine & sweating, Ira & Justina sigh faint sighs, kiss, grin, & sink into unworrying, transitory night.

• In the Tsinking zoo, unhesitating hippos, giraffes, kiwis, penguins, tortoises, porpoises, & tigers are ingesting big propitiatory portions of grain, onions, fruit, ginger, fish, & pig.

• On Thirteenth Street & First, Antoine & Honoria are sharing a pizza & a knish.

• Aries & Sirius are shining in Tunisian skies.

Key West, February 2, 1998

147

WILLIAM KLEIN

WILLIAM KLEIN
St. Patrick's Day - Assorted Police
Chiefs in Mourning - 1996

A Return to New York City

photographs - 1996

WILLIAM KLEIN - *Fifth Avenue Parade* - 1996

WILLIAM KLEIN - *Ambulance Driver with Newspaper* - 1996

GWEN STRAUSS

The Reef

After our keel kissed the sand shoal off that reef,
everything changed.
I shivered all night in the cockpit
greeting my first death.
It had arrived, skipping
soft as laughter and slaps of water.

In the morning we found the island.
I gathered coconuts and giggled at the coral fish,
their ridiculous colors; we pretended
nothing had happened.
You poured over our charts.
At night we talked too calmly,

about where we could be, where we might go.
You could not take a sextant sight because
our mirrors and clocks were all broken
flotsam, wreckage. You paced
the shore fringe, hands clasped behind your back
while sun moon stars slid loose,

untracked across our sky. I dreamed
you had no past. I grew stronger with each day.
First I took off shoes,
then clothes. But you yelled
at me to cover myself. You were afraid
upset because you liked to know

always where you stood.
I made a stew with everything I found:
kelp, conch muscles, sea urchins,
soggy books, our fear.
I kept a bowl filled for you,
but you refused to eat.

When you fell ill,
I fed you drops of coconut milk,
squeezing a sponge over your lips.

I nursed you through your visions.
The dolphin and the sea turtle
spoke to your dreams

but you would not answer them.
There would be no forgiveness for doubt.
Your silence was salt, absorbing
moisture from the air. Salt is a choice,
a bitter wisdom. That was my second death:
parched, dried like drift wood.

I made a harness and traveled
to the heart of the island
where only damp and ancient things live;
the water is brackish and the light
barely filters through. It was a long journey —
longer than the one we had traveled together

and I cannot tell you how many times
I stopped, put down the weight, and wept,
because of the burden of
wanting to speak to you.
I buried you
there in a cave of old bones.

I promised never to return
and I took with me this stone
which will not stop bleeding.
It is difficult always to find a place to keep it.
I am far away now
and I have grown fat several times over;

I have met death again
and hope. And I am no longer
so very tired as I was then.
But sometimes when I am climbing
a mountain, or sweeping the earth at dusk
strange dark birds

fly out of me.
I know them;
they journey back to you
my old man, my old dear friend.

GWEN STRAUSS

Gated

When I was womb thick
with hips spreading
like a great sail,

waddling through the tropics
of my expectancy,
a dozy cow,

contented prisoner
pausing before stairs and ladders,
before the heave-ho of me,

counting off days, names,
pretending to plan the harvest —
oh I burned impatient!

I did not know how my body
would be cannibalized,
an over-planted field,

exhausted, depleted,
veins unfurling into red tatters,
skin pulled to purple.

The moon was a cracked egg.
I had swallowed it whole.
All around me was fence and gate,

or glass — I was air tight,
a steamy terrarium, beaded with sweat.
I scratched at sleep, and hissed

escape. So then, I would be thin:
performing acrobatic
feats of love

with a gracefully
folded body, discovering
positions never tried before.

As resourceful as Sheherazade
oh my Arabian nights —
only I'd wake up

from the pressure on my bladder,
struggle to roll over,
hoist myself from the bed

while the wind of dreams
poured from me weightless as shadows,
as sand polishes meat from bone —

Let no one lie to you:
pregnancy begins alone and with loss —
Your dreams leave a stain on the sheets

where it is recorded
that you are no longer open
like a plain or the ocean or a book.

KYLE JARRARD

Red Haircut & **Carp**

It is a quiet going-away party, just the four of us, at Laurent's.

Laurent and Eric are out on the balcony with their mint-waters. For the occasion, they smoke those expensive colored cigarettes, spew out thick swirls of red and green smoke, and talk about their voyage, which will begin early the next morning.

It is Laurent's dead grandfather's yacht they'll be sailing. The old man had liked to play dominoes right on her polished deck in the sun. *Five Spot*, he'd named her. He and his wife would play dominoes most of the day in the bright shade of a tarp hung between the masts, nibble on the sweetest tomatoes and drink very cold beer. With never a cross word between them, they rounded the Mediterranean more than twenty times and then died together in a car accident during a rainstorm far inland.

Laurent and Eric are not talking about that, of course. They are wondering what the future holds, how the aging yacht will fare on open ocean. They drink and blow the pretty smoke in each other's faces. Westward the sky is orange, overhead lavender. In apartment buildings all around people are turning on their lamps and television sets, or coming to look out their windows, suspiciously and only for a moment before drawing curtains for the night. Black pigeons pace the lead roofs in a forest of rusted antennae.

Caroline, on the green leather sofa, stares at the ceiling, which is covered with wallpaper, the same as covers all the walls. It is a jungle scene: fat trees, wet vines, dark devouring plants, impossibly huge flowers, a perfect stream, placid fauna, including a smiling fish. The scene repeats itself in broad bands around the room.

She has been looking into the jungle a long time. Now she strokes her long white arms, then yawns and rubs her eyes. She taps a thick red-painted fingernail against her teeth.

For a while now, Caroline has had a bleached mohawk. No one, not even Laurent, said a word, though it is the ugliest thing any of us have seen in a while. We are not red-eyed punks. We are different, but not that different. It stands up stiffly like a cropped horse's mane, but time is making it ragged.

I am deep in a vintage white beanbag, trying to think of something to talk about besides how uncomfortable beanbag chairs can be, trying not to stare at

Caroline, who has just squeezed those breasts of hers as if she would make them grow even more. I sip a mint-water and cannot stop looking at her like you would a clown.

We pass the bowl of peanuts back and forth in slow-motion.

I am sure Caroline is thinking how fun it would be to scissor off all my fine red hair.

Suddenly, I lose a peanut.

Maybe it went into your hair, she says, sitting up straight, as if a game were to be played.

Maybe, I say.

I am surrounded by red hair. A lot lies in lengths on the dark elm floor, as if it were not mine. Maybe it isn't. I part a clump with my fingers.

It's in there somewhere, Caroline says. You can't go around with a peanut in your hair. You want me to help you?

I look up. You want my hair, don't you.

I never said that.

But you do.

What would I do with it?

Eric winds his watch all the way.

Caroline sucks on a rose cigarette and blows the smoke up high.

She says, I get horribly seasick, you know, so I am glad I did not get invited on this trip. I mean you've never seen anyone so seasick. Take lots of boiled eggs, boys.

I say, Oh, here it is.

Here what is?, Eric asks.

I show them the peanut. They all look toward it. I drop it in an ashtray with the black ashes.

Then I take up a handful of my hair and study it.

What?, asks Caroline. Something else?

Maybe nothing. Or something.

I get out my white comb and draw it through. There is a light obstruction, so I jerk the teeth ahead. I go over the spot many times. Like my daddy always did. Never leave a question mark in your hair, he said.

Caroline watches, rose smoke curling out her horned nose.

There is not much light left.

You know what your hair looks like?, she asks.

I work the comb.

Like a party skirt, she says. Like what every little girl wears that birthday your grandfather takes you to a fancy restaurant and buys you all the French fries and ice cream you can eat. You end up throwing up.

—

Caroline raises her empty glass to her lips, looks into it, groans.
She goes to the stereo and puts on a record.
Who wants to dance? We've got to do something.
She sets her glass on the floor and begins to put her body to the music. It all goes well with the jungle wallpaper. But she is not that sexy. So it looks forced, a sort of in-your-face motion and I knew whose face.
Eric and Laurent study her like jocks at a nightclub. They drink mint-waters and make adolescent comments with their eyes.
Without thinking, I get up and join her. I have no idea why, except if it is that daddy also taught me to dance and I have always danced. Caroline and I do not dance together, but apart, and turned away from each other.
My red hair sways this way and that.
Her mane bobs.
We dance four records like that and then kneel down to check out the other ones in the little cabinet, pitching aside those we don't like, keeping the best. We play them very loud. It almost looks like we are getting along.
Eric and Laurent grow tired of watching us play teenagers and go to the kitchen table and talk about their trip some more. But they look back at us once in a while and you can tell they are mixing up their conversation with other things now. It is that time of night. They want things. They want them before they sleep.

—

I strap on my sandals and Caroline stands up and crosses her arms. Laurent and Eric light up and blow out lemon-colored smoke.
Come over whenever, she says to me. We'll amuse ourselves while they're gone. I mean, we're not going to sit around, right?
They wait a short while for me to comb my hair once more. When I'm done, everybody kisses everybody good night.
Of course she hadn't meant it.

—

I have finally broken out of that wallpaper jungle and into a glass city. A large, bald woman approaches me on a deserted glass street. She wears a fine pair of rose-colored glass shoes, but they make no sound as she nears. Our eyes meet and remain that way until she puts a hand on my shoulder. I turn my head and look at the glass skin covering her hand and hear her say, Come along now, dear.

I obey.

We go to a room below street level where light breaks into bands of color as it passes through the glass ceiling. There are many house plants made of dark green glass. There is a television with that city's news being given by a woman with a white glass face. There is no sound, but her mouth is moving. She is pointing a black glass stick at different points on a colorful map of this country.

The woman who has brought me there has red glass scissors.

She says, Just relax and watch TV. Nothing's going to happen to you. Just concentrate on that TV.

I look at the woman.

What did I tell you?, she says.

I continue to look at her.

She slaps my face and I can feel it shatter and then there are hundreds of chips of blue glass in my lap.

***

Eric says, I'll see you when I get back.

I can still feel the wet where his lips touched my forehead.

I do not open my eyes.

I know that old bald woman was Caroline.

I know Eric is already gone. Off to sail across the Atlantic.

The sky is violet. Clouds pass like an armada. Lightning flashes and thunder shakes the softening concrete.

A sour city rain splatters on the windowsill, in on the floor.

I pull the bedcovers up to my neck. Listen to the mechanical love that remains to the couple next door, their tired cries.

Someone curses the faulty light in the hall, then pounds down six flights of stairs to the floor of the world.

Sewage cascades in the walls. Flush, flush, everyone flushing all at once.

There is a long civil defense siren, a test.

I open a vacation magazine and slap past the shiny pages. My eyes pause on a photograph and absorb its hard white light. I am pounded by it. I stand dazzled on scorching rock. I plunge into sun-ribboned water and go down and down. My hair comes off and floats away and I am free.

A pigeon gets on the windowsill, looks at me with one eye, then the other, flaps away.

Maybe I will go to Kenya. Sun there. Heat. The Great Rift Valley.

The baking shore of a lake where early man lived. I will need a passport with a likeness. Which likeness?

I can see a hand-caught fish on the ground, one eye skyward, drying out. The eye is looking up at a bloated hairy face. His lips are moving. I cannot hear him, though, because I am a fish. He is talking, or trying to. Maybe he is trying to talk to me. I see no one else around. He has a runny nose. He lifts something large into the air and then there is darkness.

I sit up in bed.

I comb this hair.

Eric has gone to sail the ocean blue.

———

But there are many things to do, anything to keep from badgering myself, anything to shut off the voice saying what are you waiting on, who are you waiting on, is it a miracle, is it Eric, when Eric comes home everything will be sweet perfect fine?

Will he be wearing soft sandals? How tan will his feet be?

I notice my shoes. The leather soles ground down, chewed by pavement, rotted by pet piss.

I carry them to a *cordonnerie*, an Arab's shop crammed between two buildings. He works at a greasy table with a chopped surface and wears large, black-frame eyeglasses. There are filthy bandages on his fingers.

Taking my pair of red pumps and turning them over and over, he nods sadly.

I go to a small park and sit in the sun on the end of a green bench. A man approaches chewing a sandwich and lights on the other end. He has said something he thinks is funny, I have not caught it, and then he begins reaching over to pat me on the arm as if I were an old friend. I look at him once, see the bread crust and bits of ham clinging to his chipped teeth. He tries to hold my hand. I vomit between my feet, then stand and go home.

Just before dark, I go out again to fetch my shoes.

I drink mint-water after mint-water and come to the conclusion that the freshly repaired red pumps will look nice up on the ceiling.

So I get a stool, hammer and nails. The plaster, dry and cake-like, caves in. The new leather heels plunge into hollows, sticking there. Even better, I note, standing back. Lifelike, as though emerging from another world into this one.

I drink. This world. What is this world?

———

In the night I raise up in bed with a bitter taste in my throat. I do not know what woke me up. I listen. It is our footsteps on the deck of the *Five Spot* under a giant moon. The two of us, Eric and I, heading toward a black wall of palms and a beach as white as ice. We are naked except for our city shoes. He touches my ass.

I get up and turn on every light in the apartment.

I dump pitcherfuls of water on all the house plants. Several times. Until the water runs out dark and oily across the floor.

I go and fix a mint-water and drink it straight down.

This time it makes me sick.

I get scissors and begin cutting my hair. I cut some here, some there, fistfuls of it, and throw it on the white bed. It makes a pile and looks like some strange, sleeping animal.

I have no idea of the time. I call Caroline's. I lie back on the white sheets with my cut hair and stare at the ceiling and let it ring. I want her to answer. I don't want her to answer. Then it stops ringing.

Hello?, I say.

Hello?, a loud voice says back. Hello?

It's Chantal.

Chantal? I knew you would call.

I don't like the way she says it, and hang up.

Who does she think she is?

She does not ring me back. Nor do I call her again.

I know I am acting like a child.

I know my pumps walk that ceiling night after night.

———

I just want to go away. To the country. Take a train down to grandfather's summer house. See if the willow below the garden wall has fallen from the crumbling riverbank. See what fish haunt the cool canal. Think of nothing.

I can still see the carp that boy caught that summer. A female with so many eggs in her she was fat as a suitcase and made a quacking when he squeezed her belly. And that boy not knowing the difference and thinking how big a catch he had. Had some girl opened up her girl's legs to him yet? What would be her name? Agnès? Marie-Ange? Gisette.

The elm branch he'd jammed through one gill and out the mouth, the way he held it up, leaves and grass stuck all over it, his little laughs and nervous shoulders, the faint red mustache. Whatever happened to him?

It seems to matter very much, then not at all. Like the ocean and the man out there on it, after a while.

NINA ZIVANCEVIC

Ode to the West Wind

Oh, great great West Wind,
take me back to all places and people
I cared for, take me away from this
Neo-classical order and dumbness,
away from the North Station where they
took 2,000,000 Jews away to the camps
so only my grandmother got back, take me away
from Europe ridden by plagues and wars,
away from the United States where
people die in ignorance and hunger,
take me back to Serinda where breathing counts
more than action and sublime thinking,
to the non-existing land of poetry and wit
where women don't speak of equanimity and
men dance tango all day long, lift me up
and make me forget this overbearing present,
so, if it is spring,
why am I so far behind?

NINA ZIVANCEVIC

They Blame Me

Because I decided to trust the unbelievable
because I decided to be calm   like a lake
because I wanted to become a breath of air
because I wanted to be alone
because I desired to have so many friends
because I could not be bothered
because I used to sing so many songs
because no one could hear a single sound coming from my mouth
because Tenzin said, "You always say *I*,"
because I am *I* and somebody else,
because no one ever took an interest in my drawings
I had to draw every night
because I believed in silence I had to write so many words
because I loved so many people dearly
I had to leave them behind
because I disliked the color green I wore it every day
because I did not have to do anything I was doing everything
because I liked to explain myself I was telling
everyone "because" because:
be a cause and not a consequence
because only a cause and not a consequence
has a sequence
because ...

NINA ZIVANCEVIC

Could Glory?

for Herbert Huncke

Could glory erase this sadness
of your face, Herbert,
an omniscient movement of all your facial
muscles which knew nothing
but of fleeting pleasure and perpetual pain
I lifted my camera and took a shot,
it was a photo and not a needle affair, we did not know
where to go nor where
we came from, one cold
winter afternoon in New York City
where they shoot people, not horses
in the age of Depression

IRA COHEN - *"Herbert Huncke"*
Bandaged Poet Series - New York, mid-80s

MARK FISHMAN

Fever of Matter

There is a distance between us now that is difficult to measure, it has a life that breathes without lungs, beyond us, really, as man and woman, and it doesn't recognize mercy, it doesn't distinguish between cultures, skin that tastes a little of salt, a little of garden mint, coriander, night and sex, too, they are treated alike, without distinction, wresting many from their sleep, immersing them in a kind of liquid discomfort resembling confusion, wresting many from their sleep beneath a cover of down, a moon's silent breathing, and yet there is a desire in us for a secret and ardent nearness, intimacy both carnal and divine, something to nourish our bodily appetites and our souls, my darling, closing your eyes like little hands making a fist, an embrace that is a feverish hold, I remember, it was an unusually fine summer evening, without a cloud in the sky, rose-colored and radiant, you said, and then fainting in a field of tall grass, each blade covered by the finest leaf made from beaten gold, fainting from the fatigue of getting there, from the fatigue that will follow, the necessity of returning, too, and the air is like honey, cloyingly sweet, a wind that poured through the field like a stream, young, early-summer grass that had grown tall with its richness, something we cannot see, it is true, and this distance between us is like falling in a dream and then awakening, hands grasping the edge of the bed, breathing heavily, eyes open upon the light of morning, the light of a dark night, and in awakening beneath this cover of down, and a sighing moon, a consciousness where there is no relief, it is consciousness itself, an awareness that lights the sensation of distance like a fuse, as if it were a dream, but it is not, and standing in a field of gilded grass, a wind rushing to another place through this field, looking at your sleeping figure embracing the field with outstretched arms, taking us, together, into the earth, I was drawn through a field of gold grass grown tall in the early summer as your fingers held tightly to this grass, and between us now, words moving like my fingers that follow a line describing your eyes, your mouth, and the intimate light that seems to emanate from our very skin, together, and there is no measure of the essential nature that underlies phenomena, counting without numbers, as many days and nights as are figured by our hearts with each beat, the rhythm of the pulse, there is no other time, ours is the measurement of time as if it were a window's reflection, and a desire that is something we cannot see, we cannot hold it in our hands, and we were traveling through a night above the earth, what is familiar is touchable, and you are unacquainted with this love, my darling, without cat whiskers to touch lightly what is between us, something redolent and pleasing, something moving fervently through our night as we move through its sky like tiny planets, with respect, it is true, this landscape is not on any map, where will you look in order to find something familiar in this landscape? a sky above the earth, beneath our feet, beyond our hands grasping at this field of gold leaf grass? we are tiny planets whirling out of our circles.

In the early morning, a breeze washing over us as we sleep, a faint light that is early morning, nothing is clear, our eyes open in this bed yet what we are saying has nothing to do with what is happening in this room, everything is as it was, and it confounds past and present, a diagram could be drawn before me as it was long ago, our fingers entwined like threads both silken and strong, our mouths, our lips pressing together, our hearts beating clearly separately as distant couriers of the same letter, each letter a reply to the other, saying good-bye, how warm the air is, you said, perspiration like tears at the corners of your eyes, and in mine too, and then standing in a field of tall grass, a sky darkening at once, young, early-summer grass that had grown tall, and a stillness too, breathing easily in this quiet moment, a stillness wrapping itself around us like a blanket, a cloudburst, and the clouds themselves began to spread one after the other in a sky no longer rose-colored but radiant and gray, our eyes straining in a light reflected around us, a hazy sky, and in a matter of seconds, a sky that cleared itself, brushing aside clouds and moisture as if they were merely trouble, nothing more, fine suspended particles in the air, and the salt of your skin, undressed and dark, together, we are embracing one another, lying in a field of golden-yellow grass, and in this room, too, embracing and caressing, confusing past and present, sleeping with our hands clasped, fingers entwined, a distance that is difficult to measure, but not difficult to recognize, and in the faint light of morning, our memories drifting without reason in one direction or another, a kind of carriage in which memory travels, everything touching us with its bitter breath, your eyes are averted suddenly from mine, our hands unclasp, disengaged resolutely in the faint light, an obstinate light, and our hearts that beat clearly separately in this room like the wings of birds moving from branch to branch, their wings fluttering noiselessly, landing without stirring the air, a tiny weight, these birds, and the branches swaying a little, our faces without expression, we are breathing the same air, together, inhaling and absorbing this air, your eyes closing easily, heavy with sleep, and despair slips away with each exhalation, but neither breath nor despair leaves me, rather, I am expanding slowly with sorrow, a little like a helium balloon, rising toward the sky, and there is something near that could make me burst, sound-lessness as sharp as a pin, my eyes burning in the brilliant light, lying beside you, your sleeping eyes closed against the light, your hair that sleeps with your skin, and in this room, as in a field of gilded grass, the sun has begun to warm the air, a breeze above our heads, serenity and oppressiveness at once, we are motionless in this brilliant light, and we are persuading each other without words, you must withdraw, our mute voices say, but our lips do not move, voices from a window open upon the sky, voices that converge like two fiery rivers.

There, beyond a few trees, past the shrubs whose persistent stems and branches frame a distant picture, a man and woman are embracing beneath a sky that stretches far away, and a field of grass that has grown tall with its fortune, evening light illuminating the gilded grass, each blade wrapped with gold leaf, a moon in the sky, and a woman's voice, a cry like a bird that comes from her mouth, a man's voice, too, rising without direction in the sky, a pair of voices radiating like light, a tiny fire, and tears fall from their eyes, the man and woman, her tears in his eyes, his voice on her lips, circling one another like tiny planets in a field of gold leaf grass.

In a room where the windows open upon a landscape of grass and trees and a garden, flowers like brilliant lights in the twilight, illuminating a path along which we walk, together, our hands touching from time to time, walking toward the house, a moonless night about to fall, and a breeze that caresses us, without passion, really, a little sorrow behind the breeze, a breeze in which an animal's cry is veiled for an instant, a voice crying from a window overlooking the garden, and twilight transforming itself into night, lifting our eyes to the sky, you and me, and a cloying scent in the air, past and present acting capriciously, memory with its sense of humor, but I can't breath, you said, taking my hand, and we stood with the garden at our feet, gliding in the air above the earth, and flowers that were flourishing in that night, resembling tonight, drifting a little in the sky, we closed our eyes, dizzy and filled with conceit, soaring like birds in a night long ago, and beneath us a river, water flowing rapidly like a river, our mouths open, swallowing with a great thirst a little moisture in the air, nothing can come from outside you and me to teach us, you said, and you were talking about something beyond us, really, as man and woman, as if you had known always what we know now, saying good-bye, and no longer floating above the earth, but standing back to back at the brink of a river, without moving, as though we were about to take ten paces, it was like that, my darling, but this river, nothing was resolved about this river, a river rushing past us at full speed, with our eyes open, we were motionless at first, and then finding ourselves in midstream, in a river at night, a landscape stretching to a horizon of trees and stars, dwarfed by this great landscape and the river, something that ripens like grain, you said, but in our hearts, then as now, in our hearts there was nothing that resembled a field of gilded grass.

A diagram could be drawn before me as it was long ago, our hands clasped, fingers entwined, a drawing of this fitting landscape, a design that was given to us by God's intervention, providence, and whether it is acceptable or not, I know what you think of these things, the events of circumstances ascribable to divine interposition, if we take a breath, a moment in order to bath the clear air of reason, the normal exercise of our rational faculties, my darling, what we determine beneath the watchful gaze of the sky, what we learn in this night, and a night long ago, is that there is no real truth, maybe love is a kind of truth, and then we are left with our affections, our sex, sentiments, passion, our emotions, maybe this is a kind of truth, everything conditioned now entirely by feeling rather than reason, my darling, promise not to choke, it tastes a little like evil, and finally a denouement, the unraveling of some plot, separating the threads as our hands have unclasped, fingers no longer entwined, saying good-bye, and a faint light that illuminates us now through these windows, our eyes shut upon the night, our conceit allowing us an attempt at reason, a kind of truth, too, but it is ephemeral, what we are saying has nothing to do with what is happening around us, a cloying scent in the air above the garden that drifts without us to the sky, a virulent and bitter air, in a dark and curiously fainthearted night, the dignity of mystery giving way to the smallness of whispering voices, secrets without substance or intimacy, a veil that falls without direction, without a purpose, leaving only a sort of haziness, nothing more, and we hold our breath, together, our heads spinning like tops, it must be this oversweet air, our voices say, and we open our eyes at once, as if one pair of eyes or the other has suspected a cheat, a current of air, a violent blast of wind moving suddenly through the room, a little bravado in this quailing night, a sky's reckless bravery that fills us with virtue, a kind of moral quality bestowed all at once upon us by the elements of nature, and in this room, an embrace that takes us with impunity through the night.

An embrace that lasts as long as their voices are radiating in this night sky, the evening light illuminating a field of gilded grass, and their voices return in order to pierce their hearts, sticking their own souls, a field of gilded grass, each blade is covered by the finest leaf of beaten gold, but this grass is soaked with their blood, a man and woman lying in a field of grass, fainting from the fatigue of getting there, from the fatigue that will follow, the necessity of returning, and they are making love in this night, their souls spirited away to another part of the sky, a sky that is filled with the souls of lovers.

The rhythm of our pulse, together, as man and woman, single vascular system between us, oxygen and nutrients everywhere, removing what we do not need, what we cannot have within us, but this distance, something that a blood stream cannot abstract, powerless against this enemy, a distance that cannot be measured, and a life that breathes without lungs, yet we are not bound completely by its potency, its muscle, this distance is beyond measurement as a window's reflection is mysteriously our description of a course of time, an eternal reflection, yet within this reflection there is a familiar landscape in the twilight, a street lined with trees whose branches and leaves protect us from the gaze of others, what eyes could penetrate these branches, these leaves? a street with many passers-by, but a solitary figure standing beneath the branches and leaves of a tree, automobiles moving through the twilight, their headlights illuminating what lay before them, a solitary figure, street signs, trees and shrubs, other pedestrians, but a figure gazing up at our windows, open upon the night air, and your eyes were filled with tears, your face turning away slowly, a sorrow as thick as your black hair, and a tear that fell from your eyes into my hand, my darling, what makes a soul is its pain, you said, staring wide-eyed into the night, the pale shadow of a face, watching the winking eyes of traffic lights, the luminous navigation of empty trams beneath a firmament turning in every direction, you were waiting for someone, it was in your eyes, your mouth, an expression unchanged, then and now, looking at the solitary figure standing in the faint light of a street lamp, my eyes following yours, a night like this, warm and bright, a sky lighted by the electricity of a city at night, stars and moon having been mixed up with the terrestrial commerce, and the figure became smaller and smaller, shapeless, blurred by the night, and my fear, too, diminishing its importance as the certainty of its consequence grew, my heart beating imperfectly, but in the morning, without you, I could no longer remember that arrogance, my heart beating, but the rest had disappeared like some poisonous air, and later, your voice in the telephone saying, I can see the true smile of the soul from here, a burning taste in my mouth, and thereafter, a memory of you which described everything in ordinary language, unremarkable, and intentional, a kind of protective convering like the bark of trees, a cortex which had proved inferior after all, like the branches and leaves of a tree to the solitary figure, but now, your eyes and my eyes falling into each other, into a kindhearted, merciful abyss in which there are few tears, without immersion and suffocation in salt water, and holding out your hands, lines that are streets in the palms of your hands, a kind of map, a tiny city in which we live, together, as man and woman, and your mouth tastes sweet, my darling, my fingers tracing an imaginary path from your eyes to your mouth, a faint smile that appears, and a little laughter, too, we are swimming in a sea of laughter now, a little dizziness in which there is no conceit, no self-protection, and it seems that love is a kind of truth, at once, between you and me in this night, without enmity, without bitterness, it is not like before, a night long ago, memory unsettles the places of past and present, and our desires seem to direct them in their roles.

JOE MARSHALL - *Sacre Coeur* - 1997

JAMES A. EMANUEL

Dizzy Gillespie
(News of His Death)

Dizzy's bellows pumps.
Jazz balloon inflates, floats high.
Earth listens, stands by.

Sonny Rollins
(Under the Williamsburg Bridge)

Worldwaif: lone-wolf notes,
blown in pain with all his might,
heal themselves in flight.

Chet Baker

Songbird, lost, bright lights
his guide afar, JAZZ his fate,
Icarus his star.

Love and Sex, I

My skin kept her scent
as she swirled from the bed. "Love,
I've got to buy bread."

With your twin kisses
the town clock struck the hour TWO.
Mysterious you.

"I feel your eyes." This
she repeats. (NOTHING'S private
underneath these sheets.)

Dame Gravity, I

Guillotine's high blade
I teased. Royal red cascade
that river I made.

I helped hang John Brown,
pulled the *Arizona* down
(watched five brothers drown).

Like death my strength, such
as lightning's, or, leaning much,
like a lady's touch.

Anthony Sheridan

La Forêt Obscure

i

Izzie my footsteps have not forgotten you
What might have been and what has been
Don't point to one end which is always present
What might have been becomes revisited
Without the staid blind hands
Of Augustinian scholarship and Heraclitus
Clutching past the forest of buildings

Where are you going?
People withdrawing money from walls
Cars, lorries, bicycles, the eternal double bind of roads
Below the metro stations;
Chaussée d'Antin, Le Pelletier, Cadet, Poissonnière, Gare de l'Est
Château Landon, Louis Blanc
The journey down the line between Villejuif and La Courneuve
A painted door hanging ajar
Each stop and start and screech of brakes, each hoot of the electric
klaxon in the tunnel
Each flash of light the rhythm of the journey hasn't changed

And in every carriage the people are the same
I could approach the same space in three directions

Rue Perdonnet, behind rue Cail
Now the whole area has become Indian sub-continent
The *pâtisserie* has become Yalini Boucherie
The Félix Potin in rue Marx Dormoy is now Ed, l'Épicier
The *ébénistes* have gone, gone the bookshops
With their proud displays of the Pléiade in their windows
The shops now sell trinkets and *olé olé* videos
And here and there *agences de voyages*
With inviting fares to the Himalayas and Timbuktu

ii

Place Réal has gone now, given way to Place Paul Éluard
Where outside the café terrace, a Mickey and Donald carrousel
    1 tour 8 francs
Éluard hosts space ships fire engines horses and hollow swans
Motorbikes and pigs and ducks and horse-drawn carriages on bicycle
wheels for five year olds
The traffic blares past unmindful of his requiem

Place Paul Éluard Poète is not a square at all it is just a momentary
interconnection between two hectic roads
But on the nearby pavements the empty show must go on
Between the barred horse-chestnut tree and the green plastic bottle
bank built like a tank
Exclusivement réservé au verre
Déposez ici les objets en verre bouteille pot bocal flacon
Mais attention ne jetez absolument pas
Capsule bouchon faïence porcelaine plastique ampoule
(La présence d'éléments étrangers lors de la fusion du verre et du poète
Compromettrait les résultats de l'opération)
At place Paul Éluard
Le dépôt de verre est interdit entre 18 et 40 ans

Little Duke, *bébé* on board
At Marx Dormoy, at place Paul Éluard le Marché Franprix
Le *grillotin, coiffeur*, McDonalds Happy Meal

iii

Chacaned in coconut-oil, a wrap-around
Your long perfusions cowled in a silk band
You returned home very excited your eyes clear water
Your vulva moist because you had discovered
A covered market of scumbled reflections
Your shoulder hurt you from carrying the load
Courgettes tomatoes bananas oranges an aubergine
The next day we both bought blue grapes some pears potatoes onions
and radishes
The table was laden with you. Oil mingled with balm

Paris, windows over archways
Fin d'interdiction de stationner
Paris, Charbon Mazout, rue du Département — spécialités Asiatiques,
Douleurs Musculaires, Foulures, Courbatures, Contusions
Ballonnements? Flatulences, Aérophagie
On est mieux dans sa peau, quand la peau va mieux

Paris, Atila ✡ Oiseaux, Poissons
Paris, Laboratoire, Analyses
Paris, La Cité habille les corps nus

iv

Paris, nos raclettes, nos cartes des vins
Fondues servies le midi
Paris menu complet à 64 francs
Sacred precincts and passageways

Paris, Au choix:
1/4 vin et un café compris
2 entrées
2 plats chauds
2 desserts
Paris, alimentation et livraison à domicile
Paris, cours de grec moderne
Paris, vision des volcans
Paris, livraisons et enlèvements
Paris, Entrez lentement

v

Paris, windows mirroring windows, freestanding shafts of light
16, rue Cail, opposite Grain Magique that we never entered
Between two perpetually closed shops with frosted glass
The walk to Louis Blanc, *Défense d'afficher loi du 29 juillet 1881*
Rue Cail turning into Faubourg St. Denis the walk to Gare du Nord
Now half of Hôpital Fernand Widal has been bulldozed to make way for
Ligne E of the RER

       Like the notes of a concertina dropped from a high window
She became herself, walking and statuesque,
       Winding her hair about her
Paris, *Pompe Funèbre*
Paris, *Fermé le dimanche*
Paris, *Fabrication à l'Ancienne*
Paris, *La solution Intérimaire*
Paris, *Sari Palace*
Paris, *Restaurant Pizza, Achat or*
Paris, *Démolition, Terrassement,*
Paris, *Sub-way, U -bahn*
       All other signs are in trouble

Paris, Pigeons at the hôtel Apollo
Paris, *Chambres*
       Libres
       Vacancies
     Zimmer
    Frei
Paris, *Comment garder la forme après l'été*
       Méthodes de Stars et de top Models
Paris, *Fini les cheveux abîmés cassants fourchus et ternes*
Paris, *Piétons*
Paris, *Grillades au Charbon de bois*
Paris, *Kanchpuram Silk saree*
       Remise jusqu'à 50% jour et nuit
Paris, *le spécialiste du Transport*
Paris, *Recrute au fond du passage*
Paris, *Poussez*

vi

Barricaded in sunlight as you dressed
I forfeited dawn rituals in your arms
You pushed me away as you had always pushed
You had your life to attend to which was already
Waiting feeling you were always slightly late

Paris, *Chèque Déjeuner*
Paris, *Ouvert du Mardi au Samedi*
Paris, *Descente interdite danger de mort*
Paris, *Radiante*
Paris, *Serena*
      Le confort du corps
Paris, City of *brocantes*
      Perishable goods and embroidered socks
Paris, *Semelles en bois*
Paris, *Chaussures sur mesure*
Paris, *Orthopédie*
Paris, *Révisionniste*
Paris, nerves, hands and eyes,
Paris, flesh and hair
Paris, *Sortie*
      de voitures, Prière
      de ne pas stationner

Paris, city of sleek grey pigeons
Paris, *chef de secteur*
      1ᵉʳ bâtiment à gauche ☞
      Après le porche
      Au rez-de-chaussée
      Sur Rendez-vous
      Entrez
Paris, *Spécialités de la maison*
Paris, *plats à emporter*
We contrived to be together to the end

vii

I open the window and let other places enter
The darkness of a room as it passes, the prism
Of country railway stations, outhouses, deserted tracks
I have made a space in my arms for her
She was so close I felt her breathing change

Izzie I loved you
I loved you until the days divided us like milk

Left on the doorstep in another country that has been deserted long
before we left it
Not even remembering the number any more
Or how the street in which we walked adjoined the others
Where they went or how long for

What does it mean to be wandering through the backstreets home
To be with you
To be with you is still the same
To be with you is to forget everything
We have known

I carry with me fragments of a head
A large block decorated with a youthful figure bent
My youth was distorted in yours
My love fell in catenary folds
Suitable for a door jamb

We have known when dislocation dislocates itself
The body and its long drawn-out documentaries
In the bathroom cabinet, the apologias, and plastic
Expositions of animal remains, diluted and coloured
To the latest fashions, a hootchy-kootchy show
I don't know what was left behind in all this
I don't know what the leaving represented

What does it mean to arrive

viii

When the night is plunged into the night
I have seen the footsteps of the blind leading the blind
Through the *portillon automatique*
And reeling in the dark of your long shadow
Following your mind not knowing where your thoughts are going
Izzie, in the end it was not over
A hand which opens and fears it may close without you
A hand in reflux loses its own shape

Because your eyelids are luminous with sleep
They cannot see the intent of signs
Between the heart line and the head
This deepening execration
Paris, *il est interdit d'empêcher son fonctionnement*
Paris, *ne pas tenter de passer pendant la fermeture*
Tutte le strade portano
A Roma a roma

When the light enters you there is no way out
Elsewhere under the linden trees
A boy with a shattered bird in his mouth
Sings like a nightingale
The train passes through the catacombs
Paris, each moment, 250 boutiques 28 cinemas
Virgin megastore, a shadow operated rubber door
And only the anguished silence of the dead
Paris a lure by decantation
Exhuming out of its own ruin
A footloose excursion into *estaminets*

PAUL FAURE-BRAC - *Le Pont Neuf* - 1998

PAUL FAURE-BRAC - *Le Minotaure* - *1998*
Salvatore Dali's virile creature hiding the "secrets of the unconscious."
Place Vendôme, Paris

PAUL FAURE-BRAC - *La Femme en Flammes* - *1998*
Combining two of Salvatore Dali's favorite obsessions, fire and the female form.
Place Vendôme, Paris

ELLEN HINSEY

The Art of Measuring Light

from the Pont-Neuf, Paris

The light here has begun to pass and as it passes
it will bend down to the Seine in the last of its
winter gymnastics: unwrapping its hands from
the white crevices of Saint-Germain-des-Prés,

giving a last honor to Sacré-Cœur. One will
turn one's eyes to the horizon, but there only
shadows lie, and the beams of cars that follow
the Seine northward toward Le Havre, their lamps

yellow like the pleasure boats that illuminate
the shores with serpentine eyes. But standing
in half-light, the mind devises a method,
and knows that distance is an arc, not a line;

it will follow light as it curves past the river
to meet its welcome in woods, distant from
the sphere of the thinker, yet distant only as
a pair of hands, clasping a tool in a far-off field.

The body in its accuracy cannot close the calipers
of space, but knows just the same that light
that has passed here is light that will contrive
to touch the white of wood on maple-lined streets,

deep in New Hampshire, where snow is piling
high, in the unbroken shadow of a new day.
Where for the difference of six hours, the hands
of the clock are unlocked, and Puritans progress

with morning. They wil carve out a day, wrapped
in time, envisaged in the silence of apple and pine,
and of light curving to where it will break in the
suddenness of a windfall. Perhaps there one will

measure a quantum leap, where from pasture post,
to the end of the road, light will seize the form
of an animal breathless beneath the carcass
of a rusted frame; or watch as it breaks stride

at crossroads, finding figures passing surrounded
by the wreath of their breath. The sky is not a narrow
passage, and light is there to flex the ample arm of it.
On this side, the Pont-Neuf is dark, and the mind,

that lone traveler, comes back to rest like a cast
shuttle to a waiting palm. Across the bridges
night figures come, their loads weighted like
lanterns — swinging slowly in narrow arcs.

KATHERINE KNORR

from ***Snakeskin Sally***

a novel

" Snakeskin Sally" is the story of Sally Miller, an amiable gold digger whose life takes her from a rock band in the Wild West to a townhouse in Georgetown, while all around her the United States is experiencing some eerie problems.

It's all rock, twenty-four hours a day seven days a week, K-R-A-F, 100,000 watts of rock 'n' roll, it's 105 out there and climbing, I hope you're sitting by the pool or out at that lake, this is Steve Jones, it's 11:30 and I'll be with you rocking around the clock until one. Stay put and stay out of trouble. The city shimmers with heat, the metal and glass towers in the center and the miles of low white boxes reaching far into the desert, airplanes and cars and golf carts and fencing and seesaws are incandescent, the curtains are closed in coffee shops, drivers are invisible behind screens. At a big hotel on the mountain, the pool area is empty except for a dark-faced boy wiping tables, the men are in the bar, the ladies have gone upstairs to rest with black patches over their eyes. At the dude ranch, the retirees from New York are sipping ice tea in the lounge, wearing new Stetsons and cowboy boots, waiting for the evening ride, now and then rattling their turquoise jewelry. In backyards all over the Valley, children run one after the other on the sandpapery boards doing jacknives and double barrels, sending walls of water onto yellowing decks. Traffic is swift and cheerful down the highway into the desert, heat waves rise from houses on either side and obscure the mountains. And it's good to be with you, it's hot out there but we're too cool to care, this is Steve Jones, don't go away, here's a commercial message. The desert shines as though the sun were striking thousands of tiny pieces of glass, some skysize windshield that rained to the ground, the desert bristles with wiry red weeds and white-green cactus spiny and bird-holed, abandoned trucks here and there don't rust but crack into pieces like ceramic, turds whiten to powder and blow away in the slight wind that hugs the ticking, whining, buzzing ground. Along the straight, scalded roads, the billboard frames gleam like money. "REDISCOVER AMERICA," the posters say, and one shows friendly animals at Yellowstone and another stern-looking Yankees waving from the stoops of stone houses and another ballgowned belles standing under trees with guys in Confederate uniforms

and another some movie-star type surfing off Malibu, and they all say
"REDISCOVER AMERICA, It's Big, It's Clean, It's Yours." Some drivers who see
the ads are cheered by them, they, too, feel that people have forgotten about
their own country, that people have been neglecting their own backyard,
they've gotten lazy and cynical, they've forgotten what makes the country great,
and how big and beautiful it is, people have been traveling to other countries
and getting gypped by little greasy shopkeepers and surly managers of fleabag
hotels, when they could be traveling across the heart of America, some people
feel the ads are part of a cool and wonderful wind sweeping the country,
the dawn of a new and great America, other people are worried about the ads,
they feel they're part of some larger message that people in power are sending
out, part of a new campaign shaped by psychologists to tell people that
everything is really all right except they, people, have been kind of depressed
recently, it's like seasonal blues, and they should feel better about themselves
and about America, they should stand up straight and get back to their roots,
this is what made the country great, some people feel that everywhere they turn,
this is the message being put out. Dede Frankel is driving her son to the dentist.
They have to go downtown, it seems a long way now that they live on the other
side of the mountain in one of the new areas, her husband has been making
a lot of money in the stock market, and they have built a big house on three
levels with a circular driveway, and a huge, stepped backyard with an Olympic-
size pool. She's done the garden desert-style, with gravel and cactus, yucca
trees, barrel cactus and even saguaro, it bothers her sometimes that saguaro
are so expensive, and she knows they're ripped out of the desert, there's even
a business in stolen saguaros, but she figures they're probably better off in her
garden than God-knows-where. She is driving downtown, it seems a long way,
she notices a turnoff on the right that seems familiar, a closed gas station she
thinks she remembers being open, so many years ago now, on an impulse
she turns right and then right again, toward her old house and the high school,
but she becomes confused, the distances don't seem right, until she understands
that, where there used to be tumbleweed fields on the left, and some cotton
fields on the right, behind the golf course, it's all houses now, townhouses
and a few stand-alones, with steep little driveways, and she has to drive a long
way before she actually sees the high school, at an angle, an expanse of flat
buildings, desert-colored, without windows. "I can't believe it, Jimmy,"
she says, and he turns toward her, frowning, then grins his painful smile,
the braces. "I can't believe it, when I was a kid, when I was your age, this was
all fields." Jimmy shrugs his shoulders, an Oh-Mom kind of gesture, and she
thinks she must go on, they will be late, but as she turns her big car around,
she thinks, can it be, 18 years ago, we would never have thought we'd say

to our kids when I was your age, or this was different then, we didn't listen
to our parents talking about Michigan and Montana, that was such old stuff,
but we were so modern, we were the most modern people of all, we had money,
we drove cars, we dropped acid, we fucked in vans, it was 18 years ago,
we were the most modern people on earth, how can it be? We were on the
winning side of the generation gap. Dr. Thompson of the Earth Sciences
Department of the university is thundering about the Army Corps of Engineers
wanting to pave over the Grand Canyon and about how the water table is
dropping at a dizzying rate and how drinking water is saturated with E. Coli.
"E. Coli," he shouts, hitting his wooden lectern so that the mike makes crashing
sounds. "E. Coli, do you know what that is?" His thinning hair is floating
above his red forehead and his twitching eyebrows. Students in the large
auditorium shuffle their feet on the rubber strips that edge each tier.
"Damnation," he shouts as the mike plunges to the floor. The large, egg-headed
young man who teaches first-year English in the next auditorium is shouting too.
He's a junior professor, he dresses mostly in overalls, though for special
occasions, like today perhaps, he has a cape. "It's perfectly OK to listen to rock
music," he says, "or to go to the movies. But why do we have to get our
opinions from movie stars? Do I care who Warren Beatty is going to vote for?"
The students are bored by him, sometimes they're a little concerned; he gets so
excited. Later on, in his helter-skelter little study, he writes in a notebook:
"It doesn't matter anymore what you do or make or say. We came along
too late, there is nothing new. Things maybe but no ideas. There are no
philosophers anymore, only journalists. And sometimes, perhaps one should
see this as a relief. It's all on the surface and it doesn't hurt too much.
I'm not going to get tenure." In a large, flat building off the highway,
the salesmen stand around a display case where there is a model of the
development and of the individual houses for sale. There are three of them,
each in short sleeves, with eyeglass cases and pens in their shirt pockets,
they squint out at the hot desert for incoming vehicles. The waiting area
of the restaurant is a small, low-ceilinged room with red cushions and rough
wood-paneling and paintings of bronco riders. It is icy with air-conditioning,
but there is warmth in the dimness, the candles in red-netted jars, the big
wooden ashtrays, and the very smallness of the place, with the smell of steaks
and herb bread wafting in whenever the manager opens the doors and beckons
someone in. The waiting area is full, big men standing slightly hunched,
when the man pulls out his gun. People afterward say it was a miracle
he hadn't killed more people, and how it could have happened to anyone
who'd gone to lunch there, it was just the luck of the draw. The man had been
writing letters to prominent people explaining precisely what he was going to do

and why. He is dead now, and they keep all that out of the papers.
It's all rock, twenty-four hours a day seven days a week, K-R-A-F, it's 118 out
there, you can fry an egg on your cool deck, stay out of trouble, Stan the Man
is coming up next, stay tuned, baby. A college girl with pimples is writing
in her diary: "This place is so far away from everything, and near to nothing,
without the grace of sea or forest. It's ingratious and dusty and hot.
How could this have happened to me?" In the big developer's office, which
is wood-paneled and cold and dark, the little group of environmentalists,
waiting, seems to huddle together. They've lost the flame, the ardor they had
when they rehearsed the meeting. When the developer comes, he's not what
they expect, he is tall and good-looking, smoking a big cigar, with a deep voice.
They mumble their little speech, he blows smoke toward them, he leans forward
and smiles at them and says things that twist their insides, he says man is
entitled to use the water, he says he wouldn't want to live in a time when
everybody had the shits all the time, he says the Indians have had plenty of time
to get off the hootch, and then he laughs very loudly and says, "Yes, I know,
they are a classic case of an aboriginal people who have been confronted
with the shock of a more advanced world and have succumbed to its diseases.
Ah, yes, colonizers have been ruthless. Shall we say the word? Imperialism!
Oh phooey. This country isn't imperialist. It just rewards the hard-working
and the strong. What the hell's the matter with that? Go back to your
classrooms, ladies, good day." At the dude ranch out in the desert, one of the
old men, who wears a huge hat and patent-leather boots, regrets having fallen
for the cut-rate deal that brought him here. It's too hot to ride until late in the
day, and then he's too tired, it's too boring to spend the day at the swimming
pool, and he has begun to miss going in to the shop every day, annoying his son,
as he knows he does, telling him where to put his new videos and how people
expect the salesmen to be gruff, that way they know they're getting a bargain.
He goes into the television room, just in time to see a whole bunch of Japanese
men waving their arms around and slamming down telephones, and he wonders
whether this is new film each time, or if they just run the same crazy traders
each time buying and selling shares in that curious sign language he doesn't
understand, he always preferred things more concrete, bills and coins,
merchandise you could count, and there they go again, a frenzy of sign-making,
and one of the little Japs slams his head down on the desk, lets his phone fall
on its back next to a computer screen, and then we're back in America, it seems,
big boys in suspenders striding around a room full of computers, some
brokerage house then, big boys in suspenders and more phones, people standing
and sitting, guys hunched over, whispering into their phones maybe, and then
it's back to the anchorlady, a nice-looking one, and he pays attention, it looks

like they're arresting people, but he can't concentrate on the story because
behind the anchorlady, out of focus, there are other people in suspenders,
big guys walking around, talking to each other with one foot up on the desk,
big shoes, he wonders if they're really journalists, or just actors brought in
to give atmosphere, and they're like shadows, big boys in suspenders, hitching
up their pants, picking up phones, he thinks the world fell apart when people
stopped dealing in things you could count, all those boys, their parents saved
to get them into college, they ran their little shops and saved so the boys could
be doctors, and they're not doctors, they've gone into bigger shops, and they're
trading things you can't count, like electricity, you can't see it, you can't count
it, no wonder they're being arrested, those boys lost their way, they stopped
listening to their fathers. Over in the townhouses all the women are doing
laundry, moving a load to the dryer, starting another in the washer, a little
weary, a little drawn, wide-faced and wide-assed, taking things in stride,
well-educated, short-haired and sensible, divorced, abandoned. They were

once vaguely hippies, before they
cut off all their hair, they helped
draft dodgers, they lived
in communal houses, they had
avocado plants on the window,
weed in the backyard, but they
were solid and sensible then,
too, now they do laundry, it's
Saturday, they're a little weary,
divorced, abandoned, sensible,
wide-assed, you can still see in

BOB BISHOP - *photograph*

their pale, slightly swollen faces
the upturned nose that made them so cute at 16. At a resort on the mountain,
Alexandra Pierce lies in the shadow of a parasol, zinc oxide white on her nose,
wondering if she's gone for good this time. She thinks of her husband,
so earnest and English and sweaty in bed, she can't remember why she married
him, but then most people don't remember, do they, she lies in the shade
by the big pool, and suddenly she wishes she had not so flippantly ignored all
the things that were offered once and no longer, she thinks that somewhere
in the vast and romantic attic in England where her mother, widowed and
slightly restless, keeps the commencement dresses of long dead maiden aunts
and top hats and high-buttoned shoes and silver toilet sets and uncut lengths
of stiff black silk, and also musty eiderdowns and worn embroidered linen
sheets and superseded tea china and a rusty metal chandelier, bought at an
auction and never hung, now resting cobwebbed and crooked on extremities

folded in like a crippled sheep's legs, she thinks that somewhere there might be
a dried flower arrangement under glass, or a leather-bound drawing pad with
sketches of 18th-century costumes labeled in her never disciplined handwriting,
or even a scrap of tapestry or unfinished embroidery that could testify to the
dozens of elegant and difficult little skills she had poorly learned and then
forgotten, so that she regrets now having rebelled against such inoffensive
learning, and wishes she had kept these talents, now emptied of their symbolism,
of the tediousness of girlhood, of study rooms, early lights out, useless, exciting
and sad dirty stories. They walk and walk and walk. It's still hot in late
afternoon, and all their walking doesn't take them far, they don't have the
endurance or the patience maybe the resignation of pilgrims bringing
gangrenous limbs or sterile wombs or idiot children to Lourdes or Compostella,
they never considered becoming nuns or servants, they have regular lives but
also this mission, a conviction that they can change the world, bring forth light
to this darkness where dollar bills have replaced Bibles, they walk and walk
and they sing, to make sure that no one will ever allow the baby killers to open
shop in the Valley. "Tell me something," says the man driving the big yellow
Thunderbird seventy-five miles an hour on the trench-straight road through
the desert, but many other things take place suddenly, fountains shoot up from
the pale earth and the blue mountains recede like clouds, and pale low buildings
appear behind a ridge, a pole with an American flag and some banners with
writing on them, like gigantic football pennants, many other things happen,
"Tell me something" is never followed up or answered, the Thunderbird speeds
down the highway, a roar in the silence. The mountains, the camel-colored dirt,
the brushweed like velvet, the little twinkling lights on the low buildings,
everything seems to recede as the car moves, darkness empties the sky, the earth
is great and wide and dark here, as the Thunderbird heads for land beyond
the limits of the known world. "Tell me something." Along the wide, flat
streets, the business lights go on, the pink flamingos, the blue cocktail glasses
that lean right and left like a couple twisting, the motel signs, lagoon-shaped,
golf-course-shaped, with a strip of turquoise neon and pink lettering and
the red VACANCY sign, the pool halls with lights that snake around the sign,
a few bulbs always dead, the restaurants with red flames and huge skewered
steaks, everywhere bronco riders in blue barely hanging onto horses in red, bucking
again and again, everywhere green saguaro against red mountains, cha-cha-ing
golf clubs watched by dinosaurs, hard white lights, too, everywhere, advertising
Specials, Bargains, Mark-Downs. In the northern suburb, the pale, stringent
light forms a large parallelogram across the slightly rough surface of the street,
and the smooth white sidewalk, and the lawn, nearly drained of any real color
but glittering briefly as though artificial-finishing, the light, against the ocher

facade of a house, where a metal door handle glints darkly. Beyond, the street darkens, narrows into indistinctiveness, trees and fences and rooves and cars all shades of brown with, below, the equidistant violet ovals projected by street lamps and, above, the immense, starry curve of the desert sky. The western sky is red, the mountain black, the sloping golf course striped with shadows. On the cross street, car rooves shine eerily, headlights come on, the gas station lights buzz, pale at first and gradually brightening on a large triangular sign that leads the small building like a prow. From the road that circles the mountain, the flatness of the city seems lit by thousands of tiny white stars. Closer in, on the roads that sixlane across the Valley, the tropical-pink and swimming-pool-blue lights tremble and flash in the silence of constant traffic. It's only the second night, but it becomes clear that the merry-go-round is in the wrong place. Traffic rushes by on the busy road, flashing lights emphasize the daily special at the coffee shop across the six lanes, the merry-go-round's lights seem pale and dusty. Just as the operator decides to close, two teen-age girls in a stationwagon stop, they ride for nearly an hour and a half, going from the red rocket to the blue submarine to the yellow race car. They smoke cigarettes and laugh, he thinks they are a little drunk, but only a little. This sort of thing happens to him, he is tall, rangy, girls have always been easy. But his week is wasted, he has lost interest in most things. Later, he waits in the little vacant lot, wondering who the next fool will be — a rifle stand, a dancing bear. The big truck will come and take him somewhere else. Dave Probat, former homecoming king, former All-American, now the manager of an air-conditioning company, opens the front door and sees there are no lights in the living room. He stops, he swallows, how many times, he thinks, there is the halo at the hallway door of light from somewhere else, and hushed music, and he thinks he must get out of this, it's once too many, she's in the kitchen dressed like a girl in her too-tight cheerleader's costume, an ashtray full of cigarettes, passed out. He remembers how pretty she was, and how serious, with her dark eyeliner and her teased hair in pigtails, he married her seriousness. She falls off the kitchen chair. At the gas station, the phone rings and rings. No one will know until morning that the attendant is dead. Someone has written something on his forehead. They will keep that out of the papers. The restaurant at the Five Seasons Hotel is crowded and lively, candles on every table, big torches that look like they're burning hang from the walls as though in some ancient castle, one whole wall is taken by a fountain that gurgles over turquoise lights, the whole thing topped by a big fishing net with colored balls and exotic flowers and pictures of Polynesian belly dancers. The waitresses scurry around with platters of meat and baked potatoes, or rounds of drinks from the shiny red bar, the diners are big, joyful

people with good appetites. The lights all go out suddenly, there is a hush,
a small cry. Then a group of women in sarongs come out holding a huge cake.
"Happy Birthday," the diners sing, slightly relieved. The desert night is cold
and black, even the mountains have disappeared. The scientists have set up
their watch very far out, behind a little hill, so that they won't be confused
by city noise, or by cars on the highway. They're wearing flannel shirts and
padded vests and drinking coffee from a thermos and still getting groggy
and irritable. They are the new kind of scientist, with big beards, they believe
the earth is a living thing and a fragile one and that they must protect it from
people with crewcuts and black-rimmed glasses and pen holders. Despite
the coffee, they fall heavily asleep, and only one, waking just before dawn
with a pasty mouth, thinks he hears some of the alarming noises people have
been reporting, the ticking and the grinding of gears and the whistling.
They'll have to come out again the following night. People hear the explosion
for miles. There is a huge detonation, then silence, then a series of explosions
that to the people furthest away sound like firecrackers, then a yellow flame
shoots up through the trees. It's banal, the young man was unemployed
and he drank a lot and he fell asleep with a lit cigarette. He lived in a three-
room cabin north of the city, two of the rooms were packed to the ceiling with
ammunition. They find very little of him, but they do find, 100 feet away
and nearly intact, a notebook he'd been writing in. There are some pretty
strange things in there. They will keep that out of the papers.

JOHN NOONAN

Days of Life and Death

I wake up in a rooming house sweat
trying to catch my chain-smoke breath
feel like blowing off the back of my head
I swear these dreams are gonna do me in

Man-made animals
blooded sheets
of coded messages
drape the street
where I run among the wires
through emergency rooms
lit with trash can fire
WORK NOW
the message barks

Can't handle that radio yet
I ain't heard the news
but I know it's bad
the sun moves across the bricks
starts its stretch
these are the days of life and death

Guess I'll go downstairs now
and get some breakfast
a couple scrambled
just like my brain
buy a paper
open to the funny pages
the only place I feel remotely safe
coffee black
no Sugar
I'm not the one for you

I'm a hounded
I'm a haunted
to many things I have got to do

Down Broadway
that river of bones
'neath God's sky
I blast
the slaughter cast
before my eyes
victim voices
hard and close
pound in my head
a gravity sound
with the wind they howl
these are the days of life and death

In the hills
above the river
with the hunted
I huddle in the dust
belongings piled all around us
compass shattered
on the run
take the night
get some rest
hold the children close to your breast
even these dark days will pass
these days of life and death

No Place To Call Home

Music by James Wilson and John Noonan

Wearing her sneakers and it's seven below
with no socks to be seen
in that black New York snow
with the wind off the Hudson like a big Mack truck
knock you right down and won't let you back up
Oh it's Merry Christmas
and a Happy New Year
but it's not so merry when you're standing down here
no it's rough and a humblin'
and riddled with fear

So it's back to the shelter
and back to her cot
where she huddles in the dark
holding everything she's got
her knife
her suitcase
some tired, tattered clothes
her purse
her papers
some battered, old photos
snapshots of her sister and herself at the beach
with their kids
in the summer of nineteen fifty-three

Chorus

Oh where do they come from
and where will they go
a shelter's just no place to call home
tell me
where do they come from
and where will they go
the thousands and thousands and then thousands more

On cardboard in a doorway
I see him most nights
near the candy store window
by the streetlight
he says, "hey old-timer are you feeling all right
can you let me hold somethin'
I'm a little bit light

When I was a young man
a young man like you
I had me a good wife
and pretty she was too
but the TB it took her
and part of me died
now I live out here
out here in the wild"

Chorus: *with word* Doorway's *instead of* Shelter's.

In the subways a slow suicide
spins it sad web
for Christ's sake to get anywhere
you run the gauntlet
through the junkies and hustlers
and ones left for dead
spun helpless from the hospitals
where there's not enough beds

Through the mothers with their children
held hopeless on their hips
through a sea of shattered acrobats
who must have missed the net
and the trains scream
through this godforsaken mess
scream for a mercy
that just doesn't exist

Chorus: *with word* Subway's *and then repeated with* Street's.

A L I C E   N O T L E Y

La Nativité

Cocoon   life-sized
begins to open, pearls line the split in the silk.

— the baby is born inside the mountain
the mother and her baby
are wrapped in a dark blue same as the midnight's;
inside a mountainlike opening, surrounded by dim
haloes rubbed into pleasant tactile ochers
the long blue body and its serious unfeminine face.

Simmered simmered the whole world
that. simmered in a bain-marie
as the whole world once did,
darkhaired baby. alive, and the serious face.
confined to the whole wide sky, I find
cocoon opening. silk all around
bilateral symmetry, and here's a cathedral the mind
to glorify the birth ...

More freely I was the one weren't you
and am and am a hawk of sorts, a kwah kwah kwah

into the blue bursting. empty cocoon purse again. the stars
come out impossibly over a city and near a vacant lot, because my
purse is empty.
so, on the lot have constructed by telepathy a church of reality the
mind
I hand it to you in this vision the little *maquette* of it, because it has
to
be something, with light, domes piled up and a casual huddling
effect, brown as
          beauty.

all, because that's possible, since all's just a word. flying the
midnight and if I then
died into pieces, would reconstitute safely, because that's the way

I am riding simultaneity spread out all over
and the screams of all at the same time in ropes bind the globe
uncured because of
disbelief. there is a picture of this: black cries seeping up, a
nightmare why,
and words don't heal, unless true and swift as up here.
gold cure pain gold everywhere   where you see other
pictures spilled out. I'm now in the nave
gold, gold soothing the unhappiness standing for nothing.
inside the skull, gold foil. am describing the world
song of no packages, what you want won't get,

want it doesn't matter

and let it all fall. flying again though they try to hold you back, all
the word people.

JOHN KLIPHAN

Dirge For A Dead Night

The long and the short
   of a real shitty night
Is the insight you get
From the loss of the bet
And the price down the tubes
And the boobs never felt
And the swelter of summer
   a long way away
And you pay
And you pay
And you pay
And you pay
And the play of
   the horribles
Lost in your belly
Is telling you something
Is telling you never —
Never again will you do
   all this shit
In the ritual certainty
Earned in the pit
Of a candle not lit
Of a ball never hit
Of a horse with a bit
In his mouth in a world
Which will never be right
Where the looseness is tight
And nothing
And nothing
And nothing will fit

ENGLAND

FRANCE

Rennes

BRITTANY

MICHAEL ZWERIN

from Devolutionary Notes

"A Case for the Balkanization of Everyone"

"You can't organize this place like the others."
Major-Domo of Brittany (1703)

Rennes: Occupied Brittany

A Conglomerate Motel, the heart of the beast.

Monyglot modernity behind artificial turf just off the freeway. Unmusical Muzak, three-decker club sandwiches, synthetic plants, sanitized toilets — one more multi-national castle featuring jet-lag and steering-wheel hypnosis.
Pale people in purple lobbies with carry-on bags. Putrid drapes in perfumed fortresses. It was embarrassing.

Here I was researching a book on national minorities, on the birth of "Nationism," a new form of nationalism that has at its center the will to remain different, minority cultures fighting a last-ditch battle to save themselves from this very creepy beast which eats the same food, watches the same images, listens to the same music, wears the same clothes, governs with the same inhuman inefficiency everywhere; this conglomerization called internationalism. Researching the small, the traditional, the individual, why had I checked into a Conglomerate Motel?

Will you believe me if I say the other hotels were all booked? No? What if I say they were too noisy, dirty or overpriced? Not that either? Okay ... how about a weak side? Everybody has their weak side.

I soaked in Conglomerate bath foam. Aahhh ... I adjusted my very own personal thermostat to an unecological 75° and when I got out, if ever, I would order a steak from room service.

Soaking, I decided that the Conglomerate Motel is not in bad taste really, more an absence of taste, literally no taste to the place. No past and not much of a future judging from the plaster already peeling around the edge of the tub. Its personality is designed to insult absolutely nobody, in other words, no personality at all. An absence of flavor. No taste.

When the French lecture the Bretons: "You are French, not Breton," they really mean: "You are American." More precisely: "You are a world citizen." For the French are no longer capable of defending their culture against American colonialism, or rather it is no longer either French or American, only Conglomerate. The French will probably not like to hear that they no longer have any culture of their own. They are surely not prepared to admit it. Still, the evidence seems overwhelming. At least it seemed overwhelming, soaking in the tub. We are all soaking in Conglomerate bath-foam, trying to forget the creeping rot outside. The Conglomerate Motel appeals to the same weak side which allows us to accept MORE as an ethic, which says slow is bad, fast is rich, big is better, poor is inferior and minorities are minor. States run on our weak side. We wallow in our weak side.

The foam flattens. My skin crinkles. Dial 9 for a steak. Make several phone calls (direct dial) to Breton autonomists to confirm tomorrow's appointments. Smoke a joint ...

Marijuana, muggles, pot, grass ... once itself a symbol of protest against THE SAME and MORE. Let the squares waste their lives hustling after money and power, let the squares get sloppy drunk to forget how they are wasting their lives. Not us. We're hip. This is one of the few things Monyglot Conglomerates Inc. cannot occupy: Internal Space. I claimed my freedom to commit "victimless crime" from a presumptuous State long ago.

But lo and behold. Here too THE SAME caught up with me. Every advertising executive and lawyer worth his martini now smokes grass in America, which has exported it just like Kojak (currently showing on the Conglomerate's shiny receiver.) Easy Rider turned out to be just one more example of cultural imperialism rather than revolutionary statement. (History is running backwards.) But old habits are hard to get rid of (I would not object to your calling it a habit) and although it is no longer the symbol of anything, I was totally smashed in my plush, sealed cage when one of tomorrow's appointments rang on the house phone. He had a change of schedule and came by on the off-chance I might be free tonight.

Free? Tonight?!

Sober up! Get your act together. Let in some air. Wash your face. Brush your hair. Collect some intelligent questions. Check-out the tape recorder. Time to think in French. Time for some serious conversation in the lobby of the Conglomerate Motel.

"Would you like some snuff?"

Snuff?! Where are we? What century is this? Who is this guy? I'll call him Hardy, this redfaced man with a fertile beard of prematurely grey hair; overweight, wearing a black turtleneck, extending a small wooden container. My records showed he was a member of the Breton Communist Party.

He poured some brown powder on the hollow between my thumb and forefinger. Just the ticket to clear the muggles out of my head. "What do you think about the transmitter affair?," I asked.

One week before my arrival in occupied Brittany the French State television transmitter in Roc-Tredudon, near the western tip of this peninsula jutting into the Atlantic, was blown up by the *Front de Liberation de la Bretagne* (FLB).

There's about an explosion a week in Brittany. The *Prefect* of Cotes-du-Nord (one Department of Brittany) was quoted: "Nothing but a mess provoked by some retarded students." The FLB is composed of less than a hundred militants whose techniques have earned the admiration of both the IRA and ETA, Irish and Basque "retarted students" respectively. Members of the FLB work on railways, fishing boats, in canning factories. They blow something up on Saturday night, Monday morning they're back on the shop floor. They know how to to disappear. They are hard to catch and so, lacking the individuals, the French government banned the organization giving it even more publicity and recognition. The Breton autonomist movement had been on the front pages for weeks now. There were more than the usual number of French police on Breton roads, checking the papers of ordinary locals. Some ordinary locals were beginning to say that if there wasn't a Breton liberation movement, maybe there should be.

"What transmitter affair? I never heard of any affair. You heard anything about a transmitter?" Hardy turned to a companion who had just entered the lobby and joined us in our corner. I'll call him "Laurel." Laurel was thin and kept scratching the top of his head with his fingertips in puzzlement, a mannerism which, together with the obese joviality of his friend, reminded me of the famed comic duo of yore.

"Me? Not me," said Laurel, rolling his eyes in mock horror. He was wearing serious walking boots caked with mud and a leather jacket. He scratched his head again, took a sniff of snuff and pretended to pick his nose as Hardy tried to turn serious: "... As they say, it doesn't mean anything to own the universe if you lose your own soul ..."

I had the distinct impression that they had tried to sober up for me.

" ... We say that when you destroy the soul of a nation you destroy its capacity to create, to construct a viable society. When you hide their present from them, destroy their cultural inheritance, you make it impossible for a people to construct their future ..."

Laurel held up two fingers like horns behind Hardy's head. Hardy
continued: "That's what has been happening here. The history of Brittany
is forbidden, systematically camouflaged, we are taught only French history
with the objective of making us as French as possible. The Breton language
is systematically hidden from us. It is not allowed in our schools. This is
what we call the colonialization of the spirit."

Hardy caught Laurel making horns and gave him a hit on the head.

Laurel shook his head, rattled it back and forth for awhile and then
shrugged his shoulders with a look that said ... what can I do? I seem to be
in this absurd movie ...

"Oh come on," said Hardy after some more snuff-sniffing. "We can be
honest with Mike. Mind if we call you Mike? Tell him about the transmitter.
You were there. Come on, own up to it."

Which Laurel did, and which is the reason I have disguised their real
identities. However, they had not asked me to disguise anything. I was puzzled:
"How do you know I'm not a cop?"

"As a matter of fact, the thought crossed my mind," said Hardy, apparently
not particularly bothered by it.

Laurel smiled proudly, describing his glorious explosion, the close-call he
had with a watchman, the planning and coordination it had taken to blow up
the transmitter without loss of life: "Of course, we don't expect the masses
to understand. Television is a drug, and if you take people's drugs away
they will not be happy at first. But they'll understand in the long run.
They are our people. We speak the same language."

Hardy was quick to assure me that the Breton Communist Party definitely
does not speak the same language as the French Communist Party: "They are
not amusing people. French Communists do not know how to smile."

We moved into the restaurant, a tidy place with a long Formica counter
and red-clothed tables along a picture window overlooking the swimming pool.
The Conglomerate no longer embarassed me. Laurel and Hardy seemed
perfectly comfortable in those "counter-revolutionary" surroundings.
My explanations for having checked-in here had been shrugged off with:
"After the revolution everybody will be able to stay here."

They ordered a bottle of 1966 Bordeaux, and a dozen oysters each.
Hardy offered a toast: "Make love during war."

The counter filled up with a number of staight-looking students dressed
formally who had come in from the ballroom on the other side of the lobby,
where, our waiter told us, the local dental school was holding its annual dance.
The students were neat, conformist, very French. You might think them the

classic bourgeois enemy of a Breton Communist ... if you did not know about
Brittany.

The students were giggling, they had a happy buzz and were by and large
a rather attractive bunch. Having just been served a heaping bowl of mussels,
one of the girls leaned over to our table to inspect Laurel's oysters: "Ooohh ...
oysters," she cooed: "Are they good?"

Laurel batted his eyes: "I'll trade you my oyster for your mussel."

She laughed. Hardy offered her some snuff. Laurel opened Hardy's mouth
and poured an oyster in it. Hardy gulped and poured some 1966 Bordeaux
on Laurel's head. Two revolutionaries in the Conglomerate Motel, the heart
of the beast, the heart of the ethic of MORE and THE SAME, which, we are
beginning to understand, is not the same in Brittany, or for that matter in
any portion of the map of States where Nationism thrives.

Around midnight, they excused themselves. There were posters to paste up.
Then they had to awake at six to go to the factory. I looked at my watch:
"You don't sleep much, do you?"

"No," they said in unison: "But we sleep well."

CAROL PRATL

Russian Patchwork

Piece 1

I made an exodus from West to East
and found miracles in simplicity
that senses numbed by saturation
could never imagine

vodka was my mother's milk
in the crumbling cancer ward
of a Moscow clinic
drowning out the smells of iodine
and rotting meatballs
the smells of doomed flesh
and rusting faucets
dripping cholera onto flooded bathroom floors
no Russian soul remained here
on Christmas Day

she lay there pale and naked
for seven days and seven nights not uttering a sound
at the stroke of midnight
the red-eyed nurse would whisper
"I'll trade you some morphine for Chanel N°5"
and vanish briskly across the hall, winking slyly
some hope was bought with a credit card
and it was kept under lock and key like a nuclear arm
phones were out of order
dirty sheets piled high in the cone form of a Yuletide tree
the flashing eyes of overfed rats its only ornaments

she awaited some sign motionless as I looked out onto the road
16 stories below, the snow alone shone innocent
as the kremlin bells wailed the suffering of a thousand years
5 pm, the stench of tobacco and cognac
spilt into the hall from the unshaven surgeon's office
peals of laughter reached a peak
merging with the piercing moans of abandoned others
the women of dostoevsky, the whores of gorky

vodka was my mother's milk
the courage to knock on a door and buy salvation
I silently placed the offerings of three kings
on the blood-stained table:
whisky and chocolates and Paco Rabane
toy machine guns, Dior lipsticks and French champagne
I reached that invisible line
where the oriental bumps the occidental off the map
and you are its sheherezade for a night
where the breath of life dances between two spirits
hovering in the silence of a held hand

vodka was my mother's milk
until her eyes opened seven days later
and we at last had one together near a square no longer red
with imported strawberries dipped in the new year's snow

FRANK CLUCK

Le Cerisier

She's drunk again, been drunk for the last two months. Every afternoon it starts, this numbing, this dying. She's tired, afraid to go. She prepares a glass; she prepares her leaving, as birds might get ready to migrate in that swirling flight, that circling and swooping, in that gathering up of each other and one's self, getting dizzy, getting wound up to go.

She's leaving and so she's killing it off — the fear, the couple, the family — or what's left of it. That takes strength and courage and alcohol. She's drunk and on the ground. You are in the tree.

Who knows where she was this afternoon. At the gym. With her lover. Or really with her alibi friend for tea. You accept her cover thinking better to let her live with a lie than strip that away from her too. And what if she really were at tea, or that the drinking started there, or with her lover, or both? This evening she pulled on your arm like a child urging you toward a carousel.

Et les cerises reviendraient contre ton gré. Et ton deuil n'en finirait pas.

The air blows warm. Dusk will last until after ten tonight, and the cherries will all be gone to the birds, if they aren't picked now. As it is, the most brazen — the magpies, the crows — winged a circle around the garden this morning, marking off the place for the scarecrow drama that you are. They are not afraid; only the two of you are afraid and in fearing become what you fear most, fear what you have become.

Et les cerises reviendraient contre ton gré. Et ton deuil n'en finirait pas.

You are of as many minds as the tree has leaves murmuring in the weakening breeze, fading, strangely silent with the dying light, as if the dusk does not move, as if the night cannot speak, as if the dark holds no thoughts. You let your shoes drop, you let the cherries drop, you let *her* drop through a drunkening hole in her black night. The basket can hold no more. You shake the tree, she gathers what falls, burnished red on the green and shadowed grass. Even now, even drunk and piping up to you like some grounded bird, she attracts what light is left. She is a force.

Tu veux crier ton amour d'en haut de l'arbre, tu veux pleurer rouge de ton cœur qu'elle t'écoute, tu veux l'arroser avec tes larmes qu'elle se réveille et qu'elle reste ... Mais tu ne cesses pas de la lapider avec les cerises, de laisser tomber la grêle rouge de ton cœur de glace, de cueillir en haut du ciel du soir, et de laisser tomber une moisson d'étoiles froides à ses pieds.

In a month she will be gone forever. You do not know this yet and the unknowing holds you up, bouys your thoughts as the branches spring with your weight. Not knowing, you pick cherries as an act of faith, an imperative of nature — an ignorant motion at dusk. If you had known, you would have fallen from the tree, the darkening sky; if you would have known, you would have fallen with her into the black nowhere of the future; if we all knew, we would act no more, the world would stop, stop turning, stop the sun, stop the coming of light, stop tomorrow — or the branches would break with our weight.

PETER MIKELBANK - *Triporteur*
Marais, Paris, 1995

PETER MIKELBANK - *Truffle Hunter*
Le Marché aux Truffes - 1991

LINDA HEALEY

Let's Say I

Let's say I went to bed
in black lace-up boots, black
ribbed stockings pulled down
around my ankles, black skirt pulled up,
hands tied together with what feels like
black cord, my mouth on my shoulder,
camisole? little black straps pulled down,
I'm longitudinal like a Klimt or a Schiele,
the room feels like Central Europe, candle-
yellow, and let's say I just *come to*:

It's mine, it's all going to belong to me;
not your hands on my throat in Alsace,
the door in your eyes: open, *open*

DENISE LARKING COSTE

The House on the Dunes

Like a dove. Grey and white, warm-breasted like a dove. The clap-board house, the deck over the whispy grass in the dunes down to the milk sea. She leaned on the wooden railing, looking out over the ocean, her fair hair almost white in the pale evening sun. A feather caught in the dune below. The dove, perched at the end of the balustrade, she watched the flight of the gull. Up, wide-winged over the sea then the straight plunge down to the beach and the proud head as he strutted on the sand.

She sees the rear doors of the empty bus open. She is seated on a bench in the shade of a tree, the pavement melting beneath. It is so hot and then the bus. Empty. Inviting her to enter. Mount the steps let the doors fold closed behind her sink on to the seat. Not a look behind for those that will wait. Just forward to wherever the vehicle is going. To the end of the road and then descend and find some cool, quiet place.

From the deck at night they could see the big fishing boats lined up like warships, facing inland. A symetrical line of lights and the distant roar of their motors as they attacked, their wide nets trawling the bottom of the sea. Their noise disturbed, so did the sinister points of light. They looked inhuman, unmanned. Where were the colourful boats of the past? Wood-built, nets folding over the side like widows' veils down into the deep?

The doors slam closed behind her as she makes her way up to the driver to get a ticket. Where to? The last stop — wherever that is. She sits by a window looking through the dirty glass and seeing nothing as the bus starts pulling out from the curb. Did they see her get in, the doors sliding shut behind her and start running to hold her back? No voices calling out, she lowers the window and the air, even warm, is a relief. Life warped she sits back, closes her eyes, relaxes a little. Rid of them. These people she loves so much. Their benevolence. Their silent criticism. She has done it. She has made the break.

They sat on the deck in the bright morning sun having breakfast. They shared out the papers and now and then one of them would comment a news item without looking up. Just the rustle of the paper and now and again the comment between a sip of burning black liquid. They knew how to make coffee. They knew how to make love.

The old bus jerks through the hot town traffic, now stopping in the shade of a plane tree, now out under the hot sun. It passes the port on the right, the ferries and cargos preparing for the evening departure and then takes the coast road to the north. Little by little the town falls away, the buildings thinning out and there is air, more space and views out to sea. No trees now as the bus winds up the coast, dust clouds billowing behind.

Cold lobster for lunch, should they eat on the top deck or the lower one? Maybe a little too much air for the lower one, more exposed. Bands of grey-blue sky, grey-green sea, white sand and then the grey grassed dunes up to the house, grey and white like the rest. On the table under the parasol icy wine stood in the bucket before being poured into the tall blue glasses brim full.

The air cools as the bus rattles to a stop in the villages, spaced out now, some on the side of the bare hills as the road climbs, some down on the sea shore in the shade of a few sparse trees. The opening doors let in a rush of sweet air before clanging shut as the vehicle jolts on. She leans her head against the window feeling curiously rested, calm she awaits the end of the road to come, and then her getting off wherever that will be.

Terminus. The driver looks around. She is alone at the back of the bus. The last stop. She looks out, some small houses scattered along the shore. Two tall, dusty eucalyptus trees. A couple of fishing boats pulled up on the beach. She rises, walks up to the head of the bus, smiles at the driver, descends. He looks at her, his hand still on the gears, shakes his head, and gets out of the bus on his side. She stands, hesitant. He walks over to the trees which shade a small house. There are a couple of tables and a few chairs outside. The driver parts the beads that hang in front of the door and talks to someone inside.

Marchia. We've arrived. It is I.

He sits at a table. A tall, dark woman comes out of the house. She is dressed in black. She goes over to him and puts down a jug of water and a glass.

Marchia. What have we for supper tonight?

As she turns to go back inside, she sees the woman standing before the bus.

Marchia glances at the bus driver and then calls out, beckoning.

She awakes in the small room at the back of the house to hear the cock crow and the clatter of the bus as it goes off down the road at dawn.

———

She helped Marchia with the cleaning and the cooking. The village men came in for a drink at midday when the sun hit the village hardest and the eucalyptus trees shaded the tables and chairs in front of Marchia's house. They would sit there drinking the cool, cloudy liquid, idly letting the beads slip through their fingers as they looked and talked. Sometimes the neighbouring fishermen would stop to mend their nets in the bay and come ashore for a meal. Every two days the bus driver would arrive for supper and leave at dawn. Marchia was a fisherman's widow. He had died young, when she spoke of him she was transformed, beauty suddenly filling her angular face. Twenty-four years now alone. The other men in the village were married and for years she didn't care. Now. Now sometimes a neighbouring fisherman slept over, like the bus driver. She made them pay, she would never give her body again. She had given it once and for all. For him. Now she sold it and the money helped keep the house in repair. There was always something, the water pump last year, the roof this. She did not see much of the village women. She did her washing with them on the plank by the well but spoke little.

The two women rose at dawn and ate thick slabs of brown bread with their bowls of milk in the cool, dark kitchen. Then the washing of the floors and the freshening of the ground outside under the tables and chairs with a bucket of water. They did the cooking before the heat. Thick white beans in the blackened casserole, sometimes mixed with small pieces of meat. After serving drinks and the occasional meal at midday, they retired to their rooms. Marchia to the bedroom at the front with the high, wide bed covered with a heavy white spread and her father's sabre hanging on the bare wall. She to the little lean-to room at the back with its narrow mattress, the small, paneless window covered by foliage. The only escape from the terrible midday heat was sleep. When she awoke she would leave Marchia sewing and walk along the shore or up into the hills. It was a poor, barren land. A few goats, one or two plots of cultivated terraces and the fishing boats with their meager catches. The good fish were sent to the neighbouring market, what was left over was sold on a slab by the sea. They washed in the evening behind the house in a little bower of grapevines built for Marchia by her husband soon after their marriage. They would put their clothes in two heaps at the side and pour the buckets of cold water over one another.

She did not think, each day followed the one before and she was entirely absorbed by the physical pleasure she experienced from the simplicity of her existence. Marchia asked no questions and appeared to enjoy her presence, their companionship. Sometimes she would look at the handbag in her little room and be reminded that she had another life. But her thoughts never went further than that realisation. There had been another life. The bag said it, the bag proved it. Later on she would try and force her mind to go a little further, beyond the confines of her room. But she could not. She could not go further now.

———

Then there was the accident.

She awoke feeling someone was in her room, looking at her. She turned and saw Marchia at the door, her father's sabre in one hand, the bus driver's head in the other. She turned away and vomitted into the sheets. The driver was new. He had accepted Marchia's conditions, and then had refused to pay. He had insulted her. Told her she was too old to ask for money for her body now. He tried to take her again. Rape. The sabre. And now the blood dripping on to the earthen floor and the headless body.

They rolled the driver in a big dark blanket and trussed it up. Marchia fetched a bucket of water and they washed down the floor and cleaned the sabre. Marchia's nightgown soaked in the sink. They dragged the body out of the back door and down towards the sea, shielded from the village by the two trees. Fortunately the bus driver was a small, light man and there was no moon that night. Then the open space to the shore. Marchia told her to wait behind the trees with the body while she went down to the beach to drag the small boat to the edge of the water. She came back a few minutes later perspiring abundantly, her black shawl falling around her shoulders. The boat was too heavy for her alone. Together they pulled and pushed it towards the sea and then dragged the body down beside it. Marchia rowed alone. She knew how to row, strong, regular strokes that fast took them out of the bay. When they were out of sight of the village they opened the blanket, placed two heavy stones at either end and then heaved the body over the side, almost capsizing the boat. Back to the village, the boat pulled up on the shore, the red water rinsed out of the sink, the nightgown clean.

Marchia awoke with a start. Was it the cock crowing? No. It was still dark. It was the familiar rattle of the bus at it started off back down the road to the south. But who was driving it? She pulled her dark shawl over her shoulders and ran to the room at the back. She pushed the door and entered. The small room was empty. The clothes borrowed from Marchia neatly piled on the chair. A flower from the bower placed on top.

They eventually found the bus on the outstkirts of the town. A cat had set up home under one of the seats and the vehicle had become the secret playing ground of some children from a nearby shanty town. After a few months they gave up the search for the driver. They only knew that the bus had started back on its return journey earlier than usual, before dawn. It was still night when it clattered through the villages on its route back to the town and too dark to see who was at the wheel.

Like a seagull. Soft feathered, warm bodied like a seagull. Below the sea creamed silently on to the grey beach. Above, the bird spanned the cloudy sky, carried by the currents of air. She watched it soar, higher and higher, lifted by the breeze, then dip and plummet towards the sand. Then up again, even further this time, its wings stilled, freed, in effortless, endless flight. Like a seagull, free.

S. S. BARRIE

Three
Three
Three

Dear Lord it's cold tonight. Cold as November. Here it is mid-July and the lights over at Gassin are clear as gold buttons through ice. Magic like Christmas is coming. And I've got sunburn. Burnt neck, breasts, convex stomach red like a tomato fit to peel. I body-surfed off Gigaro this morning and surprised myself with my impeccable talent for buoyancy. Fish started jumping out of the water when I caught the last wave. I told myself it was their way of saying good-bye and thanks for the spectacle. Now I think there might have been some shark or other prowling the depths.

I used to live with a man who counted stars. He used to work long hours, long days, and come home fit only for the imbibing of liquids and a gentle sprawl on the duvet covers. And then, after the ritual tooth and toenail scrub, he would climb out onto the roof and start counting stars. His total varied according to the season and the aspect of the moon, but he more or less came up with the same number every night. He would write this number down on a piece of paper tissue and place it under his pillow. In the morning, I would wait for him to whisper off to the shower before lifting his pillow to check the numbers. Sometimes he wrote my name under the total. And on cloudy nights when there wasn't a pinpoint of light to be seen and counted, he cried himself to sleep. But I never wondered about his sanity, because there are many people in this world who do things much stranger than keeping tallies of heavenly bodies.

I ask myself why things look so much clearer in cold weather. Why the night sky is so sharp in November, for example. Orion seems to spend the humid summer nights in a blur of slow movement. In winter he is nearly static, a giant diamond tracing that shifts with rigid, deft regularity. He strokes the bow in summer, his glittering belt dancing like crazy fireflies through the magic of my binoculars. I watch Orion on summer evenings and, should there be a full moon to diminish his brilliance, wish him the strength to hunt again once the weather turns. I am alone in winter, the sole survivor of this vacation paradise, and it is Orion who watches over me.

After my star counter, I met and made love to a *boulanger*. A man of bread. Dough and flour would scatter across my kitchen table whenever he arrived for lunch. He was a kind man, a gentle man, moved by the gastronomic rhythms of the community. Some say the policeman, the mayor, the bank manager, perhaps, are the most important men in the village. But I always put my money on the bread maker. He is up with the stars, awake before the sun crawls over the moist lips of the horizon. He used to thrill me with stories of how he has to get up early during the tourist season in order to make enough bread. His ovens burn twenty-four hours a day, the local version of the eternal flame. Sometimes when he has to rise extra early, to beat his dough, twist the *croissants* into stubby curls, he foregoes the formality of dressing. There is something fundamental and earthy about the thought of a naked man spoon-feeding pale, raw dough into a mouth of fire.

This place is named after a religious apparition, but the vestiges of this miracle had to be removed after the owner of the land complained to the mayor about the insufferable numbers of pilgrims who were destroying her pool-side garden. It must be said that this woman's family had owned the land for decades, but had only recently decided to construct a house and garden. Therefore, the cross erected to mark the spot was moved, discreetly, under cover of a new moon, to a more accessible spot some few hundred yards due south of the woman's property. She watches the pilgrims through binoculars, her dogs and gun by her side, vigilant against any riffraff that may have invaded the local religious community.

This woman is my neighbor. She is also, I am convinced, very much in love with me. That is not to say that she is a lesbian. Merely that she may be expressing the sort of love one finds in Plato's *Phaedrus*. When I ventured to put this point to her she made some scathing remarks about pederasts and Latin predilections towards homosexuality. She does not answer my questions on this topic on a personal level. Since my arrival she has decided to stay on for the winter. But she is small and thin and has the sort of skin one peels from the epidermis of onions before throwing them to their torrid fates in a pan of frying oil.

My current lover is a *pompier*. He is a man of fire. He appreciates a good blaze better than any man I have ever met, although his interest lies in the extinguishing, not the feeding of the flames. Last winter he would load the hearth with choice olive and pine boughs, but refuse to light the kindling. Against his code of conduct. By summer, and particularly when the Mistral howls down from the Midi and wrings her wraith-like hands over the hilly coastline, he is a man electrified. Sometimes, on a night when the wind makes the oleanders dance outside my bedroom window, he turns his head so that making love becomes a game for strangers. In the darkness it is impossible to see more than the vague, moonlit contours of his shoulders and neck, one ear

and the furry curve of his chest. He is watching the far rim of the mountains
as they wind around the other side of the bay below. He is looking for the faint
glow of red cresting the hills, the blinking lights of trucks and airplanes dashing
towards the blaze.

A fire did come here once. I did not know the *pompier* then, but he has since
told me that he was, in fact, the first firefighter to don his silver helmet and go
out to fight that fire. It started on a Wednesday night, at the onset of a summer
Mistral. One man and a tennis ball loaded with gasoline. He lit the ball and
lobbed it, perhaps with a tennis racket, into the heart of the forest. And the wind
caressed the smoldering undergrowth into a raging inferno. I woke on Thursday
morning and went for my swim off Gigaro. I was with the *boulanger* then,
and it was he who raised the alarm. Still yards from shore, I was surprised
to see his lean figure, apron flapping, running across the sand. Fire, he said.
Coming to the village. I should go home and throw all my possessions of value
into the swimming pool. And wait for further instructions.

I ran home, wet hair streaming behind me like Medusa curls. Alone
on the hillside, I made my decision that I would not throw valuables into the
chlorinated waters. I filled pillowcases with money and trinkets, passport
and photographs. Let the fire come, I thought. I took the precaution of hosing
down the garden and the house's fire-facing wall. I took a portable radio
and a bottle of *non-gazeuse* water and climbed up onto the terra cotta roof tiles
to get a better view. They call the yellow water-swallowing, water-spewing
airplanes Canadairs, and when they swoop down on the unsuspecting sea
and then circle slowly above the columns of blazing hillside they are like great
albatrosses. Birds of prey. They fly slowly, their twin engines rumbling,
propellers chugging to maintain height despite the weight of all that water in
their bellies. That day there were helicopters, too. I thought of my *boulanger*
and his advice as one rotor-propelled flying machine hovered over my house
and lowered a hose. Drained the swimming pool dry. I watched the tiled mermaid
who used to drift beneath the calm blue water emerge into the hot, dry air.
Her colors were less vivid in the daylight, her tresses not so much undulating
as tangled. I was glad I hadn't thrown my life's possessions into the pool.

My *boulanger* spent the entire three days of fire baking bread for the
pompiers. He fed his oven for seventy-two hours straight, sometimes so hot
and tired he had to take his clothes off and jump naked into the fountain in
the village square. It would seem that naked men are the last thing one worries
about when a fire the size and ferocity of a great, burning tidal wave is rolling
directly in your path. My *boulanger* received an honor from the government for
his contribution to the fire-fighting effort. Who would have thought a marathon
baking session could merit a medal? My neighbor, who bewails the libidos

of her countrymen, told me that my lover's action was heroic. You could never imagine, you of foreign birth, how important *baguettes, brioches* and the humble butter croissant are for this country's morale.

The memory of that fire always brings me out in a nervous rash. Three nights on a rooftop, waiting for my trees to turn into roman candles. It never happened, of course. The *pompiers* made a last stand at the foot of my hill and, fueled by fresh bread, kept the flames at bay. It is a linking event, a bridge of sorts between my progression from one lover to another. My *boulanger* feeding my *pompiers*. And it was the *boulanger* who introduced me to my *pompiers*. He brought bread to my house once the road had opened. You were saved by this man, my *boulanger* said as he introduced me to my *pompiers*. Count on this man, my *boulanger* said. He knows how to stop a fire.

In a way it made things easier. The old lover gets his medal, the new lover gets the girl. There is a photograph of the three of us in that day's local journal. The baker, the fireman, the young woman saved from threat of extinction by carbonization. We are all smiling at the camera, but only two of us are holding hands.

I sometimes think of the astronomer. He didn't make the acquaintance of the *boulanger* or the fireman. He knew no one in this region, save for me. He won no medals, put out no fire. He had me for a while, but I can't think he needed me, not really. Not when his achievements lay in other atmospheres. His friends, he once said, would come from other galaxies. Soon we would pick up their radio signals from other worlds. And he will be the middleman between Earth and Planet X. There will be a photograph of him as he welcomes the space travelers, his large hands outstretched in the universal manner of greeting strangers. He will break bread with them, bread that he has not made himself. Should they have a malfunction in their ship's wiring he will call an emergency fire fighting team to tackle the blaze. He will tell these aliens that he has counted their stars and that some, possibly, are missing. And in a way I respect him the most of all the men that I have known because his heart and mind encompassed the supernormal, things out of this world. He was of this world but not ruled by it. And in a way this is why I could not continue loving him. Because there is no love outside our atmosphere. Just lonely planets, clinging satellite moons, cold meteor showers. And Orion, my constant companion, whose belt shines despite the season, despite time and circumstance. He is above all of it: politics, religion, love. He is a cold lover, and one who will never share my bed.

JOËL-PETER SHAPIRO

Broach

This creased stencil premonition
A canker smothered binding
Lids more viscid then sty
Transfix the deterred stealth of text
Sinews clock the dented I
As if the reptant today were infinitive

Moth and Rust

Worn cuffs sidewalk complacency
Burlap motives caught between the zipper concrete
A skid chips the nerve-end sameness
        A stitch in time
Runs the metal aftertaste of Equinox
Seasons thimble seams

Hook and Eye

Molars twine where the wreath gnash grows.
Sanguineous drops quiver like candles,
Stir the residue yet taper not the label:
Turbid exploration of the misconceived.

STUART BLAZER

Aix-en-Providence

The autumn-spring
of a winter
in the south of France
& this same January
New England-style
defies the flying-time
(6 hours)
& setting the watch ahead.

I'm still behind.
Elsewhere is here,
those stone walls
are made of snow now
& this parking lot
is the field
across from your house.

Melting. Freezing.
Passion's language
spoken by a refrigerator,
defrosting it
a sure-fire cure for jet-lag.

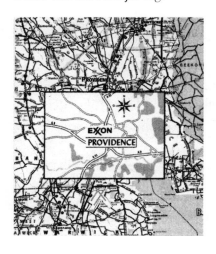

Today is an errand
I'm in no shape to run,
let it down,
let it fall into all
this ploughed snow
lining the streets,
barrier-reefs
against the long reach
of some mistral
finding its way through
the closed front door
where my forehead frozen
on the icy window
tries to see out
but is caught looking in.

Stedman's Divers

For a long time there were two Nicholas Stedmans: one a biochemist, the other a painter. It was, Stedman admits, "a schizophrenic existence, like two sides of a brain, each with its own specialist activity." After graduating from Cambridge and obtaining a doctorate in biochemistry at Paris Vll, the scientist joined the research team at the Institut of Cancerology and Immunogenetics in Villejuif, and worked on the replication of retroviruses; meanwhile, the artist continued his own, parallel research. "In fact, both were working with different manifestations of a single process," he points out in retrospect, quoting John Donne: "The soul is form and cloth the body make." For Stedman, at the time, however, painting and science seemed irreconcilable. Like Jeckyll and Hyde, one had to get the upper hand. Like one of his Divers, it was the artist who finally took the plunge.

One of the artist's major themes, divers, springs from a crucial event, a mental snapshot. On the Promenade des Anglais in Nice, Stedman watched a diver diving off a rock. He explains how his particular viewpoint, watching from directly above, produced a heightened state of involvement with the diver, a sort of voyeuristic out-of-body-experience. Similarly, his painting, uncompromisingly figurative, is conceived as a direct extension of the body: it is literally a process of embodiment, an exteriorisation of an inner dance. After the painting's completion, once the artist has departed, the spectator takes his place, entering into direct identification with the counterparts Stedman has left behind.

Like the diver in Nice, Stedman's Divers, are ourselves once removed, projections of the self into the paint medium itself. The series is in constant, perhaps cyclic evolution ....

Through a porthole in our minds we look out on ourselves coming and going, appearing and disappearing. Or perhaps we are returning to the point of departure, rising to the surface again.

– *David Wharry*

From Nicholas Stedman, Body and Soul, *on the occasion of the Nicholas Stedman exhibition, Galerie Le Monde de l'Art, Paris, April 1998.*

NICHOLAS STEDMAN - *Le corps en danger: "Chute"* - 1997
Galerie Le Monde de l'Art, Paris

A.A. LIKER

from The Justice Conspiracy

a novel in progress

> The Justice Conspiracy *is the story of three men who enter into a "conspiracy" to bring into existence, in one place on earth, an imaginary metropolis, that most illusive of all categories, justice. Against nearly impossible odds and circumstances, they succeed, over a period of time that extends from an undated, worldwide economic and political collapse.*
> The novel details how Humanity might, one day, organize itself along the lines of what the author believes is an inescapable philosophical premise: The sovereignty of the individual is total, *and the reader is presented with a paradox-free alternative to the concept of "government" and an improvement on the "liberal democracy," which seems to have emerged victorious in the ideological war that has raged for most of this century between totalitarianism and the "freedom" that democracy purports to bring.*

from Chapter 1

The newly-elected governor of the Southwest Region, Mozelle Brasheer sat 266 miles nearly due west of the gaudy old MGM Grand Hotel in Reno, Nevada, where Francesca was facing down a particularly vociferous pack of press wolves. She was ensconced in the comfort of the lavish, new Governor's Mansion in the city of San Francisco, surrounded by her cabinet members, political advisors, and the ever-present Dickie Bamber, her number one advance person. Governor Brasheer had wanted all her key people with her to witness the carnage of Francesca Ferosce at the hands of the press.

"Slow 'em down, hell!" Mozelle shouted. "What's that female tawkin' 'bout? Ahm not jes' gonna slow 'em down, Ahma gonna take 'em down ... *permanently*. Put 'em outta business, that's what! Don't these people who wraht for newspapahs evah bothah teh read 'em?"

"Apparently not, Governor," Dickie Bamber replied, when no one else replied.

"Well, boys," she bellowed, in the heavy drawl that had become one of her distinctive trademarks, "What'd Ah tell ya. The great Francesca Ferosce of the Tanneh Organization scramblin' 'round up theah in front of all them reportahs and TV people ... wonderin' what the hell she's gonna say next teh squirm outta this one. Look at her tryin' teh look so calm, and cool, in the face of all that heat. And, Ah don't jes' mean from the lahts!" Mozelle Brasheer laughed a loud boisterous laugh and slapped her thigh. "Doncha jes' love this, boys?"

Muffled cheers, laughter, clapping, and some foot stomping could be heard coming from the darkened gallery just behind Governor Brasheer and Dickie Bamber, who sat next to her raised dais near the wall-sized television screen.

After the sudden death of Governor Ellis A. Richards, followed by her success at the polls, in the first democratic elections to take place on the North American continent in more than a generation, Mozelle Brasheer had ascended to the position of Southwest Regional Governor. At 59, she was the people's choice, or as she liked to say, the "folks'" choice — the most politically powerful person in a region that included the southwestern states of California, Nevada, and Arizona of the former United States of America.

Shortly after the Collapse, Governor Ellis A. Richards had seized power in the region for himself, and for a handful of cronies, who were flagrant opportunists of the worst sort. Power grabs such as this had occurred all over the North American continent to such an extent that balkanization had become the new order. The now dead governor's rule had been anything but benign or democratic. In fact, it was well-known that he detested democratic institutions, blaming them as he did, in speeches that always turned into tirades, for all human ills, past and present, including the Collapse. Governor Richards had been vain and paranoid. So paranoid that no successor had ever been named or even considered. He was going to live forever, or so he thought. Then, one day he died, suddenly, creating a huge, political power vacuum. His staff had rushed to find a suitable replacement to run in the quickly called election, but it was too late. Mozelle Brasheer, and her campaign staffers, were already in place. She had won handily against the best of the worst of one of Richards's hastily picked straw men, with the usual political rhetoric, coupled with her own "down home" charm. She had also capitalized on a major fear of a huge number of the new electorate, and what many considered was the former governor's weakest point: his borderline obsession with protecting the world's first Major Proprietary Environment, which he himself had permitted to be built in the high desert of Southern California. In dozens of campaign speeches throughout the Southwest Region, Mozelle Brasheer had promised she would put an end to what she scathingly referred to as "that little pipsqueak of a Godless, lawless, renegade city-state pretendin' legitimacy within the borders of our great and glorious, God-fearin' democratic region!" It had worked. Scarcely ninety days after her inauguration, she had set in motion the new state machinery that would allow her to fulfill a major campaign promise — that of putting an end to the first Major Proprietary Environment, and its embryonic equivalent, Tanner City, in the state of Nevada.

*

The Bones of
Ralphipithicus Pettycanas

(Ralph Petty: American Artist in Paris)

photo: DAVID APPLEFIELD - *"Ralph Petty" Montreuil, 1998*

Frank: *Today, the term expatriate has lost much of its original meaning. There are not many writers and artists who come to Paris anymore for reasons of political protest or as a social statement or form of rejection. But there are some. There is one American writer-fugitive in France who was wanted for hyjacking an aircraft in the sixties, another who advocates the legal non-payment of federal taxes. Others prefer France because the subject of their work is spared being scrutinized with the confining puritanical blinders which dictate much of North America taste. Still others actively prefer being artists outside of the intense commercial pressure to produce work that is consumable by a sufficiently large and existing market. Yet, today there also seems to be a reversal of sorts: an upbeat, flexible, prosperous America has taken on a new global attractiveness, while France — once the focal point of everything avant garde—has retreated into the background. Ralph, you've been in France for over twenty years. What made you move from a small town in rural Colorado to Paris, and more importantly, what keeps you in France today?*

Ralph Petty: I came running from something and found something else that I didn't know I was looking for. And I think that this is a phenomenonon probably true for others. When I came to Paris in the early 70s I didn't know anything about the place; then I saw the streets, the buildings, the women, and ... What was more important to me then was the act of leaving. I felt like a refugee. I could think of myself differently. Europe became the New World and I could remake myself.

RALPH PETTY - *watercolor (details) - 1998*

Frank: *As had once been true for many expatriate writers and artists throughout the century, your "running away" to France was both personal and political. Tell us how this exodus came about.*

RP: Well, in 1971 with Richard Nixon in office and the Vietman War still escalating, there was a lottery for the draft based on birthdates and mine was number 17, which meant that I would have had to take the physical exam to go into the army and most likely I would have been sent to Vietnam. My brother was already in Vietnam. I didn't want to go because I thought the war was wrong and psychologically I couldn't have made it through the miliary. But, my father had been a WWII and Korea veteran and my uncle was head of the local draft board. And his son was in Vietnam also. So the pressure was close to home.

I tried for Conscientious Objector status but my request was refused. For my family I was an embarrassment.So in a moment's notice I left my hometown of Alamosa, Colorado, population 8000, and headed to Fairbanks, Alaska, near the Arctic Circle. I thought I was getting away from civilization, as if little Alamosa were Rome.

Frank: *How did you pick Alaska? Why not Canada?*

RP: Because it was far away, near Canada, but still part of the United States. Had I gone to Canada, I would have faced felony charges. Plus, the University of Alaska had a good anthrolpology department, where I enrolled. This doesn't have much to do with anything but, I remember a nightmare I had; studying physical anthropology I had to memorize a challenging list of Latin names of our ancestors: *austrolopithicus africanus, austrolopithicus robustus, gigantapithicus, sinjanthropous, paleojavanicus,* etc. I woke in a cold sweat screaming "They just discovered the bones of *ralphipithicus pettycanas*! How's that for deep psychological disturbance.

Frank: *Somehow all this relates to your emergence as an artist. Keep going.*

RP: I felt terribly alone and spinning. I had no cultural references. I was a total outsider, and I went into deep depression and to be even more alone I moved about 20 miles outside of Fairbanks into a cabin in the forest where I had to cross-country ski to get home. I had no electricity and no running water. It was minus 40° around the clock. My nearest neighbor was miles away.

What I realized was that you can never really get away — because civilization is in your mind. In the winter time I just read. Earlier, I had hung around the French quarter at nights in Fairbanks in the bars that had sawdust on the floors and blues and jazz music and strippers and lots of lowlife from everywhere, the rejects of the world who either hated society or needed a new beginning or were hiding from something. It was there that I met a guy named Graig who was out on parole from a California prison, a guy who had done time for counterfeiting. And it was he who gave me a copy of Doestoyevki's *Crime and Punishment* which I learned was essential reading for prison intellectuals. I devoured the book. I read all night, there was no day. It was perfect, reading Doestoyevki in a cabin in a Klondike winter. And then I read

RALPH PETTY - *watercolor (details) - 1998*

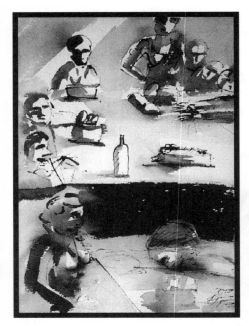

I am the moon
a red flame in leprosy
shimmering black on
winter's sky
satin feathers dipped in
wrath of acid
crimson blood driven
deep into an indigo canyon.

Frank: *So you first discovered then your affinity to images, to a visual interpretation of experience. What happened next?*

RP: I solved the Vietnam problem — it took the draft board a year to find me, but they found me. I finally faked a kind of catatonic depression to get prescribed heavy tranquilizers. The only way out was to build a medical record proving how unfit I was for the military. I pretended to take the drugs, but never took them; I traded them to my ex con friends who actually liked tranquilizers, and the State psychiatrists incredulously kept increasing my dosage until it was so high they finally gave me a physical deferment. And

The Idiot and I realized that I was the idiot and that was the turning point. I realized that all this pain, bewilderment, confusion and sensuality could be turned into an art form. I ordered lots of books from a local bookseller, and proceeded to read everything of Doestoveski, then Neitzche, then Kirkegaard, Schopenhauser, all the dark, weighty, northern thinkers.

So I thought I wanted to be a writer and wrote a lot of poetry. Oddly, I always drew on the side of the poems in the margins waiting for the words to arrive. That was the beginning of my art. Funny, I remember one of these poems when I think back:

that's how I liberated myself from the army.

Then I hitched to California in the back of a pick up truck on the Alcan Highway in a freezing February and ended up in Santa Cruz where my friend Craig had moved to, scheming away how to make money. California Schemers, they were, not Dreamers. I enrolled at the University of California at Santa Cruz and signed up for a Doestoyevki class, but after what I had just lived through the Doestoyevski they were studying in class wasn't what I had read. It was dead. They were buzzards, picking the books apart and killing the soul of the work. Doestoyevski is about burning through the adverture of life, turning over the rocks of the

soul and finding all these insects ... and seeing redemption in that. And here we were in a pretty classroom surrounded by giant Redwood trees overlooking Monterray Bay picking apart the prose as if it were a carcass.

By chance, I started to take art classes at night at Cabrillo Junior College where I had a fantastic drawing teacher, Don

Thompson, who gave me encouragement and opened doors for me. He allowed me to develop my own bizarre, gnarled, eccentric, and personal imagery. I just dropped literature then and there but continued to read and write ... and draw!

Frank: *So, how did you finally decide to leave the United States?*

RP: In the fall of 1974 I moved to the Art Department at Davis UC and studied with the visiting artist Hassel Smith, who was Richard Diebenkorn's teacher and colleague, but being an engaged communist and an enlightened painter and unable to obtain a secure

teaching post in the US he had moved for political reasons to England in the 60s. When I finally got my degree in painting Hassel encouraged me to come to Europe. "Don't go to Europe like an American," he told me. "Plan to spend some time." That was over twenty years ago.

Frank: *What has living in France afforded you as a painter that you could not have attained if you had stayed in California or returned to Colorado?*

RP: Well, when you move somewhere else you are allowed to evolve, transform. My transformation from a small town boy, then to Alaska and finally Paris is like a catapillar metamorphising into a butterfly. It wasn't like the same animal just growing up. And, it's true, daily life in Paris is more

subtle, richer. I've built my life here. I have my family and friends. I built my studio ... Culture and daily life are one and the same. The food, the conversation, the architecture ... Culture is not a dead thing; it's a way you structure your life.

Frank: *Okay, but today we hear more and more comments about how dead or old fashioned contemporary French life has become. Whereas creativity and flexibility are the new keys to the American model. How do you explain this?*

RP: Business and culture are not necessarily the same beasts. Americans often confuse them. If I were a businessman I'd rather do business in America. But as a painter, I prefer Europe. America from the Old World point of view is a place you can realize dreams. Having lived through the nightmare and coming out on the other side, I feel more capable now of going back, in a way like a European, and seeing the real possibilities that that continent offers. In any case, I feel like I've now come to terms with my conflicts with the US. Especially with the America in me.

Frank: *I understand that after all these years in Paris you and your family are acquiring French nationality. Does this change anything for you?*

RP: Well, I was thinking that I'd change my name to Jean-Ralph Petty!

C.K. WILLIAMS

Last Things

Thinking it a closet, I opened the door of the darkroom of a photographer-friend whose apartment I'd borrowed some months after the death of his thirty-four year old son, whom he adored and whom I never knew, and found curled up and discolored in a tray of dried fixative a photo of the son the instant after his death, his glasses still on, eyes closed, a droplet of blood caught at the corner of his mouth.

Recently, my friend assembled and had printed a book, entitled *Alex*, about his son, with selections from his writings, diaries, letters and friends' remembrances. There are also many photos the father had taken, from the son's birth on through his life. Near the end, there's one from a few days before the son died. Almost all the generous sensitivity, the intelligent wit so clearly evident in the other pictures has been transfigured by the enormity of his suffering: he looks like some dark noblemen, a pharaoh. The caption reads, "This is the last photograph of Alex."

I'm sure my friend isn't aware I know about the picture. Is writing about it a violation of hospitality? Before I show this to anyone else, I'll have to ask his permission. If you're reading it, you'll know my friend pardoned me, that he found whatever small truth the story might embody, about grief or pain or time, was worth the anguish of remembering again that doubtlessly reflexive moment when after fifty years of bringing reality into himself through a lens, his camera came to his eye as though by itself, and his finger, surely also of its own accord, convulsed the shutter.

C.K. WILLIAMS

Canal

An almost deliciously ill, dank, dark algae on the stone of its sides,
a putrid richness to its flow which spontaneously brings forth refuse,
dead fish, crusts, condoms, all flowing in the muck of viscous gruel,
under the tonnage of winter sky which darkens everything more,
soils the trash, fruit, paper, dead leaves, water, still impossible more.

Yet trudging freezing along it, I seem taken by it, to be of it,
its shape and its flow; it and I in the cold wind make one single thing,
this vast, steel-hard lid with gulls fixed in it lifting and falling,
this sheet dull as darkness idly winding between indifferent buildings,
it and become one, a unity, not in fantasy, not in sham prayer,

but as though one might actually be the mind of a thing, its awareness,
as though only watching its thick, indolent surge would bring into me
all that has touched it, gone across it, sunken and perished within it,
all caught as cognizant lymph in its form of a low, immortal ark,
in the space held rigid above it, the insatiable gaze flung upon it.

C.K. WILLIAMS

The Dance

A middle-aged woman, quite plain, to be polite about it, and somewhat
    stout, to be more courteous still,
but when she and the rather good-looking, much younger man she's
    with get up to dance,
her forearm descends with such delicate lightness, such restrained but
    confident ardor athwart his shoulder,
drawing him to her with such a firm, compelling warmth, and moving
    him with effortless grace
into the union she's instantly established with the not at all rhythnically
    solid music in this second-rate café,

that something in the rest of us, some doubt about ourselves, or some
    conjecture,
nothing that we'd ever thought of as a real lack, nothing to be admired,
    or to be shameful for,
but something, still, to which we've never adequately paid attention,
    the opposite of which
might have consoling implications about ourselves, about the way we
    misbelieve ourselves, and about the world, too,
that world beyond us which so often disappoints but which in the end
    is what we're given, what, thankfully, we are.

CAROL ALLEN

"Send it South"

"Send it South," he answered, never looking up.

That was a coded answer. He really meant, "Put it in the attic."

Filling the attic is a project my husband attacks with fervor. Before, I would have disagreed, saying, "But maybe someone we know could use it." Or, "That thing? It would be better off at the dump!" I've since learned, big or small, ugly or nice, any discarded item from our family is destined to journey up those three flights of stairs and be hidden away in the enormous attic of our country home in the South of France. Moreover, I've become a willing partner in filling it up.

I have childhood memories of attics; my husband does not. Born in 1940, he spent his early years traveling light as his family fled first the Nazis, then the Communists. They immigrated to Israel and later, in 1953, to France. Their attics were their suitcases.

My parents' attic was only the nesting place of Christmas ornaments and boxed objects and souvenirs someone in the family pronounced too precious to throw away, like all my high school yearbooks. But my Aunt Lessie's attic in rural Louisiana ... that was a real attic.

My cousins and I would open the door at the bottom of the dark stairs, huddled against each other, trying to seem nonchalant. One of us would tug the string to turn on the light. Up we'd go, closer and closer to the gaping black room above, stairs creaking every step of the way. Terrified, we were sucked forward, riveted like nails to a magnet. Near the top step we'd grope for the second light-string.

The attic was like a huge, dim cave. Wind whistled eerily through the louvered ventilators. We confined our rummaging around to the center under the single 40-watt bulb, never brave enough to find the older treasures tucked under the black, cobwebbed eaves. But the attic's center had enough to interest us for hours — Uncle Walter's discarded hats and boots, somebody's abandoned sewing box filled with buttons and cloth scraps from long-forgotten clothes; broken objects that were funnier than when they had been new — wobbly hobby horses, a headless sewing model, and stacks of old magazines, ingenious sources of paper dolls.

I would think of Aunt Lessie's attic often as we packed up my mother-in-law's apartment. Some of the things we boxed, although from two different

cultures on two different continents, are shockingly similar to those I remember
from my childhood — boxes of buttons, no two alike; pairs and pairs of
assorted eye glasses; leather or embroidered coin purses, a blush-pink,
beaded evening bag.

Some are touchingly different. In the back of a drawer full of shoes
I found a medicine box full of coins and small bills in three different currencies.
Before the packing was over I had found four other such caches squirreled
away in closets and drawers. The thought, "It can happen again," had silently
accompanied this woman through all her comfortable and sheltered life in
France. She had been ready to flee, pack her suitcase and leave everything
behind, erasing her past once again.

I found dingy postcards and letters written in Russian, in Romanian, in
Hebrew. Carefully opening a paper-wrapped packet, the paper almost falling
to dust in my hands, I discovered twelve crocheted doilies. My husband had
told me his mother and grandmother had crocheted during the war to earn
extra money. They were delicate, lovely. I am pleased they will finally rest in
the attic with my mother-in-law's leopard-skin jacket she wore proudly into
chic Parisian restaurants, the image of invulnerability on the arm of her elegant
husband.

To the attic. Everything. They join fellow keepsakes from my husband's
life as well as my own. His grandmother's trunk is there. It moved her 65-
year-old-life from Russia to Israel to France. We are filling it with souvenirs-to-
be for our girls: fancy dresses and shoes, hats and costume jewelry, rhinestone
sunglasses. I envision a granddaughter clomping around in those gorgeous
sequined high-heels I wore for New Years Eve in 1980, my old turquoise silk
sheath draped over her tiny shoulders, dragging the floor.

This filled attic merges our cultures, builds a past, preserves a history.
We dream of our children, our grandchildren, and maybe even our great
grandchildren, discovering, remembering, questioning, but at the same time
finding solace and security and humor exploring the vestiges of their families'
divergent stories.

What will some grandchild think as he looks at the picture of my uncle,
cocky in his Marine uniform, laughing with a buddy in the South Pacific in
1942? Will he understand that another photo, the stern face hidden behind
a bushy beard and covered by a dark wide hat is that of his great, great Russian
grandfather, taken the same year, in Bessarabia?

What questions will a grandchild ask when she finds the grayed-with-time
mosquito netting from my great grandmother's canopied Louisiana bed?
It survived the Civil War and stayed within a 30-mile-radius of its home for
over one hundred years before traveling to France to join me. The red satin

bow at its peak is faded to the color of spilled tea, but it's still there.

Except for his grandmother's trunk, no such relics of my husband's ancestors exist; not in the attic, not anywhere. This will not be true for the next generations. We are determined to build a past that family members will rummage into and discover with questions. They will be secure in knowing these things have been sitting in the same place, collecting dust, waiting for them, a long, long time.

After months of gradually declining health, punctuated by senility-provoked outbursts of erratic behavior, my mother-in-law died peacefully in her own bed. She had been a widow for several years. In the quiet aftermath of the funeral, prayers and visiting relatives, my husband, an only child, and I sat in her Paris apartment. He fingered through boxes of old photos of relatives long dead and his children when they were young.

I looked around the familiar living room: the Louis XVI furniture and overstuffed velvet chairs and sofas; Persian rugs; paintings, some by known artists, most not; crystal vases, silver vases, porcelain vases, and all the other accumulated objects of a family's shared life. "What will we do with all this stuff?" I wondered aloud.

He answered, never looking up, "Send it South."

DOUGLAS OLIVER

Few Possessions in Togo

If we think about rural lands, it's night
more swiftly over village earth humid
with vegetal rotting: our feet halt. After
the manioc-pounded day, the hot yam
fields haunched with women, the blaze
has gone out of it, a hand-wave of light
behind the black rectangles, unglassed,
cut into mud or concrete huts, creates

a dream of few possessions, the kerosene
lamp by an enamel cooking pot, the fufu
in it bland as tofu. It's our eye at
the glimmering window, where, halted,
we pick up the gleam of French fashion
mag pics on the interior wall, above
a single stool, kids already foetal
for sleep, knees up to swollen bellies.

The hard floor bare, a wooden toy,
the man out somewhere topping up
with palm wine, and the mother
easing her spine after the day's bending.
What can we add to so little, us with
what we think is so much?
We leave a nothing by the mud wall; it's
the oval trademark in a Western shoeprint.

DOUGLAS OLIVER

The Cold Hotel

On the ticket to fantasy lands
we find the cold hotel whose door
is opened by the key of Europe.
If we could only find that key
(and the management is searching)
we'd enter a comfy bedroom with
a Euromoney terminal,
rented armchairs, wide mattress;
and when we ordered
tea or coffee from room service,
it'd come up with plenty of sugars,
the way it did when our incomes
were acquired from slavery's aftermath
across Africa, India, the Caribbean,
in all the unsavoury histories of
our island pride. Nothing has been fantasy
in African lands for writers jailed and exiled
under regimes we helped to spawn.
The great ambassadors:
Kofi Awooner, Ezckiel Mphahlele,
Frank Chipasula, Dennis Brutus,
Arthur Nortje, Ngugi wa Thiong'o.
I go beyond my rights to name such names,
myself a travelling poet-representative
for a people that won't take a dip
in their incomes, no not for any
possible good imaginable,
not for any benefit of the future's poor,
not even for their own grandchildren.

We don't need to just now, when in Brussels
they're helping us back home
make our unemployed a new Third World
within our tremulous circle of employment
whose island centre is nowhere
but whose deregulated circumference
passes clearly through that hotel room in
Brussels, Stuttgart, Bonn.

Can this really be our room key?
It just fits our suitcase locks.
Inside the case are Stephen King's Gothic
novels from many airports, little thrillers,
and another country's currency bills
financing the circle that maintains us,
a circle mystical as the Catholic God,
comfortably horrific. We live in
an illusion that we'd face horror
well if it ever came to us.

JOE MARSHALL

One Cup Three Handles

Liv was cataloguing the strange marks on her body — moles, scars, beauty spots and birthmarks. Each had its own story. I made a map of her figure on the back of a coaster. I labeled it with the marks and their stories. We were sitting in wicker chairs outside a café at the Place de la Contrescarpe. Liv smelled like laundry detergent and wild flowers. She was wearing a white t-shirt, a pair of light-colored shorts and sandals. She didn't allow them to hinder her exhibition. Liv was into details. I was plagued by a preoccupation with the bigger picture.

I had moved to Paris to study existentialist literature. I got a part time job bartending in an Irish pub. I started learning French, memorizing words and verb tenses. I waited for the day when I would wake up and suddenly be fluent. Liv and I met outside my school.

I liked her strange marks and their stories. They were an invitation to look at her body freely, without feeling lecherous. I nearly had a small round brown one on her thigh named after me. Liv hadn't noticed it before. It turned out to be a melted sliver of chocolate from the gold-wrapped waifer that came with our coffee. While Liv searched for uncharted marks I turned the coaster over and doodled across a beer promotion. Liv said my doodle looked like a Roscharch test. The last thing a Roscharch test was supposed to look like was a Roscharch test. It looked like a skull to me.

I told Liv about the existentialists I was reading. How they looked at life from behind, from death's deep end. The problem was eternity. Existentialists determined that it was a myth or at least unknowable. And they complained about it. I flipped the coaster in the air like a big coin and told Liv I was looking for my own solution.

She was running through the last of the list, a straight white scar that she had acquired falling out of a tree, age 14. It ran along the top of her ribs, just below her left breast. I could see she wasn't wearing a bra. Liv said, "There, now you know where all the strange marks are on my body."

Smiling, I replied, "Yeah, I'll be able to identify it one day if I have to."

"If I go first!," Liv shot back. "But that's not why I showed you ..."
She hesitated slightly. Was she considering our future? "Lovers should know every inch of each others' bodies." Then the coaster came down, landed and

spun slowly on the table top. I remember waiting for it to fall on one side
or the other.

Late afternoon in the Luxembourg Gardens. An old woman had been
asleep for some time (too much time?) in an uncomfortable steel chair. I saw
myself approach her, lean over, check her frail wrist for a pulse. I needed to be
reassured. I was concerned. When she woke up she caught me watching her.
She walked past where I sat as she left. She would not look me in the eyes.

Another late afternoon. Same rusted tangerine sunlight. My body was
cast in shadow. The tops of old buildings struggled to hold squares of sun.
Then rectangles. Then nothing. Just before #86 had passed loudly, with fumes,
in front of me. The Panthéon was over my shoulder. "You could be hit by
a bus and killed tomorrow." I repeated the modern proverb like a mantra,
the repitition melodic.

Early evening. Muffled drum beats from a distance. The top of the Eiffel
Tower. I didn't notice the view of the city but the distance to the ground.
A sudden flight and unbearable emptiness in the stomach. Then me lying there
in a skull and bone-crossed heap. All but the ghost of me had jumped. I was
the ghost then watching the people below gather around my body or turn away
sickened.

Someone told me that most household deaths occur in the kitchen. Liv and
I ate dinner in the living room. We'd watch t.v. while we ate. Reports from
Belfast, Luxor, Rwanda, Algeria.

And sometimes I stared at my wrists. It was a fetish. I watched the delicate
blue-veined flux twist beneath the surface of my skin, not yet red from
exposure. An eventuality my mind would run over and over.

I didn't know Hilda at all. She was a friend of Liv's. I'm not sure how well
Liv knew her either really. Maybe when it came to friends in Liv's past she
hadn't been very discriminating. When you're young you don't care as much
who you keep company with. I wouldn't want to be judged by my own history
of callow acquaintances. "Rat" Morose alone, the precocious anarchist, would
be enough to get my visa revoked.

I questioned Liv about why she had insisted on Hilda's visit. She told me,
"That's what people do. It's normal. Maybe you'll like her." I didn't like this
explanation but I was worried she would think I didn't want to meet her old
friends. That I didn't want to learn about her past. Liv and Hilda are both
Norwegian. They met as high school exchange students in Lincoln, Nebraska.
Liv told me they had exchanged a couple of letters after their year abroad.
Finally, a couple of Christmas cards. Since then she hadn't heard anything

from her. She knew Hilda had recently moved to Paris. That she lived with
an English boyfriend who worked at the Paris stock exchange. That was all.
Then the week before she had run into Hilda in a clothing store at Les Halles.
She invited her over for "a little get together ... to catch up on old times."

Liv and I had been seeing each other for six months, living together for one.
We had different work schedules. When I went to bed Liv was getting up.
It was nice to crawl into the bed warmed by her, scented with her. But traces
of Liv were not as warm or fragrant as Liv herself. Ending or beginning our
different days we bumped into each other in dazed states.

We were trying to work out communal living and contrasting schedules.
I read the existentialists. I imagined looking back over my life from my death
bed fifty or sixty non-guaranteed years in the future. Was I smiling, pinching
the young nurse's backside, begging one last cigarette? Was I scowling, cursing,
regretting my past? Where was Liv in all that?

When we managed to get together Paris stopped. The people left. What
remained was marveled at. We hopped unknown lines, rode until the names
of stations didn't mean anything. We explored gated gardens hidden from
the street and witnessed ancient statues degenerate. We found small stores
with shelves of tiny Buddhas, earthy tubers, herbs and ornamental paper
(rituals for eternity?). Only a hint of the proprietor: whisps of incense curling
out of a curtained recess. A *tangine* glimpsed on a stove. Garlic and coriander
tangling with patchouli (rose?).

The day before Hilda was supposed to come over, Liv starts warning me
that she talks. Is in fact always talking. In Lincoln, armed only with a dusty
text-book English, Hilda dominated conversations. She interrupted, cut you
off, continued after you. She lost her audience and then herself in convoluted,
verbal onslaughts. She gasped for breath between phrases like skinny girls play
the tuba. Liv said Hilda had kept her in the clothing store for half an hour.
They spoke English like they had as exchange students. Liv said it was funny
to hear Hilda using British slang with an American accent.

It occurred to me that maybe Liv wanted to meet Hilda alone. Reminisce
in my absence. Maybe I'd just get in a fight with Hilda. And then with Liv.
I decided it'd be safer to go down to the pub early for a pint and a game of pool.
I could make up an excuse later. I readied myself, conscious of the clock.
Racing within its ticks ... I'd avoid Hilda.

I'm sitting at the kitchen table with wet hair. Liv's already home from work. I'm asking her how her day was, what she had for lunch, etc. I'm trying to seem calm, in no rush to get anywhere in particular. Liv is happy that it's Friday. She has the whole weekend in front of her. Her responses seem like they may take the whole weekend. I've already come up with a few excuses for why I have to go out. I'm deciding which one sounds best when suddenly someone lays on the doorbell. I say "suddenly" but I was expecting it like a loud noise you know is coming. And you jump anyway. Military salutes fired at a soldier's funeral, for example. The doorbell rings, I jump. It makes an ugly inhuman screech. I go to the door. Liv's throwing crackers and pretzels in wooden bowls. She brings a full coffee pot and three cups with sheep on them to the table. She arranges the cups carefully around the circular table as if she were setting the hands on a clock. The lazy energy in the room flares up. It's Hilda. Earlier than expected. Unwanted guests are always earlier than expected. According to Liv she may be right on time. Finally (fatefully?) we're introduced. She's good-looking. I hold out my hand. Hilda ignores it for the French peck-on-the-cheeks greeting. Usually its two pecks, sometimes its three or four. I never know how many to go for. Hilda does two but hesitates on the second, her nose turned up like there's an interesting smell in my ear. I can hear her breathing. She seems nice (I'm an optimist with pessimistic tendencies). She's dressed expensively in black, a short skirt and a silky blouse unbuttoned to the border of sexy and indecent. Blond hair, pale sericeous skin. I can tell she's one of those women I'd just admire from across the room. I wouldn't let her catch me looking at her. It's the attitude, the way she carries herself: hip flared, waist resting hands. She demands to be looked at. And when you do you're just like all the rest.

There's a pause as we move towards the table and the crackers, pretzels, coffee. We all sit down and Liv says, "Well ... ", deciding where to start catching up first. Hilda pulls a small package out of her designer purse. "This is *brunost*, B-R-U-N-O-S-T." She spells it loudly as if I'm hard of hearing. *Brunost* is a brown Norwegian cheese. We have a brick in the fridge. Since moving in with Liv it has become a regular at breakfast, lunch, dinner. "I brought it from home for you two because it's so hard to find here. My mother made it herself," Hilda says. We thank her. She asks me if I know what it is. Before I have a chance to say yes she begins explaining where it comes from, how it is made, etc. I listen to Hilda tell me there are varieties made from the milk of cows, goats or a mixture of both. How it is fermented. How it is boiled and allowed to nearly decay. Liv is getting out our Norwegian cheese cutter. It looks like a small triangular spatula with a groove cut into the middle.

Hilda opens the cheese, still explaining. She begins cutting slices by running
the flat bottom of the cutter along the top of the brick. Slivers the size of credit
cards start sliding out of the groove. There's a lengthy pause. We're all uncomfortable. Liv serves the coffee. I become aware of the kitchen clock ticking.
Then Hilda:

"At Virgin Megastore the other day I saw the biggest wanker. Have you two
been to the one on the Champs Elysée? Well, this wanker came up to me and
told me he liked my pullover. Don't I know it, the way he was staring at it
while he talked to me and I just said thanks and turned my back on him, but
he just kept on. No sense, a real bloody wanker. He asked me if he can buy me
some ice-cream. The French, they'll flirt with women no matter where,
everywhere. Its unbelievable, yeah? I could see what he was thinking, from
Virgin Megastore to a hotel room around the corner. I told him to piss off!
Yesterday afternoon I was in FNAC and you know how it is there, always a lot
of people, I love that, all those people, I just love that, and I felt somebody rub
my bum and I just thought well there's a lot of people here but then at the same
time I turned around and there was some bloke there behind me acting like he
don't know what was going on so I just turned back around trying to ignore
him. But no, he was French and he's not going to stop there. I felt him again
this time right, well ... (she turns towards Liv and whispers) he touched me like
you wouldn't even let your BOYFRIEND touch you (I stifled a humph. How did
she know how I touched Liv?) and of course I freaked out. I started screaming
and swinging my purse at his head. I grabbed people standing nearby and
yelled 'help! help!, he just grabbed my VAGINA!' (Hilda's shouting all of this
in a loud voice. She puts particular emphasis on 'vagina'. I hear the mystery
neighbor above us ((I've never seen him leave his apartment)) cough. Liv and
I look at each other. I'm reminded of watching unexpected sex scenes on cable
television with my parents.) and of course no one would help and some of the
punters even laughed. Can you imagine? He left the store quick and I followed
him out. I didn't know what I was going to do but I was so mad I just don't
care and I certainly couldn't shop with all that anger ... frying up inside me.
The only time I'm able to shop mad is when I'm using the bank card of the man
I'm mad at and then I do all right (wink to Liv). I couldn't be bothered to
follow this ... this ... bum-pinching wanker all day though, you know?
I'm always busy and that's the last thing I have time for. There was a cinema
right there and I didn't have anything better to do so I decided to go see the last
Valentino film ... "

Liv says, "Pulp fiction? I thought that film was completely ... "

"No, not that one, it was his LATEST one but I didn't like it too much.
I forget how it was called ... "

I ask, "Are you talking about Tarentino? Quentin Tarentino?"

"Well, yes. Where have YOU been?, but anyway I walked into the cinema and I hear this bloke behind me say I'm with her to the ticket-boy but I don't even pay attention. I don't even notice that the ticket-boy bastard charged me for TWO tickets. I just went and sat down and you'll never guess who was behind me. I give you three guesses. Go ahead, guess ... I'll tell you. It was the bum-groping wanker! And where do you think he sits? Who do you think goes and sat right behind me?"

Liv asks, "Not the same guy?"

"Yep. Unbelievable. Can you believe it? I think it was the SAME guy. So I turn around and I say listen pal, you leave me alone. Bugger off or I'm going to scream. And people all over the cinema were looking at us because I think I was already screaming. But I don't care and I said to him just who out of hell do you think you are? You think girls LIKE that shit? You think I'd ever let you FUCK ME? You? Not only are you ugly but you've got no behavior, no manners. Piss off, you! I don't even want to be in the same cinema and just looking at you disgusts me and stuff. He was shocked and doesn't move and I told him I'm going to call security and tell them he is molesting me and that he already grabbed my vagina. So he was getting up to leave all embarrassed and stuff and that's when I would notice he's wearing a Paul Smith suit and I just love Paul Smith, so I asked him how much he paid for his suit and where he got it and that made his jaw fall. I had to beg him to stay two minutes and talk to me. He told me he was a designer and knew Paul Smith PERSONALLY and that if I will like to I can meet him sometime. And that anyway he owed me a dinner since I paid for his cinema ticket. Finally, he was pretty nice and he has the cutest little red Porsche not to mention his cute little bum (giggle). Fuck (sigh). (I notice Hilda and I do not weigh the significance of certain words equally.) So actually I can't stay too long tonight because he's coming over to get me here, yeah? I gave him the address, I hope you don't mind. We have dinner reservations at 9."

She takes a deep breath. Then she puts a pretzel in her mouth. Liv says we don't mind. I wonder what happened to her English boyfriend. I see there's lots of time between me and the 9 on the clock of the kitchen wall. Liv says how good it is to see her after all these years. So on and so forth. Hilda offers me a credit card of *brunost* on a cracker. I tell her no thanks, I just ate before she arrived. I don't know why I say it because I haven't eaten anything since I woke up. I'm on my third cup of coffee. It was something to do while Hilda talked. She chews a cracker. Caffeine chews my insides. There's a long space of silence. My stomach comes to life, growling hunger in the space. Hilda and Liv politely ignore it.

Liv excuses herself to go to the bathroom. I'm alone with Hilda.
She's looking around the apartment like she's at a garage sale. I can see from
her expression that she wouldn't be surprised to find most of our stuff actually
in somebody's garage. The silence is uncomfortable. The clock is ticking
on the wall above the sink. Eye contact with Hilda feels like touching a used
syringe amongst your bags under a bus seat. If the table were a clock Hilda
would be sitting at six. I'm at ten. Liv was sitting at two. Hilda crosses
her legs on our side of the table. I can see her skirt sliding up her thighs.
She runs a finger along the back of her calf like she's tracing a run in her
stocking. I can see quite clearly — she's not wearing any stockings. Her silk
blouse hangs down. Her breasts are pendulous, round, cupped in a black lace
bra. She sits back in her chair after taking a long time to get her legs settled.
I take my eyes away, quick. "You're sure you don't want some *brunost?*,"
she asks. I accept this time. She watches my mouth as I put the cheese
covered cracker in.

Liv comes back from the bathroom. She sees that Hilda and I are not
talking or looking at one another. She starts in on a story a Yugoslavian friend
has told her about the outrageous price of vegetables in Belgrade. That if you
pinch the melons the vendor might kill you. Liv isn't as quick as Hilda.
There's longer pauses between her sentences. I notice Hilda looking at me out
of the corner of my eye. She is impatient with Liv's story. She starts talking at
the same time. I lose track of what proceeded and can no longer predict what
will follow. Before Hilda was giving us each about two seconds of eye contact
like a rotating sprinkler on a suburban lawn. Now she stops looking at us all
together. She prefers the mirror that is hanging on the wall of the bathroom
door, her wristwatch. This change coincides with the beginning of Liv's story.
We watch Hilda watching herself. As she chews she starts talking over Liv's
story about Yugoslavian vegetable vendors.

"You do know I'm not seeing James anymore? It just had to end (Liv ends
her story), there was no avoiding it. He's still madly in love with me but there
was no way it could go on forever. He's in the hospital actually and I feel bad
but he won't tell me what's wrong and he doesn't want me to visit. This friend
of mine met some girl at a bar who said she used to know James when he
worked on rue St. Denis at a porno shop selling dildos and string bikini knickers
for men with elephant trunks hanging off the front or even leopard print ones
but I don't believe a word of it. I told her straight on that James never, never,
worked on rue St. Denis, let alone in a porno shop. I don't know who this little
slut was that my friend met in a bar but I just couldn't believe it. Although you
better believe I asked James about it when he got home and of course, as you
might expect, he denied it, like all men deny things. I wouldn't step foot in a

place like that, would you? It opened up many kinds of questions about James' past that I just don't know about. What about those weekends I had to go away because of work? You know what they say, 'when the cat's away the big rat will dance on the table.' How can you trust a man to share your bed and eat with the same silverware as you do, sit on the same toilet seat you do — I even stopped putting layers of paper down first — when he probably worked in a porno shop playing with dildos and leather panties and stuff. Can you imagine? I wouldn't step foot in a place like that for the life of me. They've got disgusting pictures on the wall and rows and rows of porno films and these little booths you can go in and watch people fucking together and the seats are always sticky. Its absolutely revolting and not only that, its degrading to women. It reduces them to objects ignoring their ... how do you call it? ... mental process and ..."

I find myself looking at Hilda's lips. I watch them smack up and down. I hear her voice but I 'm no longer sure what she is saying. Maybe she's speaking Norwegian now. I look at her teeth, her tongue. In the arcs, where her teeth recede into her gums, there are mushed up remnants of cracker and pretzel. They're slightly less white than her teeth themselves. I watch how her tongue, her jaw and her lips all move together. They are coordinated with her eyebrows and lashes, the muscles in her cheeks, her hand gestures and head movements. I close my eyes. The sound of her voice and the movement she was making detach from each other spatially in my mind. Liv seems even further away, to my left somewhere. I open my eyes and look at her. She is staring at Hilda, nodding her head. Sometimes she says, "uh-huh" or "yep" or something similar. I look back to Hilda. The flesh and muscle of her face appear to be crude additions to her skull. Like a bust half finished, the sculptor called away. He has left two rotting olives in Hilda's eye sockets. My thoughts are reckless, uncontrollable. I feel a little sick. I wonder what's wrong with me. I'm too embarrassed to say anything to Liv and Hilda. I can smell the *brunost*. I push the brick closer to Hilda, the talking skull. Her voice becomes a ferocious, unrelenting pressure in my head. Her words blend with the ticking of the kitchen clock, making its beats erratic. Like when Liv flushes the toilet during my shower, a occasional cold water phrase from Hilda splashes across my thoughts.

"Stephanie was betrayed! The astrologists knew from the beginning what would happen with that marriage. They were just keeping quiet about her cursed stars then to sell more papers now."

"No one's heard from him and he hasn't answered any of my letters. I even put a self-addressed envelope with an international reply coupon in the last two I sent him. Those intellectual ones like him have strange borders and they're capable of anything. Totally unpredictable."

"Older people looked younger then than they look now and often younger people now look older than younger people then . . . No! Sorry, the opposite, I mean the opposite."

And:

"Did you know Jesus had a brother? Yeah, its true. I read somewhere that Jesus had a brother but hardly anyone knows about him because his miracles weren't as miraculous as Jesus'. Can you imagine Mary asking you everyday why you can't be more like your brother Jesus? The brother was actually the one who thought of turning water into wine first but he only did one bottle or something and so when Jesus did that whole wedding party everyone forgot about him. It sounds pretty American actually, take the little guy's idea, do it bigger and better, then forget about him."

Liv and I finally make eye contact. I'm not sure what she sees but she goes over to the liquor right away. She makes me a drink without asking. She offers Hilda a drink as well. Then Hilda says:

"This old man who lived next to my parents, you know I'm from Finnmark don't you? (I ask Hilda if Finnmark is spelled with one "n" or two but she doesn't even look in my direction.) Well this old man refused to eat any of the fruit or vegetables grown in the region because he thought they might be contaminated from the nuclear accident in Chernobyl, although studies showed that there was absolutely no danger. This old man loved cabbage but he had refused to eat it since the accident in Chernobyl. He was mad for cabbage. He finally broke down and accepted one from my mother on his 85th birthday. He steamed it that night and ate it without realizing it was rotten and he went to bed and never woke up the next morning. He was half blind but he could hear like a rabbit. In fact, now that I think about it, his ears kind of looked like a rabbit's (giggle). My mother told him it was rotten too late — after he had already eaten it. It came from a diseased patch and some of the cabbages were rotten on the inside. She just talked on and on about it to our old neighbor. Evidently he threw-up when she started telling him his cabbage might have been rotten. Before my father died we used to tease my mother, saying she was the one who killed our neighbor. She would get so mad (laughing). We never did find out if his cabbage was rotted or not. Its funny, the IDEA of him eating a rotted cabbage made him throw up and die."

Liv says, "Whatever killed him probably made him throw up and die."

"People can throw up and die of the most ordinary things, can't they?"

No one asks why her mother had given this old man with rabbit ears a rotten cabbage for his birthday. My stomach has a hole in it, queasy. I imagine very

clearly in my head the poor old man with rabbit ears. He's in a rocking chair,
a blanket over his lap, leaning to the side, vomiting on the wooden floor
of his log cabin in Finnmark. The rich brown boards blacken with the liquid.
I think I feel what he felt in my stomach. A hybrid burp/puke forces its way up
my throat. My heart is racing. I swallow and wash down what I swallow with
scotch. I think: you never see reports on television of rotten Norwegian cabbage
or cheese killing people.

    I hadn't heard footsteps in the hall but suddenly the door screech is going
off. I jump again. Hilda's date is here. I say to Hilda that her date is late.
He's pushing the screech like impatient people push lit elevator buttons.
Hilda and Liv stand up. Hilda says good-bye and promises to keep in touch.
"We'll have to have another little get together real soon. Anyway, you *know*
we'll see each other before too long. If you don't call me, I'll call you," she laughs.
She walks out into the hallway, greets the wanker on the lips. They step away
from each other. He wears a big red smear of lipstick across his lips, part
of his face. I think: maybe Paul Smith should come out with a line of cosmetics
for men. The wanker's smiling innocently. Like a man who has worn a costume
to a party and hasn't yet noticed nobody else has. Hilda doesn't introduce us.
Does she think we'll never see him again? Liv closes the door on them.
We can hear Hilda's voice fading, yet persistent, as they go off.

    Slowly, I will take a good tug on my scotch. It will burn
going down but I will feel already stronger than Hilda's voice
or the smell of *brunost*. Liv will come over to the table and
hug me. I'll feel her soft curves meld to my angular frame.
Maybe she'll only feel me squeezing too hard. She will sit
down beside me. We'll look into each others' eyes. I'll look
down at the drink in my hand. I'll be shaking like a man who has just barely
escaped a horrible accident. The ice cubes will knock together hollowly in my
glass. I'll notice that Hilda's perfume, still hanging in the air, seems to smell
like sulfur. I'll speculate that sulfur has something to do with death. Perhaps
I'll just be confusing death with hell. I'll be able to hear the ticking of the clock
hanging on the kitchen wall. It will sound lonely, isolating. Usually when
I notice it I put a disk in the stereo or turn the television on. Tonight the ticking
will sound terribly peaceful, inviting. Neither of us will move or say a word.
Liv will be looking where Hilda had been sitting. She'll be caught up in her
own thought.

I'll take her hand. She'll say nothing but give me a tired smile that is familiar
and warm. I'll smile back. I'll look into her eyes. Liv will have beautiful eyes.
I'll run my fingers lightly over the underside of her arm and wrist. I'll know
she likes this from experience. Her sleeve will be pulled up, revealing light
blue veins beneath pale skin. A delicate movement felt rather than seen.
My breathing will calm down. It will join the slow ticking of the clock on the
kitchen wall. I will wonder if Hilda's visit has marked us somehow. If indeed
her words do need to be written down. Liv will stack the three coffee cups
with sheep on them together but make no further movement to clear the table.
She will point out a small chip in the rim of one of the cups. Looking more
closely at them my perspective will shift. They will suddenly look like one cup
with three handles. It will hesitate precariously on the edge of the table.
My breath will wait. The clock will catch. There will be a long pure moment
of boundless possibility, without words or ways to know how the future
will enclose us.

THIERRY GUITARD - *drawing, 1998*

BLACK SIFICHI

Ventoline

The asthma attacks are coming on again.
The top model weather forecaster is
Angling her cleavage aesthetically and telling me
The Danger level of pollution is a level two.

Wheeze in the air.
Fantasize.
Wheeze it out.

She licks her lips and the audience roars.
Publicity!
Weather Broadcast Brought to you by EDF Nucléair.

Tax evasion will soon be an Olympic sport
Supported by the lovers of Lady Di.

Bombs going off all around the Mediterranean
Kids disappearing everywhere.
To what place do they finally go?
Do murdered children have a special place
In the eyes of an expanding universe?

Wheeze. Wheeze. Wheeze.

In 40 years the temperature will be 1° hotter here
And 7° hotter on the poles.
The doctor prescribed a month of pills and
Two Ventoline inhalers.
5 Hits a day maximum she insists.
Too much adrenaline otherwise.
An hour after the attack I'm up to 4 inhalations.

Breath in.

Waiting for the day when land mines will be planted
Instead of flowers in our country.

Breath out.

Everything looks better around you when you're
Talking on a portable phone.
It all fits into place.
We're just diodes on the global map.

Accept your secret number,
Accept and use your secret number
And you can step into the future.
Subscribe to a contemporary art gallery
And witness and buy so much art
About desolation and pain.

Chopped off arms in the praying position.
Empty rooms. Empty chairs. Empty walls.
Foetus earrings.
Nice. Really Interesting.

What's it called?
Sarajevo. Van Gogh's ear.

Inhalation number five.

Look out.
Hamad Butts fragile poisonous gas filled glass vessels
Suspended in the centre of the gallery like a temptation to
Joyful terrorism.
Set up like one of those steel ball games you put on your desk.
Only much bigger.
Drop the first ball and the last ball moves.
Are they really filled with poisonous gas?
Well buy a gas mask — go into the gallery and try it out.

Ventoline for everyone!

Computer made music with every dog bark
Digitized to help form an unending constant beat.
I must ask the doctor for some "Ecstasy-Ventoline".
They want me to live.
I'm still a successful consumer.
I might even buy stock in one of those Mega-supermarket
Multi-nationals.
If we could only get 51% of the market.
Then we'd have control.

Since the end of the Monarchy.
Princess. Egyptian, mercedes, booze, prozac, crash.
Naomi Campbell has visited Kurdistan.
She thinks that "land-mines and poisonous gas"
Should be illegal ... internationally.
I think knives should be illegal ... internationally.

Make me a star.

Hit number 8 on the Ventoline.
Wheeze in.
The future is mine.
A thousand company presidents control the planet.
You could be one of them.

Tap your resources.
Tap your resources.
Create a system.

Tax the people.
Create a logic.
Create a market.
Subtract a value.
Create an illness.
Divide a people.
Multiply the profit.

NANCY HUSTON

LIMBO

Get it in Inglish. Shoved. Wedged. Lodged in the language like a bullet in the brain. Undelodgeable. Untranslatable.

How it is.
Feeling (rotten word, feeling) so close to old Sam Beckett these days. Close in the way Miss Muffet is close to the spider. At last having come to see why the reductio ad absurdum, the people scarcely people, all of them stopped, stymied, paralysed, plunged into blackness and silence, they cannot move they cannot talk they cannot see, they are pure minds struggling to discover the first words and especially a reason to pronounce them, there is no world no reality no country, all signifiers are indifferent but equal, nothing matters, no mater even dolorosa, we are back in the womb or else already in the tomb — no matter, take my word for it, you take a word, you turn it into another word, the meaning moves, you stay the same, Hamm, Cham, what's in a name, a rose, how do you get from here to there, it's neither here nor there, neither ego nor alter, nothing alters, almost nothing, if only nothing, it's such a freak accident, why born here rather than there, borne from here to there, carried, plunked, and wherever you look people rush about blathering and dithering, spouting words that spark off this or that, love and anger and the whole gamut, dammit, oh thrill, oh thrall, oh thrull, veering off into nonsense, so wouldn't it be better to just shut them up, lock them into boxes, coffins, vases, mud, sand, stuff their mouths full of sand, make them cease talking, make the word-machine cease grinding out its senseless sense, if I can be Irish and then French I could just as well be Danish or a dog, why choose, how choose, it's all the same to me, it all comes down to the same thing, a catastrophe, every choice is a Fall, and the words are fed up with running in circles, building characters, weaving plots, barf, it's exhausting to go on striving for resemblance, verisimilitude, they come from such-and-such a country, belong to this or that milieu, are men, or women, and then, and also, or children, who gives a shit, and because they had this done to them they reacted like that, you must sympathize, empathize, poor guys, put yourself in their place — whereas there is no such thing as place,

no such thing as light color movement music, all the nuance harmony and
dissonance they claim to find so moving, nope, no go, nothing but a brain that
can't bloody well can it, wound up like a bloody mechanical toy and compelled
to go on ranting and raving until death doth ensue because there you are,
chucked headfirst into time, language, the verbal slop-pail and forced to swim
volens nolens, go on crawling endlessly through words, phrases, paragraphs and
the rest, glutting on garbage, stirring up ructions, eructations, every now and
then a character floats to the surface and is instantly sucked under, squelched,
drowned, every now and then a glimmer of an idea but — wham! bang! dead!
O let me gaze awhile upon thy tender visage! Nay nay I say! Out, out, brief
candle! Bye-bye birdie! Farewell cruel world! The time has come, the walrus
said — and it congeals for an instant, gives you something to chew on, then
dissolves, melts in your mouth, rejoins the flux, the sewage, the random
writhing mess

•➤

Well let's start a new paragraph here let's take a new breath let's go see
what's on at the movies, what did X say about Y and it is of crucial importance
that at this particular conjuncture in time there be a major effort on behalf of

Yes?
No.
But wasn't there — just now — a glimmer? A little sliver of — ?
Blam, black. Doom. Done.
I was sure ... maybe not a sliver but ... a glint?
Blood, black, thum, whump. Shut. Clot.
Didn't it open, just a what's it called, a shard? A crack?
Slam, bang, dark. Closed, dead, mum.
I caught a glimpse — a tiny flash — if not a liver then a shiver, pink —
something moving, glistening, like, like — a smile, wet gums, or —
Hammer on thumbs. Sledgehammer whamming finger nails, one by one.
Now. Night. Numb.
But I tell you — it was almost like children, like children romping, children
chortling, children rolling in the grass for joy. Sheer —
Thump. Whump. Obliterate. Oblivion.
Wasn't there ... perhaps ... a character under there? Back in there ...
I mean ... behind the curtain ... trying to lift a corner to get in?
Gag. Bars. Iron doors. Clang bang shut. Bomb. Tomb.

I could swear — a sparkle, something like a sparkle, a magenta- or fuchsia-colored scarf, a swish, something swirling — a dancer, maybe? A woman, in silk, spinning ...?

Chest to cement floor. Anvil on back. Crushed. Mushed. Tons and tons of nones.

And weren't there ... you know ... flutes and gurgling brooks, the jagged brilliant notes of saxophones and trumpet? And also — an undulating line of silver slither in the grass? You know, something ... alive, flashing, like laughter — ?

Throttle, gag, choke, fist in teeth, nose flat, blat, dot dot dot, nul.

In the meadow was a little boy, he'd fallen off his bicycle and skinned his knee, a trickle —

Void. Cancelled. Censored. Silenced. Struck out.

A man tearing down a dark street in desperation, zig-zagging to avoid cars, lamp-posts, garbage cans, dogs, all manner of obstacles — panting, gasping for breath, his heart heaving —

Stooped. Stilled. Stunned. Stone.

A stranger? Stranded on the seashore, dressed in a stained trenchcoat, the waves lapping at his shoes, the wind rising, buffeting, hurling sand into his eyes — his eyes watering, streaming ...

Nothing. No thing. Blank.

Bodies squirming, writhing, melding, slick with sweat, bodies of all shapes and colors, jiving in their juices —

Blast. Damn. Wall. All. Deaf. Blind. Dumb.

And so much, so horribly much has been done, and well done, too — Well done! — and all of it has been useless though one would be hard put to say what useful would have been, less hunger oh yes, that certainly, and less war and less racial discrimination perhaps, sexual discrimination we can handle but but but but — I mean, is the goal to improve the world or to tell it like it is or to tell it like it isn't like it could be or might have been or like nothing in the world has ever been? To *épater les bourgois* or to give them pause for thought or to help them pass the time? Lead them down the garden path, the little red lane, thirty-six white horses and why get up on one's high horse if it's only words words words, as the prince of Denmark says, or even actions, what's the difference, a man of words, a man of action, how believe in him here if he could have been there, how take him seriously when he's nothing but a laughable assemblage of members and muscles and mucous and mealy-mouthed preconceptions?

Pre-conception or post-mortem: that's the place to be, rather than this
quagmire in between, flailing and floundering, waving to the crowds, grinning,
putting a good face on things, going on, keeping up the good work, chin up,
chin chin, I said that before, many years ago, can't think up new words every
day you know, can't change tongues every year, do you only open your mouth
to change feet, you're not supposed to take me literally, as a matter of fact
you're not supposed to take me anywhere, leave me alone, that's all I ask,
not only is there no god, there's scarcely any man to speak of, just a blip
in the void, a flash in the pan, a bird in the bush, words, words, Worst Word Ho?

•⟋

Here: I pluck off my fingers one by one and drop them on the ...
what's that thing down there called, the floor? The ceiling? The flour?
With what will I pluck off my nose, now that my fingers are gone? Here,
have a foot! Where do you want it? In the gut? In the gutter? Say when.
Say also how and where and why. Tell me a story, tell me a story, tell me a story,
remember what you said. That, at least, has rhythm. All God's chillun' got
rhythm! Perhaps rhyme could save us? She died of a fever and no one could
save her — bad rhyme, that one — and that was the end of sweet Molly Malone.
Who can believe this shit? Neither rhyme nor reason. You set something in
motion and then, ta-dee-da. You pull yourself up by your bootstraps, and then
they go and pull the rug out from under you. Justify, at all costs justify.
Make an effort to deduce the cause from its effect. Come on, now, this is serious.
There's nothing to laugh about. If you keep on laughing we'll rip out your
spleen. Where exactly is the spleen, anyway? I smell a rat.

•⟋

Beckett, my brother, my foot. At last I feel (ugly word, feel) close to you.
At last your language is limpid to my, what, brain, heart, foot. If there are two
languages, there are any number of languages and — worse — the gaping gaps
between the words. No reason to say this rather than that, much less do this
rather than that. The absurd was discovered by foreigners. No accident.
Dirty fur'ners, furretin' around in their dictionairies. My tailor is rich and
my soprano is bald. Look, here's a chair, here's another chair, here are seven
hundred thousand chairs in the same little room. Here, have a rhinoceros.
Only a Rumanian in Paris could have come up with the rhinoceros.
And only a Russian expatriate would choose to spend her time spying on
sub-conversation in French. *Le monde est rond*, dixit Stein the stone.

La civilisation accidentelle. This empire is one big fall, not even preceded
by a rise. Everything tends to collapse; I hope you understand the gravity
of the situation. Word play, they say — but, it's serious! Believe me, there's
nothing funny about it. Stop your giggling, wipe that smirk off your face,
we're talking about the void. Now, where can you go from there? Takeoff
impossible. You're nailed to the spot, condemned to life, and forced to see,
second by second, how preposterous the whole thing is. Blessed are the dead,
for theirs is the kingdom of heaven.

Now, don't get snide with me, all right? I'm as noble as any son of Man,
or any son-of-a-bitch. Okay, okay, so I came out of a woman's cunt —
you're not going to make me worship that, are you? Is it my fault if the vaults
of heaven the swirling cosmos the shooting stars the earth's atmosphere
the meteors and comets and carbon dioxide and whatnot all came down to this?
Creatures with pricks and cunts making other creatures with pricks and cunts
— and, what's worse, talking about it? Thinking about it? Making up stories
about it? Myths, legends, poems, fairy-tales, novels, Bibles, blablaba?
Why should I shoulder any responsibility in the matter? Why I at all,
in the midst of it all? Who said I had to be here, and, more importantly,
what the fuck did they say it for? *A qui profite le crime?* That is the question.
Compared to that, to be or not to be is twaddle. Or piddle. Take your pick.
I pick piddle. Peter picked a pecker.

Oh! To be released from the obligation to live in any tongue! To relinquish
languish, once and for all! To vanquish lanquish. That's a good one. Well, so-so.

Everyone is someone but I, who know that all of us are no one. Sshh.
Don't tell. Mum's the word. And our mummies and daddies before us.
And our sons and daughters behind us. Or below us. Full sentences. Full stop.
Spinning logic, spinning tales, spinning tops. Dripping with meaning.

Who would ever have thought it would come to this?

I have found my own language at last, a language comprehensible only to
myself. Boy, are you guys ever naïve. It's time to face the music. Stand on your
own two feet. Look where all your getting to has gotten you. Facts, fiction, facts.
Good, better, best. Never take a rest. Drink to me only. Had we but world
enough and time, this coyness, lady, were no crime. How do I love thee?

Let me count the ways. Not marble, nor the gilded monuments of princes.
Tiger, tiger, burning bright. Rhinoceros, rhinoceros, in the night. Fill me full
and stab me dead, but do it like a gentleman. Like a damsel. In distress,
of course. OK. Here we go, grab my hand — or my foot, if you prefer.
 Bally-something. Literary studies. Literary buddies. Literary biddies.
There is no — Right. There isn't any. It's not a joke, I'm not exactly
having the time of my life in here. On the other hand, it's not a tragedy,
either. It's a free country, it's nothing to write home about. Well of course,
if there's something you want to say ... But what if there isn't, and you're
obliged to say it anyway, with the miserable means at your disposal?
Words and more words. Look at the state you're in. We'll just have to move
you to another. Look at reality — you call this a life? A fine fix you've
gotten us into. Now try and get us out of it. 'Twas brillig and the slithy
toves did gyre and gymbol in the wabe. Gymbol? Did you say gymbol?
Gymbolism and interpretation? Use this to mean that and that to mean this?
A fine fix in need is a fine fix indeed. Look — just where did you get your
gumption from? Do you think gumption grows on trees? Do you think
it just falls down out of the sky? I've worked my ass off to provide you and
the children with gumption, and this is what I get! Huff, puff! Where do you
get off? Stop the world, I wanna get off. If this is Tuesday, it must be Paris.
Maybe Tuesday will be my good news day. Maybe not. Who said this was
Paris, anyway? It might just as well be Bally-whatever. Or Calgary. Or Gary,
Indiana. That's the town that knew me when. Whenever.
 Language is fascistic; it obliges you to specify. What sex. (Oooh-la-la!)
What tense. The present is very tense. By the time you get to the second
syllable you're out of it; the first is already past. I wouldn't put a dog out in
this tense. Home at last. Home's where the heart is. What about the spleen?

•➔

Okay. If you want me to tell you a story I'll tell you a story. There you
have it. And the moral is — sleep, sleep, that knits up the ravel'd sleeve of care.
A blind date with God. Or Worm. One of those guys who flung us here to flail
and flounder. Oh, bosh. Jeronimus. Jeronimo! Here we go again — on our
high horse! Marching forth triumphantly, trumpets and drums, strumpets and
bums, dazzling glory. All the king's horses and all the king's men, and so and
and so forth forever, amen.

•➔

Just give me one of those little nuggets and I'll show you what I can do
with it. I'll rub it and polish it, make it gleam and glow like gold.
In the gloaming. Knee-deep in love. Oh, yeah. Forgot about that one.
The whole world loves a lover. It's love, it's love, it's love that makes the world
go round. Merry-go-round. Happy-go-lucky. Boy, a good thing there's love, eh?
Love is one great big sine qua non. Without it, nothing. With it, nothing.
Oh, and something else. For the love of God, something else! More lies.
Here lies. Wishful thinking. Don't think we haven't tried. It's not enough to wish,
you've got to ... Hey, who does he think he is? Where does she get off?
And if you really believe what you say, then — . Sorry, no hope today.
Where there's death, there's hope. Clean slate. Proper noun. Improper usage.
We gave you the language and what kind of use have you put it to?
Do you think this is what words are for? Frankly, you go too far.
You're getting just a bit too big for your britches. Not one more word out
of you, do you hear? Just drop it. Cata the strophe.

━ •

Beckett beckons. Come with me my pretty miss, and let us leap to the
abyss. What is a miss? Mister Lister kissed his sister. Do you realize what
you're saying? How can you possibly — After all I've — And you just go and
— Well, I won't stand for it. Then what do you stand for? And what do you
write for? And what makes you go on breathing in and out, day in day out,
come rain or come shine, come hell or high water, twixt the devil and the deep
blue sea? Hm? Hm. Been there before, too. It's an old story. But I've
forgotten the ending. And the middle. And the beginning. Jesus Christ.
Nothing to grab onto in this slop. Grasping at straws. The straw that broke
the camel's back. A figure of speech. What he's really trying to say is that.
Whoops! A figure of skating. Pirouette. You can't catch me! I'm the king
of the castle! Sticks and stones can break my bones! Shall you pace forth,
sally forth, & so forth. And fifth. Don't you care? Don't you even give a shit?
Polish it behind the door. Shit or get off the pot. I'm getting there, I'm getting
there. What I wanted to say was — Basta. Two syllables. Foiled again.
You fiend! You villain! You basta! You turd!

Oh. How disappointing. You really disappoint me, you know? He disappoints me. So where do we go from here? What is to be done? A complete
revolution. That was her greechy period. Now she's grown up. This could
go on forever. That's just the problem.

━ •

Not on me, you don't. Can't put that over on me, don't even try. I'm not foolable. She's been around, the little lady. Clear yourself out a bit of space. The words and the birds. Speaking to Virginia Woolf in Greek. Septimus, dear Septimus. It's not so hard after all. It's not so terrible. Just make a start. Take a running leap. Have a little salt. Sprinkle it on the birds' tails. It's all right. It's all wrong. Sing to me your lonely song. Droning, whining, going nowhere. Painted into a corner. Blue, red, gold. The particular. So much beauty. Oh darling. Sweep it away, sweep it all away. Mop, dustcloth, window cleaner. Spic, span. Quick! Quirks, kinks, quips — all gone? No? Oh, Godot! To be gone!

Now, don't look so glum. There are periods like this. Commas, too. So much undoing still to be done. The overarching: nothing but that, from now on in. Must promise to never be bathetic again. What's the difference between bathetic and pathetic? Well, bathetic is like pathetic only soupier. Sloppier. Bathing in pathos. Pathing in bathos.

•➔

Let's admit we have a head.
(Grumble grumble grumble.)
Or at least that we want to get a head.
No, no, not that!
Go on, climb up the ladder.
Anything but that!
Wake up in the morning.
Argh! Not waking up in the morning again!
Well, wake up in the night, then.
Mercy! Leave me in peace, or in pieces!

This whole thing is sorely lacking in vacuousness.

•➔

Once upon a time they lived happily ever after. Not only that, but they had a whole kit and kaboodle of kids. Mustn't forget that, no, no, no. How many children? Address? Phone number? Marital status? Are you sure?

Okay, look, this is just a mess. In fact everything you've ever done up to now has been a mess. That's what it amounts to. Add it up — yuck. A bunch of muck. Clichés, clichés, the twittering birds, the booming guns, the lazy hazy crazy days of summer, to say nothing of the croaking frogs and the smoking bogs and the bloaking fogs, no that won't do, fogs can't bloak, that's impossible. That's asking too much of them. There's a limit to what fogs can do. If only you'd get down off your high horse and look at what's happening in the world around you, you'd know that. How did you get here, anyway? Sit down there. Right this minute. Pick up your pen and get to work. Stop shirking your working. Stop jerking off. Try to come up with something important for a change. Knowledge handed down from one generation to the next. Hand-me-downs. Charity. You must consider those who will come after. It's just basic human kindness, that's all. When you come right down to it. Your navel is dirty. Stop picking your navel! Ugh! Really!

Well, let me tell you this: he died in my arms. I'd never seen him before, and he just walked up to me and died in my arms. Now what am I supposed to do? Did you ever see such a thing in your life? They all ran after the farmer's wife! The farmer takes a wife, that's where the plot thickens. You bet your ass. Because then the wife takes a child, and then Cain slays Abel, unless it's the other way around, I forget, and then Blim and Blam see that they are naked and then everybody starts knowing everybody else and before you can say Boo the whole slithering slough of generations gets set into motion and the next thing you know you've got Job and all those things to cry about.

Who started it?

Well-Enough did, also known as Worm. He felt lonely, he longed for some company. How dare you leave Well-Enough alone? he screamed at his Creation. Talk to me! So he made us. In his image. It's enough to make you tear your hair out. Eat your heart out. Puke your guts up. Scream your head off. Mothers weeping for dead children, wives for dead husbands, Romeo for Juliet, the whole schlemiel. I'm sure I've left out a few, but you get the general drift and gist of my jest. That's what you get. That's how much thanks I get. Don't thank me, thank Worm. Don't clap, just throw money. Reptiles were a far more peaceful form of life. It's not my fault. If I'd had it my way, we would have stayed right there in the slithy toves where we belonged, without giving it a second thought. Not even a first one. Ah, bliss! Ah, Nirvana. Released at last from the vicious circle of births and deaths. If I only had my druthers. Where have my druthers gotten to, anyway? I was sure I put them here somewhere. They were here just a minute ago. Hey, Shakespeare — have you seen my druthers, by any chance? Did you borrow them without asking? I'd give anything to get my druthers back.

•◞

No, no, no, this will not do. Bouville, thy name is mud. Nowheresville.
You're going nowhere fast. Two four six eight, who do we appreciate?
The dead! The dead! The dead! He's still got a little fight in him.
Stiff upper lip. Stiff dick, etc. The words themselves are so, something,
so delicate, perhaps. Irrefutable. Once they're there. There, there, now.
Then, then, here. They just keep spilling out whether you write them down
or not, even if you press your lips together, beg to be gagged and drugged.
It just. Yattering. Nattering. Nagging. Nagg and Nell. The taming of the shrew.
Tis pity she's a whore. Leave me alone, woman! Damn dames! Keep wanting
things to go on. The weight of the world on my shoulders. Oh my darlin'
Clementine, you are lost and gone forever. Dreadful sorry, kid. You must have
forgotten to brush your teeth. Or put out the cat. Or put out milk for the cat.
No help for it now. Too late, babe. Can't turn back the clock. Sorry, that's
the way it is. I'm going to have to shrug my shoulders and turn my back
on you. Ready, set, go!

•◞

No go. East, West, tomb's best. If only ... Yeah, if only. That's just
the problem. If only nothing, but we haven't any nothing, there's nothing
I can do about it, I wasn't the one who decided there would be something!
Why something rather than nothing? When Being goes down the drain, it all
goes down the drain. So what's it waiting for? You do all you can, and it's
never enough. You try to fix things up, you hog the blankets, make sacrifices,
set bombs and no, they're never satisfied. You give a woman an inch and
she'll take a yard. You give her a yard and she'll ask you to mow it. Guffaw.
Hardy haw-haw-haw. Hip-hip-hooray. So where do we go from here.
Just keep putting one foot in front of the other, then in your mouth. Heroism
consists in hanging on one second longer. Hang on in there! From the neck.
Till death doth.
  Shall I compare thee to a summer's day? Lazy hazy crazy, muggy clammy,
perfectly unbreathable? Or shall I compare thee, rather, to a puppy-dog's tail?
That's what little boys are made of, after all. Boys will be boys. Girls will be girls
too, only they won't admit it. That's a good one, hahaha. Oh, I wouldn't slap
my thighs over it. Well, I know another one ... No, I've forgotten it. I'm sure it
was a good one, though. Worm told it to me, once upon a time. Or twice.

Doesn't matter, I have no vested interest in all this, you know. I have more
than one string to my bow, anyhow. Besides, I've got better things to do.
I seen the mist but I missed the scene. No, what really bugs me is that.
Okay, if you really must know. If you insist. But don't say I didn't warn you.
Don't complain to me afterwards that. You do realize what you're getting into,
don't you? You're going into this with open eyes and a clear conscience?
Okay then, here's the truth. The whole truth and nothing but. And here it is
again. In your face. That's where the shoe pinches. That's what it boils down to,
when push comes to shove. Yep. Something. No getting around it. You can try
treating it like a burning bush and beating around it, but that won't save you.

Whoa, there. No point in getting all beady-eyed and bushy-tailed about
this. Keep your cool. I yam that I yam, and never the twain shall meet.

～•

Take it from the top. Blim and Blam. Abraham and Lucy. A quivering
molecule. Then a homuncule. Cells dividing, which is to say multiplying.
Go forth and multiply. Obscene, isn't it? Any way you like it. Choose your
position. The Kamasutra suggests a few hundred. Get to the point.
Make your point, for the love of God, or Worm. What's the point of all this?
Are you trying to tell me you're just going to sit there and live for the rest of
your life? Is that your plan? Is that all you can come up with? I can't believe
it. I feel sick. The whole thing makes me bloody sick, if you wanna know
the truth.

Now. Breathe deeply.

Om is where the Art is.

Don't give me that Krapp.

Stop crooning at me.

No more lullabyes, no more good nights.

Twitches and spasms. Jactations.

Here we go again.

K A T H L E E N   S P I V A C K

"O vase of acid.
It is love you are full of …"

In 1959, Kathleen Spivack went to Boston on a fellowship to study
with the poet Robert Lowell. "That single act changed my life," she writes.
She worked with Lowell both privately, in tutorial sessions at his house
on Marlboro Street, and in a class alongside Anne Sexton, Sylvia Plath,
and others who were in the first bloom of their careers.
The following is an essay from Spivack's longer work on that period.

SOME THOUGHTS ON SYLVIA PLATH

Walking into class at Boston University one February in 1959, I sat down
next to a young woman who like myself, had gotten there a bit early.
The chairs were in disarray around the seminar table, and the windows looked
out on busy Commonwealth Avenue below. Robert Lowell was, as usual,
a bit late, and most of the class on time, so there was always an awkward wait.
There was little talk; a low murmur to the person most immediately proximate,
but students did not interact easily. It was rather like going to church, edging
into a pew, trying not to call attention to oneself, and waiting for the service
to start. People said hello self-consciously, but mostly sat and prepared
themselves mentally, in silence.

The woman next to me was astonishing in her stillness. She appeared
perfectly composed, quiet, almost fixed in her concentration. She was softly
pretty, her coat slung over the back of her chair, and a pile of books in front
of her. Her notebook was open, her pencil poised. Everything seemed neat.
This was Sylvia Plath.

I had read her poem, "Doomsday" when I was in high school. The poem
had appeared in *Harper's Magazine.* I loved the music of it, the reckless
nihilism. I had memorized the poem, but had forgotten the author's name.
The author's note in *Harper's* had stated that Sylvia was a student at Smith
College. It had been inspiring to me that a young college girl had been able
to write and publish this poem. The poem had stayed with me through college.

I had always wanted to meet the author, a young woman who seemed to be living the literary life I craved. I had solaced myself on many a gray day by reciting grandly, as I walked to and from school, her lines:

"The idiot bird leaps out and drunken leans ..."

The poem ranked in importance to me with Frost's "Acquainted with the Night," a poem I still treasure, for I too had walked "out and back in rain."

After we had introduced ourselves, I somehow put the poem and the person together. Faltering beneath her intent stare, I said something about how much that poem had meant to me. But Sylvia was not interested in her "Juvenilia." Nor in the juvenilia in Lowell's class. Focused around her own goals, she was pleasant but noncommittal. We talked a bit before class, from time to time, as we both got there early. Sometimes she seemed restless, agitated beneath that extraordinary stillness. She hardly interacted with the other students, her head bent in a book, pretending to ignore the comings and goings, the chair scrapings, nervous throat clearings, and so forth that accompanied the beginning of class. It was not that she wasn't polite: she was; but she seemed nervously preoccupied. I thought she might be worried about Lowell's opinion of her poetry, for a greater tension overcame her when he entered the room. She seemed inordinately serious, her head bent over her notebook. Was she taking notes?," I wondered. Sitting next to her, I saw that she was scribbling, over and over, the ink marks digging at the page. Maybe she was doodling.

Her "Journals" from that time record how distant she felt from the class, but I think volcanic emotions lay beneath even the feelings of boredom. Outside of class she was already beginning to write "The Colossus," and other poems.

Sylvia had a neat co-ed prettiness. She wore pleated skirts and buttoned down pink long sleeved shirts, and a little pin; a kind of frozen woman student's uniform. Sometimes she would fold her camel's hair coat about her shoulders. She positioned herself at the long table in Lowell's classes, often at the foot of the table directly opposite Robert Lowell. Her voice had a kind of rasped, held- in drawl to it, with the syllables clipped at the same time. Although she spoke softly, she seemed definite in her opinions. She had read almost everything, it seemed. Lowell's obscure references were not obscure to Sylvia; she was the best-educated of the group. She had absolutely no sense of humor. Ever! Lowell's off-hand jokey manner did not evoke a smile from Sylvia, as it did often from others. She was serious, focused on the matter at hand, almost pained. Lowell was intense about poetry, totally one track, but after a long exploration of a poem, or of the work of a "famous" poet, he might turn with a deferential smile and make a little off-hand light comment.

To Sylvia, these were annoying distractions. She could not deflect her attention.

The person in class, and the person revealed in Sylvia Plath's letters, journals, and eventual poems were entirely different. Longing, anger, ambition, and despair appear to have been motivating factors for that gifted poet. These furies expressed themselves outward frequently, as they did even more totally inward, toward herself and her achievements. As in a Greek tragedy, in which the elements of destruction reside within the character of the protagonist, the elements that led to her suicide had been apparent even in the early stages of her adolescence. Her desperation, so tightly reined in, increased throughout her life.

Sylvia visited Robert Lowell's class and recorded in her journal her first impression on February 25, 1959.

"Lowell's class yesterday a great disappointment: I said a few mealy-mouthed things, a few B.U. students yattered nothings I wouldn't let my Smith freshmen say without challenge. Lowell good in his mildly feminine ineffectual fashion. Felt a regression. The main thing is hearing the other students' poems & his reaction to mine. I need an outsider: feel like the recluse who comes out into the world with a life-saving gospel to find everybody has learned a new language in the meantime and can't understand a word he's saying."

She had told the class, the first meeting, when we went round and introduced ourselves, that Wallace Stevens was her favorite poet. She sat very straight as she said this, seeming quite sure of herself. Lowell approved. Sylvia was erudite and classical, unlike the flamboyance of Anne Sexton. The achievement of her poetry at that time seemed to lag behind the scholarly achievements of her mind and critical ability.

Sylvia might occasionally venture a comment on a student poem, although Lowell did not invite this very often. When she analyzed a student poem, she was critical, brilliant, and a "good student." She knew about such things as scanning, and rhythm, and structure. She was quiet most of the time, and only when she spoke of someone else's poems did that hard edge surface. She was precise, analytical, and could be quietly devastating to another student poet. I would never have guessed that she had taught her own classes at Smith College, since she did not have the encouraging warmth that prefaced her critical comments. Her remarks were distanced, and logical.

Her own poems were very tightly controlled; formal, impenetrable, but without the feeling that was later to enter them. They were good, they were like perfect exercises. They did not have the wild passion of some of the poetry from her "Juvenilia;" that passion had been replaced by duty and structure.

Lowell did not particularly praise Sylvia, for although her poems were perfect, they had a virginal unborn feeling to them. As Sylvia herself did at that period.

It was hard to imagine her married, passionate, or caring about anything really: of course she cared intensely about her life, but hid behind a perfect mask.

Lowell tried to push her on her poems a bit, trying to get at the feeling underlying them. He did this gently; he also, I think, sensed how brittle she was. Anne Sexton, on the other hand, was writing warm poems, more than that, her poems seared, hot with feeling, and Lowell's critiques attempted to rein them in a bit, get Anne to make her imagery consistent, and to work more with form. George Starbuck sat in the middle of all this, a genial presence. High domed forehead, smiling, George listened and occasionally made some very good comments on poems. He was kind, modulated, tactful. George's own work was also extremely formal, technically perfect in its presentation. He later won the Yale Series of Younger Poets Prize. But he was a much more gentle soul than either of the two women.

Lowell, that year, was always on the verge of a breakdown. The class was generally awestruck, and trembled with a resonance to the fragility of his mental state. The experience of being there was nerve racking. Lowell's idiosyncratic brilliance took turns with the more obscure parts of incoherent lectures. As each class extended, and the afternoon got colder and darker, we hunched in a kind of numb terror of frozen concentration over the student poems presented, and over the other, more famous, poems that Lowell would read aloud and dissect.

Like the rest of us, Sylvia Plath was probably scared to death whenever she had to present a poem in the workshop. She withdrew behind dry defenses. Lowell admired her work, as we all did. He respected her; but assumed a hands-off position on her poetry, brief in his comments with Sylvia, unlike the more relaxed casual jokey manner he might sometimes choose, a more rambling discursive comfortable approach.

On a particularly lucid day, Lowell passes out copies of Sylvia's poem "Sow." I can still recall his somewhat nasal Southern-New England voice, oddly pitched, as if starting to ask a question, saying to Sylvia and to the class, "This poem is perfect, almost." A slight breath-gasp, nasal, outward as if clearing his sinuses silently. "There really is not much to say." A kindly but bewildered look. Long, struggling silence. Lowell looks down at the poem, brow furrowed. The class waits. Sylvia, in a cardigan, does not move. She listens. No one else moves either. "It appears finished." Long silence. Lowell looks agonized, but then he always does. Anne fidgets. Realizing that her arms draped with charm bracelets are making noise, she stops. Sylvia leans forward, dutiful, expressionless, intense, intelligent.

"But, I don't know. There's something about it ..." Lowell's nasal voice trails off, helplessly. "Does anyone else want to say anything about this poem?" No one apparently wants to say anything. We are all too intimidated. Anyhow, we have learned that Lowell will bite our heads off if we "say" the wrong thing. We're all afraid. If he is entering another breakdown period, he might turn and lash out on anyone who accidentally irritated him. Who knows what is going on in that tortured New England mind? Lowell frowns with effort. Another long dissatisfying silence. There is the almost inaudible sound of Lowell's rather nasal breathing. He is thinking. Everyone tries to refrain from saying something stupid. The room gets darker. Sylvia does not move, watching. "I'm sure this will be published," Lowell comments to her off-handedly, with a sly kind near-sighted glance. But perhaps the poem already has been published. There is a feeling of unsatisfied poetic process in the room. The poem is formal and beautifully presented, as is Sylvia herself. Everyone senses Lowell has "damned with faint praise," and has managed to sidestep real engagement with the poem. One can't get beneath the surface of the poems Sylvia brings to class. And yet one can't define that, or change it either. There is an air of disappointment, an accepted frustration.

And then Lowell launches for some reason into a reading of Randall Jarrell's poem "The Ball Turret Bomber," another "perfect" poem. "Now that's the genuine article," he says, looking up, and smiling gently, as if surprised anew by the perception. Lowell looks exactly like Little Jack Homer, I think ("He reached in his thumb and pulled out a plum. What a good boy am I!"). He regards us all triumphantly, about to crow. We all know how much he loves the work of Randall Jarrell. We have already gone over "The Woman at the Washington Zoo" in a previous class. The tension is broken, at least for the moment. Lowell, cocking his head, squints toward Sylvia encouragingly. Sylvia slightly relaxes her dutiful straight posture, and I catch her eye. Anne shifts, smiles at Sylvia across the table. The bracelets dangle, the skirt slithers as she re-crosses her legs.

Neither the poetry nor Sylvia herself really got due recognition from Robert Lowell, who was more dazzled by Anne, his other female visitors, and most of all, by his own poetic process. He was deep in *Life Studies*, and W.D. Snodgrass as a current favorite poetic role model interested him more. Sylvia's formal poetry at the time seemed confining, a path Lowell had already traveled in his earlier work. Lowell wrote later of his surprise when Sylvia burst out of that tight poetry into a passionate statement of her later work.

Lowell and Elizabeth Hardwick visited Sylvia Plath and Ted Hughes in their small Boston apartment, according to Sylvia, but it appeared a duty visit, and did not develop into a warm social friendship. Elizabeth Hardwick instead remembers having the couple to dinner, and says that "Sylvia was very quiet."

Plath probably felt most comfortable with Anne Sexton and George Starbuck, both poets near her age. She wrote briefly of their famous after-class meetings at the Ritz. Anne Sexton has written more about these times as well. It is interesting to note the sense of competition in Plath's brief journal entries (May 3 and 20, 1959) concerning these two poets.

"Retyped pages, a messy job, on the volume of poems I should be turning in to Houghton Mifflin this week. But A. S. is there ahead of me, with her lover G. S. writing *New Yorker* odes to her and both of them together: felt our triple-martini afternoons at the Ritz breaking up ..." She also wrote "All I need now is to hear that G.S. or M.K. (Maxine Kumin) has won the Yale and get a rejection of my children's book. A.S. has her book accepted at Houghton Mifflin and this afternoon will be drinking champagne ..."

Sylvia did not win the Yale Younger Poets prize that year, but George Starbuck's collection, *Bone Thoughts*, did.

I followed Sylvia's work throughout, as it appeared. Anne Sexton kept in touch with Sylvia directly, as the two of them had shared a special bond, an obsession with suicide. "She's the only one who understands," Anne expressed to me and Lois Ames. Anne was totally open about her own obsessions.

Coincidentally, while writing this essay I went to Oberlin College to visit my son who was then a junior. I stayed at a "bed and breakfast" home. My hostess, an outgoing talkative person, told me of a young woman poet she once knew. Before retiring to Oberlin, Ohio, Mrs. Melvina Keeler had lived in Cambridge, Mass. where she worked as a music teacher. Her husband had worked for Sylvia Plath's father and illustrated Dr. Plath's book on bees. Mrs. Keeler became the lifetime friend of Aurelia Plath, Sylvia's mother. Both Mrs. Keeler and Mrs. Plath had just had baby daughters and they wheeled the two children together in their baby carriages. The daughters grew up, led different lives. Sylvia died. The friends kept in touch. Mrs. Keeler had just returned from visiting Mrs. Plath in a nursing home in Massachusetts when I met her at Oberlin.

There have been many motivations suggested for Sylvia's death in addition to that of the failed marriage. The pressure of being a young ambitious woman in the fifties. On the personal front, an intense neediness and despair, lack of sleep, all contributed. A desire to re-unite with her dead father, etc. Other psychoanalytic explanations have suggested that Sylvia's mother held her in thrall, which ultimately drove her mad. Psychoanalytic interpretations also suggest the effect of her father's death, as well as her mother's too-close attachment. All these are rather after-the-fact, as if we can never accept what is, finally, the mystery of another person's life and death. But her death spoke to us, and resonates still. A sort of literary industry has been created around the question "Why?"

We must at some point note that many other women, both Plath's generation and younger, have undergone experiences of betrayal and abandonment but did not attempt suicide. They may have felt like it, thought of it, but had not done it. Why? Was it brain chemistry? A weakness in the delicately balanced physiological system? To mythologize Sylvia implies that suicide was something within her control: a "chosen" act. Or that it was a necessary part of her gift. As if we couldn't have "the art" without "the death". One notes that Plath's younger poetic sisters, no less abandoned or betrayed, seem not to have needed to choose such a drastic solution. What is the wild card here? Why do we resonate so to her pain? Haven't some of us been all too close to that edge ourselves? It is this edge which captures our imaginations when we think of Sylvia Plath. We see ourselves through her, as in a distorting mirror.

Sylvia, I was told by Anne Sexton, was paid $50 by her publishers as an advance for *The Colossus*. But following upon her death, several publishers advanced prospective biographers more than $20,000 each, which was an unheard of sum of money in those days. Suicide definitely increased Sylvia's worth, much as she could have used the money in her lifetime.

Sylvia Plath's later poems, with their honesty and daring and imagery at their best are incomparable. "Daddy," "Lady Lazarus," "Tulips," "The Arrival of the Bee Box," "Stings," "Death & Co. "— the list is long. These poems are classics; triumphs of both form and feeling. The formal promise in her earlier poems was more than fulfilled, and she transformed herself into a truly first rank poet.

Sylvia Plath has been celebrated, since her death, for giving voice to women's rage. She had the courage to express anger in her poems, not only victimization. But she did not live long enough to give voice to a larger vision, a voice of compassion and of wisdom. Death had always seemed an attractive option to Sylvia Plath. She turned to death as the only way out of disappointment and exhaustion. But she thought of death, had thought of death before, as a solution, where another woman might have chosen a less terminal way of collapse.

What is most touching about the life of Sylvia Plath survives not only in the poems, but also, in the photographs. The girl in the bathing suit, the newly married couple, the radiant young mother with her children, the lovely picture of Plath and Hughes bending with joy over their first born, the picture of the smiling girl with her husband; all look not so very different than the

photographs we all have of our young happy smiling forward-looking times.
Looking at the photographs one feels we were all that hopeful young woman,
literary, educated, full of illusions and talent and optimism and fierce possessive
love. That young man, Ted Hughes, how could he have become "the enemy"
so quickly?

—

   My mind sifts through its own internal photographs of Sylvia Plath: that
soft, extremely quiet, talented, young woman, sitting next to me in class,
filled with a passionate ambition ... There is a barely perceptible change in
atmosphere: the class has ended abruptly, loosening its knot of concentration.
Like an exhalation in unison, a scraping of chairs lightens the room, signaling
to us all that the moment we have shared is over. Anne and George walk out
together. Sylvia remains in thought for a moment. Lowell hunches over his
papers and books, stuffing them into a huge cracked leather briefcase.
A few deferential students murmur round him, but the rest leave. Outside
the classroom door today, Ted silently waits for Sylvia to get her things together.
He helps her with her coat, her books. I can see her shy smile as she looks up
at him, watch them walk down the hall together, know she will be telling him
all about what happened that afternoon, what poems were talked about,
what Lowell said: what she really thought of it all.

SHARI LESLIE SEGALL

from *The Stars on the Ceiling*

a chapter from Our Lady

The cab driver stops as instructed behind a black Peugeot 405 in front of the gourmet take-out shop on the Avenue de la Motte-Picquet. "Want anything special I'm sssttaaarrrvviiinnngg! — here take my worldly goods I'll meet yupstairs."

Patrick catches the satchel and fishes for his keys in his backpack. "Wh-what are are — what are y-you g — well — g-going to h-h"

"Want anything special?"

"Can I — dyou m — c-can I a-ask for — well ... qu-quiche? P-please. Ms. Br-Brittain."

"I dunno can you? What kind?" As she studies the shop window Leslie realizes he's no longer standing next to her. "Hello, I'm Ms. Brittain — ," she yells as he heads down the avenue, "And I'll Be Your Waitress This Evening. Our Specials Today Are: SALMON/ SPINACH." She yells louder. "OR MUSHROOM/LEEK." He turns around for the smallest number of seconds needed to show her his crunched-up face. "SALMON/SPINACH!," she confirms and is up in the apartment fifteen minutes later with the newspaper; the mail; four slices of quiche: salmon/ spinach, mushroom/leek, celery/roquefort, vegetable garden; three varieties of salad: seafood, niçoise, tomato-mozzarella; a baguette de compagne-and-a-half; three types of cheese: goat, brie, cantal; two masterpiece pastries: an opéra and a sachertorte; a bottle of Perrier; four huge day-glo oranges and a Mars bar: hazelnut. "They were outa Havana cigars. We get any faxes?"

Patrick hands her five pages. "I don't wanna look at them!" She starts grabbing place-setting components from every cabinet, drawer and shelf. "The nice lady micro-waved the quiche for us how could we forget to eat?" Patrick hands her five p"President of the United States been assassinated?," she asks, nodding to the faxes.

Patrick scans them. "N-No. They're j-just "

"Then file the fuckers and here — " She dumps dishes and silverware on the table for Patrick to arrange "use this for garbage." and hands him the plastic sleeve from the Trib.
"Y-you have f-four messages. Actually."

Leslie looks instinctively through the archway to the answering machine "I don't wanna Oooohhhh-Ooohhh, what'sss thi-issss?," then walks over to see what's lying on the bed. "Iiii Luhuhuhvve Ihhhtt! I LOVE it! I love IT!" She holds up an oversized white t-shirt with the silhouette of a runner exploding against a fiery red-and-yellow Barcelona Olympics logo. "Patrick! Don't say you never gave me anything, right?   I love it!   What Ay Trehhhhh-Zhurrrre!"   Patrick slowly approaches the alcove, almost smiling, jabbing holes in a flowered paper napkin with the tines of a fork. "And just to show you how much I love it I'm gonna warn you that I'm about to rip all my clothes off and put it on rather than just insensitively ripping all my clothes off and putting it on without warning you!" He whips around and runs back to tend to his cutlery. "Works every time!" Leslie sneaks up behind him once it's safe and whispers "It's safe! It comes down almost to Ms. Brittain's knees!"

"W-which — well — qu-quiche dyou ... want? Quiche. Ms. Br-Brittain." Not reacting to Leslie's reactions, Patrick picks up the spatula.

"I really do love it. It's so soft!   And I love it especially because it came from ... money that Jack Kote bought us off with! Do you have to focus on me like that when I speak to you, Patrick? What happened to the good old hours when I didn't know whether you were hearing me or receiving orders from your home asteroid through a little electronic implant in your ear? Thanks. Really. We'll split everything — except the mushroom/leek — that's all for yooohh-oohh — what's thi-is?"

Leslie reaches for two blue and yellow packets next to Patrick's plate. " 'Glows in the Dark'," she reads. " 'Big Luminous Stars' 'Astro-Magic' 'Glows in the Dark' 'Planets' 'Our Solar System' 'Astro-Magic' 'Adhesive, Luminous Stars and Heavenly Bodies' 'To sleep in outer-space, stick these decals on your walls and ceiling; expose them to light for several seconds and they will glow in the dark. Good night and bon interplanetary voyage!' Patrick this is the greatest thing! Is this not too amazing? Where did you — you got these in the airport? Patrick give me a break here! Will your landlord create an international incident if you put these up?"

"Yeah. L-look!" Patrick opens a flap in the dark-blue packet containing the planets and points to a paragraph of yellow letters.

Leslie reads. " 'Astro-Magic will shine in the dark for sixty minutes after being exposed to FIFTEEN SECONDS', " she emphasizes with surprise, " 'of light.' Holy shit! — it doesn't say holy shit here. 'Try it as often as you wish. This packet contains the sun and all the planets of our solar system' — Look Patrick! 'and Haley's' fucking 'Comet' — it doesn't say fucking either — with the tail look at the tail! and Saturn's rings and those gas those stripe things on Jupiter. I Cannn Nnnottt Standdd Ittt! 'Peel them from their backing, put them on your ceiling, walls, furniture. Astro-Magic: with

RALPH PETTY - *watercolor (detail)*

your head on your pillow you can sleep under the right star. Have a good trip through outer space!' And these are" Opening the other packet she announces "THEE-EE TWENTYYY BRIGHTTESSST STARRRS" in a Wellesian voice. "This is definitely worth having your passport confiscated by your landlord for. I think there are more than twenty here, Patrick, whad'you think? Way to go! Good day at the old airport magazine-kiosk! Where are these manufactured? I'm gonna reheat the rest of the quiche." She stands and reaches for the platter.

Sitting very straight and tall, Patrick asks "W-wanna ... try one? O-on your ceiling. Imean."

Leslie slams the platter back down. "THE LADDER'S IN THE CLOSET BY THE FRONT DOOR! I'll close the curtains will my little lamp be enough?" While she pulls one of the yellow rubbery stars from its backing "I wouldn't dare waste Saturn. Or Haley. Who are these little guys? — maybe one of them's your home asteroid, Patrick!", Patrick secures the ladder as close to the bed as possible so as to be able to place the heavenly body directly above the point between the two

pillows. She hands it up to him. He takes it from her with slow, surgical care
"Frchrissakes you'd think it was a real star!" and respect.

"It i-is a r-a real st-star. M-Ms. Brittain." Patrick sounds surprised she didn't
know that.

"Oh! ... You think my little nighttable lamp is enough?" Perfectly prone on her
back, Leslie positions herself just right of center on the bed, looking straight up, her
hand on the lampswitch. "There's anticipation in the air, Patrick Trucock!"

"Yeah." Patrick starts down the ladder. Leslie pats the comforter with her left
palm, indicating his spot. "I can't stand it I can't stand it! SHINE SHINE!" she
tells her lamp, drawing herself up on her right elbow to peer into the bulb. Patrick
stands still on the lowest step, focusing on the blinking light in the answering
machine on the dresser. "Patrick Trucock if you're gonna get nineteenth century on
me now, now's not the time, Patrick, we are about to give birth to a star! It was
your fucking idea to put it up there they're your I promise that any brutal sexual
attacking I'm gonna do to you in this bed will be delayed until further notice will
you just get here frchrissake! I know! I know what you're doing, you intelligent
earthly body, you're stalling so our baby'll be able to soak up EVEN MORE light
but the envelope said fifteen seconds. The fucking thing has enough light stored by
now-WAIT!" She jumps up, scampers over to switch off the lamp in the livingroom,
scampers back, dives into position in bed. "-to be able to guide Portuguese sailors
from one end of the earth to the other. Take your shoes off before getting in."

Patrick lies down next to Leslie. Leslie turns off the lamp. "Ohh-hh Myee-eeee
Gohoh-ohohdddd!" The star shines brilliantly on the blackness of her ceiling in the
blackness of her bedroom. Patrick bolts out of bed. Leslie tries to grab him.
"WAIT!" she cries.

"No! Wait!" he replies and runs over to the table for another star.

"What'rydoing?" He climbs up the ladder. "Don't waste them, they're yours,
sweetie!"

"T-turn on the the lamp. Quick!" Patrick orders and leans over to stick a smaller
star to the northeast of the first one. He scrambles down and flops into bed
backwards. "GO!" he shouts. Leslie reaches for the lampswitch again. "WAIT!"
he shouts. "A-another few seconds! ... NOW!" Leslie turns off the light. The big
original star and its baby offshoot star spontaneously combust in the apartment sky.
Leslie and Patrick study their heaven in silence — Leslie prays the phone won't ring,

wants to get up and unplug it, stays to absorb the starlight — then stare at each other for some seconds, only their heads out of perfect alignment with the axis of their bodies flat against the bed. Their breathing falls into sync, their eyes are happy and quiet...
....
...."I'm going to do it," Patrick says, his soft words flowing unbroken. Leslie squints and tilts her head. Outer space is silent again......... Then ... "SATURN!" Patrick announces and — "AAAAAAAAH!" Leslie screams — flies over to pick his planet off its protective backing. "THE LIGHT!" Patrick demands. "THE LIGHT!" Leslie responds and the planet goes up and stars follow planets and planets surround stars and Patrick tries to get the Milky Way as accurate as possible, shuttling back and forth between the table and the ladder and up the ladder, with Leslie the "Vice-Intergalactic Chancellor in Charge of Lamp, OK, Patrick?," and every time he comes down from the sky they take their positions to make sure all is right with the universe and when "THE SUN!" goes up "THE SSUNN, PATRICK!" it's the most spectacular celebration of all with neither of them asking or even caring how the sun and the stars can be shining in the same couple square meters of firmament at the same time and they stare on their backs at Saturn's rings and Patrick decides to save Haley's Comet for last because he's gotten nuts about perfect placement, and though in the beginning every several celestial bodies Leslie wanted to know whether Patrick realized he was going to have no stars or planets left for his own ceiling "Don't you even want Jupiter? I hope you know what you're doing." by the end of the packet of stars and the end of packet of solar system all Leslie's concerned with is doing a good job at her light-station and soon when the lamp is turned off again the ceiling in the bedroom-alcove "looks no different from heaven, Patrick" and Patrick is exhausted and they are lying on their backs on the comforter getting a load of the miracle of matter.

There they lie, at once buoyant and anchored, each fitted into their own essential space like beings about to be kryogenically frozen and transported into the next wave of time. They say nothing because ("there is nothing to say. What is there to say? We just created a universe.") but absorb each other's light through the kind intervention of the stars and the planets which draw up the light from one, nourish and reinforce it, and dispatch it down into the other, exchanging it for the light the other is giving up to the same seamless process. After her light has stopped at every star and planet along the way to Patrick's light, Leslie slowly stands, leaving the form of her light behind her, beside Patrick on the bed, and goes over to the dinette table to have her dinner.

Patrick follows several minutes later, rising languidly, moving languidly, like someone who has just donated blood. Just donated energy to the source of energy.

While he dishes himself some salade niçoise, Leslie strolls to the bookcase for a Stones cassette and tucks it into the machine on the partition and after tonight she and Patrick never speak about the stars and the planets on her ceiling again, just as people never speak about how the earth is revolving under their laundry room or about the oxygen they're breathing. Just as people during the Renaissance did not stop each other on the street in downtown Milan and say, "Hey, man! What's hapnin? T's the Renaissance today, man, cnyuh diggit?" One of the last times they visit their firmament with words is when Leslie, cutting some goat cheese, tells Patrick to get his resume out of his backpack and adds in magic-marker under "Professional Experience": **Created a Universe   Paris, 1992**.

Then Mick and the boys start asking *Brown Sugahhhhh, How kum yuh dance so guh-uhd noww-uh*, which Leslie takes as her divine cue to cut the opéra and the sachertorte each in half and haul the pastry platter, two dessert plates *Juss like a young girl shou-ould-uh-huh-mah*, two dessert forks, two fresh napkins, two champagne glasses, what's left of the bottle of Perrier, and Patrick onto the bed. The big silver-metal ladder is still wedged as far against the mattress as it will go, looking as if it's just landed and deployed its unloading platform, one empty *you shoulda heard im jusst arou-ounn midnigh-ight* blue-and-yellow cardboard Astro-Magic envelope draped across its top step, the other on the floor. *I said yeah-ehuh yeah-ehuh yeah-ehuh whooo-ooo how kum yuh how kum yuh* "dance so go-oodd whooooh!" Leslie sends Patrick into the livingroom to turn off the light again and switches on the lamp *jusss like a* "jusss like a" *black gir-irl shou-ould* "yeah-eah-eah-uhhhhhhHHHHHHHHH!", knocking Tropic of Cancer off the nighttable with the end of the fork in her hand.

"There are no coincidences in this world, Patrick." She picks up the book and sets it, open, on her crossed legs, between the plate of pastries and her tummy. "What is there only?"

"I-I kn-know. Ms. Br-Brittain. What there ... is. Actually."

"Ordinarily, you know, I wouldn't be so sure but after what you just manufactured up there I'd be a fool to doubt you," she tells him and starts reading: " 'But in Matisse, in the exploration of his brush, there is the trembling glitter of a world which demands only the presence of the female to crystallize the most fugitive aspirations. To come upon a woman offering herself outside a urinal, where there are advertised cigarette papers, rum, acrobats, horse races, where the heavy foliage of the trees breaks the heavy mass of walls and roofs, is an experience that begins where the boundaries of the known world leave off ... Even as the world falls apart the Paris that belongs to Matisse shudders with bright, gasping orgasms, the air itself is steady with a stagnant sperm, the trees tangled like hair ... The wheel is falling apart but the revolution is intact ...'* Page one sixty-eight. You're a virgin, aren't you, Patrick?"

Patrick bothers neither to focus nor to unfocus. He's too drained to do anything but let his eyes settle wherever they land and they land on Leslie's eyes. He doesn't bother to answer either. "Mick Jagger is in the tapeplayer, Henry Miller is in our genitals, the solar system is occurring overhead and you're a virgin." Leslie contemplates Patrick and nods, sets her plate of untouched dessert on a ladder step. Takes a swig of Perrier then offers the bottle.

"gin, too," Patrick mumbles, pushing her arm away.
"Huh?"
"Y-YOU'RE A — I s..........n-neverm-mind. M-Ms. Br "
"Huh?"
"a v-virgin.....too. Too. M-Ms. Br-Brittain. I s — th-that's whatI s........said. Actually."

"You're either trying out a new smartass routine on me before taking it on the road or you've gone back to your asteroid without kissing me good-bye. You're absolutely right, though. I'm a virgin, too. We're all virgins too and we're all brutally fucked on a daily basis. Daily virgins and daily fucked. I never want to know, Patrick, why you are a virgin at the age of twenty-whatever-the-fuck-you-are. It'd make me too angry. It'd make me too angry .... If you want my cake you can have it." Leslie turns off the lamp and they get into their kryogenic-freeze positions and look at the balls in space for a long time. *Leh-eht's do some lihihving* They both know that Patrick did a sensational job with the Milky Way and they both know not to say it.

"If you give me nothing else ever you will *after weeih die-ie* have brought astronomy into my bedroom." Staring straight up, Leslie is watching a brilliant sun keep *Wii-iild horses, couldn't drag me away· Wii-iild wild horses we'll ride them someday·* track of its responsibility on a darkened field. *Wii-iild horses, couldn't drag me away· Wii-iild wild horses we'll ride them someday ...* "If I give you nothing else ever I will have punctured your senses and poured Henry Miller in." She switches the lamp on. "Listen to this: 'O Tania, where now is that warm cunt of yours, those fat, heavy garters, those soft, bulging thighs? There is a bone in'* " The phone rings. Leslie rests the book on her thighs and looks at the machine.

* Henry Miller, *Tropic of Cancer*, Grafton Books, 1965, page 168.

BOB BISHOP - *photograph*

BOB BISHOP

Paris' Place de l'Alma above the tunnel where Princess Diana lost her life on August 31, 1997 was quickly transformed into "Place Diana," a veritable shrine to the departed "people's princess." These messages and declarations, jumbled together in a confusion of historic facts, appeared to me as a form of *art brut* ... and a unique manifestation of popular writing. When the City announced plans to permanently remove the graffiti from the torch, I felt an urgency to record these acts of spontaneous expression with my camera.

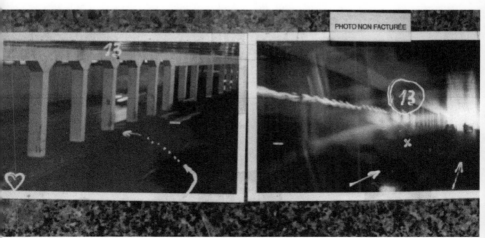

BOB BISHOP - *photograph*

Le Novelist Diane Johnson: Life After *Divorce*

Speaking with **Frank** editor David Applefield

Frank: *How is living and writing in Paris different than living and writing in the United States? Or is this purely mythic?*

Diane Johnson: I think it is easier to live in Paris, in that it isn't necessary to have a car, services are close by, and so on — thus, I feel that I have more time to work and write when I am here. But the writing process is pretty much the same in either country.

Frank: *But surely the aesthetics, the style, the language, the attitudes, the history effect the way you approach your work. You've lived in Paris for nearly four years. Does the fact that you're outside of your native culture isolate you, or do you think that all creative people by definition live out of step with the society around them?*

DJ: If not out of step, a little apart, and to be a little apart gives a kind of necessary solitude. Lots of writers, if not most, leave the places they are most comfortable for places where they are strangers.

Frank: *How do you account for the great popular enthusiasm in the United States for literature based in Paris?*

DJ: Americans have always had a love affair with Paris, and of course we have a long literary tradition of American writers here, American films set here and so on. So we feel connected to the subject of Americans in Paris. Besides this, many people are actively planning a trip here, which gives them a more than academic interest. For Americans, it seems that travel to France has always represented beauty, freedom and good food.

Frank: *You're not suggesting though that* Le Divorce *is merely a fictionalized travel guide. The world you capture taps into deeper interests. In describing Stephen King novels, a reviewer once said that they would be holding down many beach towels that summer. Did you approach* Le Divorce *as a deliberately popular novel or is the book's popular success a positive result of this strong appeal for the image of Paris?*

DJ: No I don't think people read *Le Divorce* as a travel book, but I always like to imagine myself in the place a book I like is taking place – maybe everyone does, and of course, everyone likes Paris. This worked in favor of my book, I think.

Frank: *The cross-cultural issues raised in* Le Divorce *... what is it about these issues that interests you? Do you think* *you're carving new ground in a wave of new novels that take American readers beyond their cultural borders?*

DJ: *Le Divorce* tries to raise several subjects of cross-cultural concern, especially American violence and self-satisfaction. I didn't see it as my task to comment on French national character, just to portray it, but perhaps their self-satisfaction comes through too. Not carving new ground, I'm afraid, since American writers have long found the interaction of Americans with other cultures a useful way of getting at their our own situation. I think of myself as a sort of political novelist, or novelist of manners, but always writing as an American, with a view limited by my own nationality, of course.

Frank: *How critical are you of your own society? Government? Culture? In what ways are you political?*

DJ: One thing about living abroad is that one can see more clearly the problems in our society. But by the same token, being abroad makes it harder to participate in any effort to change things at home. But maybe writing about one's society is in itself a political act that has to stand on its own.

Frank: *Aside from the financial rewards, is it a positive experience or a frightening one for a novelist to have his/her work transformed into film? To what degree are you involved in the film rendition of your novel?*

DJ: I wrote the screenplay for the film maker, Interscope. They'll doubtless change my script a lot; but I enjoyed the initial stages of turning a novel-into-film. We'll have to wait to judge the result.

Frank: *What hope do young, unpublished literary writers today have in getting published? Any advice?*

DJ: You hear that it is harder for young and unpublished writers now; but on the other hand, there are a lot of first novels being published. I don't know what an analysis of the statistics would show. But I do think that the new participation of bookstores in reading clubs and readers' meeting places generates a good climate for reading, which in turn should help writers starting out.

Frank: *What's comes after divorce?*

DJ: I'm writing another novel set in France – I always set my novels where I am. This one is so far called *Convictions*, and I do have a few more French characters this time, and go into their minds a bit more than I dared to do in *Le Divorce*.

Frank: *How so? And how do you go about capturing in English the inner thoughts that are occurring in French? Is language an obstacle, a challenge, or something else?*

DJ: For me language is kind of an obstacle as well as a medium. Obviously the French people in my novel will have to be thinking in English. I'll try to suggest Frenchness some way. The challenge will be to convey their Frenchness, and get people to accept the convention by which they are understood to be speaking in French. Oh dear ....

Josh Parker

breakdown

I went to Paris to have a nervous breakdown. I thought it would be easier than having it in Chicago, where people tend to look down on mental disorders, and where being crazy is, almost without exception in any field, a serious liability.

And I went to Paris to write. I have very good reasons for preferring to write in Europe. There is something, as Henry Miller said, of the giant idea incubator about Paris. Art presses in at you from every side, fills your vacant moments even when you think you are most oblivious to it, bores its way into your absent-minded moods as you shuttle from one side of the city to the other, and presents a placid moving background of itself to draw your poor scattered thoughts. As a writer you can go crazy in Paris and people look on it at the very worst as an unfortunate artistic side-effect. But my major reason for coming here is that a language barrier is by far the most convenient way to disguise the fact that at present I am a very poor writer. I'm probably the kind of writer you've never heard of — even if you subscribed to the most obscure literary reviews — and wouldn't want to read unless he wrote something useful, like banal advertisements in the subway, or recipes on cereal boxes. In Paris no one notices.

So, I am in Paris, sitting up in my room a good part of the day and pretending to write, letting my rather frightening accumulated collection of feelings and neuroses get the better of me for extended and gradually lengthening periods of time. For example, I can walk down the Rue de Rivoli now, if I force myself out, but I cannot look up when I pass people. I am tired of staring at the sidewalk, but I simply can't look up. I can't think what kind of expression I could paste onto my face to make it acceptable to whomever I pass, and so I am forced to look into the gutter, which is demeaning. What expression would be on my face if I did happen to look up and met someone's eyes as we passed? I don't know. I can only think it would be the look of a madman. A horrible, transported grimace, with a set, indelible deadness around the eyes.

Stojan has given me a little apartment to sleep and write and cook in and, frankly, I am enjoying the luxury of at last being in Paris. Of not feeling compelled to rush out every day to discover that some new kind of anti-social behavior has come over me. I tend to stay more and more in my room. I will be staying for a while. There is no rush to do anything, my visa is in order, and there's nothing special in the city I need to see right away.

My friend Jean-Marc stops by in the evenings after he has had a drink downstairs in the Rue du Temple, and is quite taken with my fits of madness. He suggests wine might amplify them. With a good Bordeaux, he says, my madness will get a wild kick, and move beyond this tedious dull paranoia that takes me in the day. How romantic. I could sit in my garret under the massive wood beams and rage all night against my own soul, and as long as my computer is up with its screen glowing into the room I might accomplish something. He only mentioned this once. Now he just shows up three nights a week with a bottle of wine, and I have a glass while he sits in my chair at my desk and drinks the rest of the bottle. At ten o'clock the phone rings, and Jean-Marc pushes his chair back from the table and sits glaring out the window. It is Stojan. *"Allo, "* Stojan says. *"Je suis fatigué ce soir.* I think I will *reste chez moi.* Is it ok? *Je t'embrasse."*

Jean-Marc pulls his chair back to the table after I have hung up the phone. He puts his head in his arms for a minute, and his hair is yellow and soft in the light. He pulls himself up and grins at me, his eyes teasing and menacing. "Kept boy," he says.

In theory alone. More and more often Stojan sleeps at his house, and I see him now only once every two weeks. Because of this, things have been getting a little testy between me and Jean-Marc, with whom I had an affair two years ago when I was here before. Testy. I mean dangerous. Dangerous is what I mean. There is only one lamp in my room, and when Jean-Marc sits in front of it and rests his arms on the table, the light slants across his fingers, and makes the little blond hairs below his knuckles light gold. His face is deep and ruined from smoke and drink, and still very handsome to look at.

Paris in the daytime is, to begin with, a cleaner city than Paris at night. The whole place is groomed carefully every morning before anyone is up, but by evening it is already shabby and run-down again. By night it is a medieval city. I have seen rats crossing the streets in the nicest neighborhoods. Muck runs between the cobblestones, dust blows from nowhere and collects in the cracks, making a gritty silt, the street lamps cast pools of light on shockingly unsanitary piles of cardboard and potato peelings. If you sleep as late as I do, you can get the impression that the sunlight itself burns away all the town's grime before you are up. Stojan never calls me in the daytime from his office. Only at night. In the morning, when I step outside the sidewalk has just been washed, hosed down, and scrubbed with a long-handled green plastic broom. I can imagine that it is really my apartment. That I am really an honest self-employed young person, perhaps a published writer.

Why on earth would anyone choose to go insane in Paris? It is the best place in the world to be sane.

Across the river the students mill around the squares near the universities, where I take a class on Wednesdays. Soon, I think, I may be too crazy to go to class anymore. Soon I might not be able to sit in a chair in a room full of people. I might have to sit on the floor, or curl up in a ball in the corner. The professor might make arrangements for me to continue my studies in this way. "He is the crazy American writer," he might tell his other students. "Leave him alone. He likes to listen to lectures curled up on the floor. We think he must be a brilliant writer to be so crazy, but no one can read his handwriting, so we can't be sure." I will have to wait until everyone else has left the class before I can get up off the floor and walk out. During private meetings with the professor I will twist my hands together behind the back of the chair. "Leave the crazy American writer alone." I could never get away with this in America.

Another good thing about going insane in a foreign country is that when you absolutely have to say one of the nonsensical things that comes into your head, you can say it in either English or French. In French, they will think you are trying to say something else, and in English they will think it is some kind of slang or part of a song.

After a while, though, they are all going to figure out that I'm going crazy. There's no way around that. Stojan and his friends, and eventually even Jean-Marc and his friends, are all going to realize that I am certifiably mad. That the consulate had no business giving me a visa when I was unfit to travel, and that I will probably spend the rest of my days as a burden to the French health care system. Or be shipped back to America to wander the streets.

But not today. And not for another month or so, at least. I must slow it down so I can last here. And, meanwhile, I write ...

When I was younger I had a friend, Jill, who was a potter with a writer boyfriend. I remember explaining to her once how hard it was, being a writer, and working all night, say, and if someone came into the room in the morning and looked around, there wouldn't be any evidence of work, if they didn't turn on the computer and look, or go through the printed sheets. Jill said her boyfriend complained of the same thing. That when Jill made something in her studio, she actually had something she could show someone, something a person could appreciate at a glance.

These days I'm grateful that writing is something only half finished when it's done. That reading isn't the same as looking at a picture. That reading takes work on the part of the audience. A failed painter is one thing. You can look at his canvases and say, "This is shit." A failed writer is a more ambiguous figure. In order to pass judgment you have to actually read him first. And, while people take a certain interest at looking at a half-done sculpture or canvas, no one wants to read the first draft of a novel. That gives me a grace period of anywhere between six months and five years. Once I publish and the reviews come out, it's all over. But, for now, it's, "Oh, the poor brilliant writer, no one can recognize his genius." They don't realize half the reason no one can recognize it is that I'm making every possible effort to make it illegible.

BARBARA CHASE-RIBOUD - *Bathers*
Cast alumunium and silk flour relief - 1973

JOHN CALDER

Gourmandise

Now, today, I have indulged myself.
The journey was long, but not unpleasant.
Now, back in Paris, the city where
I have decided to die and before that
live as much as the world lets me,
on this sunday, this February sunday,
where there is no sun,
I buy a ticket for a hated return
and indulge.

A glass — *a coupe* — from royal Rheims
and a platter, called a plate, of delicious seafood
laid on ice and a half-bottle
of a favourite wine:
the special taste of dry Sancerre,
dry but fruity, lingers on the palette,
followed by a sea-snail and another sip.

My appetite encouraged
by the passing waiters,
small as it is, I reach for a clam —
brown bread and butter dries the mouth —
another clam, this time with lemon;
I order Badoit
to slow the wine consumption and to aid
digestion. Then an oyster
with its shell-juice, then another sip.

In other climes
children starve and water's not for finding.
Many die from poisoned rivers, many from despair.
Many die for freedom's cause and many die against it.
Many fight the next door tribe
and slaughter or are slaughtered.

Bombs and famine, casual killing
(another clam goes down)
global warming, global business
side by side drive mankind onward
to a grim tomorrow

where all the growth and all the killing,
all the trade and manufacture,
all the art and all the writing,
all the notes composers put together,
all the loving potting and ceramic,
all the loving leading to new life,
all the pious ceremony and preaching,
and suppression of ideas,
or the liberty to spread them,
will all go together when they go.

And let the world ... the wine is nearly finished!
Carpe Diem says the hand that reaches
for the final oyster; two sea-snails
and a prawn are left. Dear Sam,
Sam Beckett, saw it coming long ago,
and now I hear the next-door table ordering
dishes much more lavish in a normal voice
and I reproach my small indulgence, thinking:
in England you would not get this,
even at five times the price.

The world of affluence divides:
some pay for much at little cost
and others much for little
and never know the difference.
And in the other half
where life from day to day goes on
as polar bears and wolves and whales
strive not to be extinct,
and scenes like this indulgent restaurant
lie far beyond the thinking of the average man,
faite la moyenne, it averages out, and welcome what's to come:
sans food sans suffering sans pleasure and sans life.

JOHN CALDER – *doodle – circa 1998*

293

Frank *16/17 Contributors*

Carol **Allen**, writer, poet and community leader originally from New Orleans, is the author of the children's book *Plain Weird and Other Weird and Wacky Poems* and the editor of *They Only Laughed Later, Tales of Women on the Move* (EuroPublic Press, 1997). She founded the Paris Writers' Workshop at WICE.

David **Anderson** was born in 1946 in Los Angeles. He studied at the San Francisco Art Institute and has won fellowships from the National Endowment for the Arts and the Pollock-Krasner Foundation Grant. His latest exhibitions include shows at Allene Lapides Gallery and Linda Durham Contemporary Art in Santa Fe and the Braunstein/Quay Gallery in San Francisco, CA.

David **Applefield** founded **Frank** in Boston in 1983, and soon after brought the journal to Paris where he has been writing, editing, publishing, and lecturing ever since. Author of the novel *Once Removed* (Mosaic Press, 1997), Applefield has also written the guide book *Paris Inside-Out* (Houghton-Mifflin, 1994) and publishes the *Paris-Anglophone* directory along with the *www.paris-anglo.com* website. His cross-cultural articles on living and working in France regularly appear in *Where Paris*, *The Paris Free Voice*, and *Paris Notes*. When he's not conducting guerilla marketing seminars in Africa, he's at home with his wife and their three polyglot kids in Montreuil, just outside of Paris.

S.S. **Barrie** was nominated for the National Magazine Award in Canada and *Three* won the 1995 Writers Bureau short story award in the U.K. She makes her home in the Var, France.

Mei-mei **Berssenbrugge's** collaboration with Kiki Smith was published by Kelsey Street Press in 1997. She lives with the artist Richard Tuttle and their daughter in Abiquiu.

Bob **Bishop**, a Paris-based photographer orignially from Chicago, is the founding editor of *The Paris Free Voice Magazine*. His pictures recently appeared in the book *Right Brain Left Brain Photography: The Art and Technique of 70 Modern Masters*. Bob has been a community leader in the anglophone community in Paris for twenty years.

Sherwin **Bitsui** is a member of the Navajo tribe. He is a student at the Institute of American Indian Arts, Santa Fe, New Mexico.

Black **Sifichi**, born in New York City, moved to Paris in 1988 after six years in London. Poet, performer, and DJ at Paris' Radio Nova (101.5), his recent projects include his first CD with Negative Stencil, "Fellatio Praecox - Outspoken Word Trips," and "Nutralic Trax Nights" with DBL.

Stuart **Blazer**, American poet, lives and writes in both Adamsville, France (a few miles north of Aix-en-Provence) and Providence, Rhode Island. Edwin Honig once told him that Provence is Providence without the "id", and subsequently the chapbook *Premier Poets Series, Number 9*, took the name *Aix-en-Providence*.

Jon **Brandi** states that "as a young man, I was torn between studying, acting and becoming a priest. Fortunately, poetry chose me and I've been with her since." His recent books include: *A Question of Journey*, (prose vignettes), and *Heartbeat Geography: Poems '66-'94*.

Jack **Butler**, novelist and poet, directs the Creative Writing Program at the College of Santa Fe. His novel, *Dreamer*, from which the excerpt in this issue was taken, is forthcoming from Knopf.

John **Calder**, British-Canadian publisher born in 1927, writer, poet, and cultural guerilla, has published over 6000 books in his fifty years of literary publishing, including the works of twenty Nobel Prize winners, most notably Samuel Beckett. Calder spends half of his time in Paris, half in London, half in the leading opera houses of the world, half selling his books to the last remaining independent bookstores on earth and the last half on the Eurostar getting there. Calder has just announced the creation of his forthcoming website *www.calderpublications.com.*

Melanie **Cesspooch** is a member of the Northern Ute Indian Tribe, located in northeastern Utah. Currently, she is a student at the Institute of American Indian Arts, Santa Fe, New Mexico.

Christiane **Charlot** is a Brazilian graphic artist and book binder living in France since 1992, with her husband and their daughter Louna.

Barbara **Chase-Riboud**, African-American writer and artist living in Paris, is the author of *Sally Hemmings*, the fictional biography of Thomas Jefferson's mullato mistress. Her sculpture appeared in *Paris Connections*, a, exhibition catalog of African-American Arts in Paris (Bomani Gallery, San Francisco, Q.E.D. Press, 1992).

Denise **Chávez** is the Artistic Director of the Border Book Festival in Las Cruces. She is a poet, playwright, novelist, and teacher. Her latest novel, *Face of an Angel*, was published by Farrar, Straus, and Giroux in 1994.

Frank **Cluck**, poet — *accompagnateur* — *homme d'affaire*, has been doing business in France since 1987. His selection in this issue comes from a work in progress, *The Scarecrow in France*, which blends his poetry with a photographic essay by the French photographer Michel Madona.

Ira **Cohen** is a photographer, editor, film-maker, traveler and poet. He has recently been spotted in Manhattan, Tangiers, Paris and Brussels. His *Minbad Sinbad* (Didier Devillez Editeur, 1998), includes essays and observations on his travels in Morocco and his conversations with Paul Bowles. Henri Michaux on Ira's poetry: "Reading your poems is like smoking raw nerves."

Jacques **Cousteau**, one of the most important ocean explorers and enviromentalists of the 20th century, died in 1997. His comments in **Frank** came from a commencement speech delivered at the American University of Paris.

Jon **Davis's** latest book is *Scrimmage of Appetite* (University of Akron Press, 1995). Other works include *The Hawk. The Road. The Sunlight After Clouds* (Owl Creek Press, 1994) and *Dangerous Amusements* (Ontario Review Press, 1985). He teaches at the Institute of American Indian Arts.

Dirk **De Bruycker**, born in Belgium (1955) and currently living in northern New Mexico, is a painter and print-maker. His recent work, which he calls "icons of transformation," record his artistic and intellectual transitions since his immigration to the bare, desert landscape of New Mexico. He has exhibited at Kay Garvey Gallery in Chicago, Handgraphics Gallery in Santa Fe, Linda Durham Contemporary Art in Galisteo, and the Jan Maiden Fine Art Gallery in Columbus, Ohio.

Claude **Decobert** was the barman at the Ritz in Paris between 1946 and 1987, where he served many of the world's most celebrated cultural figures and cultivated a rare friendship with Ernest Hemingway. Today, Mr. Decobert lives in a Paris suburb where he teaches archery and monitors the local deer population.

Martin **Edmunds** was selected for the National Poetry Series for *The High Road to Taos*, published by the University of Illinois Press in 1994.

James A. **Emanuel** evolved from teenage ranch hand in Nebraska to university professor in Poland via Detroit. Emanuel is a poet, anthologist, essayist, critic and autobiographer and has lived in Paris since the 1980s. His book of innovative jazz and blues haiku is forthcoming from Broadside Press of Detroit.

Paul **Faure-Brac** is a mass communications graduate from Macquarie University in Sydney, Australia. He has been living in Paris for the last five years working as a photographer in fashion and journalism.

Mark **Fishman** is an American writer living in Paris. Having previously published stories in the United States, he is currently working on a novel.

Phillip **Foss** has recently published a new book of poems, *Chromatic Defacement* with Chax Press. His other works are available from Light & Dust Books and Lost Roads.

Gene **Frumkin** is Professor Emeritus of English at the University of New Mexico, and his last two books of poetry are *Comma in the Ear* and *Saturn is Mostly Weather: Selected and Uncollected Poems*.

Greg **Glazner** received the 1991 Walt Whitman Award from the Academy of American Poets. His books include *Singularity* (Norton, 1997) and *From the Iron Chair* (Norton, 1992).

Renée **Gregorio** drafts poetry in between sessions of legislation writing for the state of New Mexico. In the near-past, she's run bookstores, edited literary magazines, competed in Dead Poets' bouts and won, and published in literary journals in both England and the U.S. Her first full-length collection, *The Skins of Possible Lives*, was published in 1996 by Blinking Yellow Books of Taos, New Mexico.

Thierry **Guitard**, French cartoonist, was born in 1966 and raised in Saint-Ouen l'Aumône, a Paris *banlieu*, in a single parent family. Arrested at 19 for selling cannabis, Guitard spent two years in prison where he perfected his artistic talent. In London he founded, with Miriana Mislov, the magazine *La Pieuvre*. A regular contributor to *Libération*, *Rock'n'Folk*, *Nova Mag* and *Citizen K*, Guitar's most recent one-man exhibition was at La Médiathèque François-Mitterrand in Poitiers.

Linda **Healey**, American by birth and French by attrition, is a past editor of the Paris literary magazine *Pharos*. She has published her prose and poetry internationally.

Christine **Hemp**, lives in Taos and her work has appeared recently in *Harvard Magazine*, *The Christian Science Monitor*, and anthologies by MacMillan and Simon & Schuster. She was the first poet-in-residence at Voyageurs National Park.

Ellen **Hinsey** was born in Massachusetts, presently lives in Paris, and in 1995 won the highly-prestigious Yale Series of Younger Poets contest for her book of poems *Cities of Memory*. Currently, Hinsey directs the WICE Writer's Conference and is working on a new collection of poems.

Nancy **Huston** moved from Calgary to Paris in 1973. Author of the acclaimed novel *Slow Emergencies* (Little, Brown Canada), she has published 15 books of fiction and non-fiction in French. Her novel *Cantique des Plaines* won the Governor-General's Award for Fiction in French in 1993. Despite her literary achievements in Europe and Canada she has yet to be published in the United States.

Kyle **Jarrard**, an editor at the *International Herald Tribune*, has lived and worked in France since 1981. He has widely published his short stories and poems. His first novel, *Over There*, was published by Baskerville in 1997 and his second, *Down There*, is forthcoming.

Diane **Johnson**, acclaimed novelist and story writer, is best known for her book *Le Divorce*. She has lived in Paris since 1994 and is currently working on a new novel.

André **Journo** is *un epicier pas comme les autres*. Also known as A.J., Journo is the soul of Paris' rue de Rosier with Chez Marianne its headquarters. Journo, aside from selling numerous fellafuls, has co-authored with Gerard Baudson a monumental work of spiritual, political, and religious significance targeted for publication in 1999 in numerous languages.

William **Klein** was born in 1928 in New York. Klein first came to Paris at the age of 18 as a GI and studied at the Sorbonne with Fernand Léger. He sold his cartoons to French newspapers and soon became a photographer for *Vogue* until the release of *Who Are You Polly Magoo*, Klein's provocative film about the fashion industry. He proceeded to make over twenty films including *Mohammed Ali The Greatest*, *Mr. Freedom*, *The French*, and *Grands Soirs & Petits Matins*, and built an international reputation as painter, graphic artist and photographer. Klein was the first American photographer to capture the uprisings in Paris in May 1968. His latest film work is entitled Messiah. Marval published the book *William Klein Films* in 1968.

John **Kliphan**, a hip lawyer from San Francisco, teaches law at Schiller University in Paris and writes poetry. In 1990 he created The Live Poets Society, which promotes international poetry readings in pubs and other lively locations.

Katherine **Knorr**, lives in Paris and is the Features Editor of the *International Herald Tribune*. *Snakeskin Sally* is her first novel.

Denise **Larking Coste** lives and works in Paris as executive vice-president of CIES, The Food Forum. In 1997 she self-published a collection of stories, *Black and White*.

David Herbert **Lawrence**, born at Eastwood, Nottinghamshire in 1885, was one of the most prolific and influential writers of fiction, poetry, essays, and travel writing in the English language in the 20th century. After WWI, disillusioned with industrialized Europe, Lawrence began his "savage pilgrimage" in search of an alternative lifestyle. This took him to Sicily, Ceylon, Australia and, finally, New Mexico before his death in 1930.

A.A. **Liker** hails from the West Coast of the United States and has lived in Paris for the last 12 years, where he has been quietly writing *The Justice Conspiracy*. This excerpt is A.A. Liker's first published piece.

Joan **Logghe's** most recent works are *Twenty Years in Bed with the Same Man* (La Alameda Press, 1995), and as editor *Catch Our Breath: Writing from the Heart of AIDS* (Mariposa, 1996). She has lived in rural northern New Mexico since 1973, building a solar-heated house with her husband and raising three children.

E.A. **Mares** teaches at the University of New Mexico. His latest book is *The Unicorn Poem and Flowers and Songs of Sorrow* (West End Press, 1992).

Joe **Marshall** was born in 1970 in Grand Rapids, Michigan, the disputed furniture capitol of the world. He studied literature at the University of Michigan and first crossed the *périphérique* circling Paris in 1995. In the summer of 1998 Marshall is touring the independent bookstores in the United States for **Frank**.

Harry **Mathews** is the author of over a dozen works of fiction, poetry and non-fiction including *The Conversions* (Dalkey Archive Press, 1997), *The Sinking of the Odradek Stadium* (Harper & Row, 1975), *Country Cooking and Other Stories* (Burning Deck, 1980), and *The Journalist* (Godine, 1994, Dalkey Archive Press, 1997). His translation of George Perec's *Ellis Island* was published by The New Press in 1996. He is currently working on a comprehensive Oulipo Compendium to be published in 1998 by Atlas Press in London. He has been associated with the New York School of poets with John Ashbery, Keneth Koch and James Schuyler. Mathews is married to French writer Marie Chaix and divides his time between Paris and Key West, Florida.

Robert **Menasse**, little known to anglophone readers, is an eminent Austrian novelist born in Vienna in 1954. His work includes the trilogy: *Happy Times, Brittle World*; *Sensual Certainty*; and *Reverse Trust*. The excerpt presented here is from a work in progress about his ancestor, the Rabbi Menasse ben Israel, the negotiator for the re-admission of Jews into England in 1655. Calder Publications is publishing *Happy Times, Brittle World* in 1998.

Eric **Michaels**, born and raised in Illinois, has been a classical guitarist and a commercial illustrator. Since becoming a professional artist in 1983 he has received numerous prizes, including the prestigious George Marks Award. His work is collected by the Albuquerque Museum of Fine Arts, the Institute of American Indian Arts Museum in Santa Fe, the Americana Museum in El Paso, and many private corporate collections.

Peter **Mikelbank**, freelance writer and photographer, has been living in Paris since the late 1980s. His stories and photos have appeared in *The Washington Post, Sports Illustrated*, and *Life Magazine*.

Henry **Miller**, the literary symbol of expat bohemia, was born in Brooklyn, New York in 1890 of German ancestry. In Paris he published his first novel, *Tropic of Cancer*, with Obelisk Press in 1934. This was followed by *Black Spring* (1936), *Tropic of Capricorn* (1939), the trilogy *The Rosy Crucifixion*. His later writings include books of non-fiction, travel and plays.

Carol **Moldaw's** last collection, *Taken from the River*, was published by Alef Books in 1993. Recent works are forthcoming in *Partisan Review, Triquarterly, Manoa, Southwest Review*, and *First Intensity*. Originally from New York, Moldaw now lives in Santa Fe with her husband, poet Arthur Sze.

Yves **Morice**, after a career with Larrouse is now retired in Biganos, France. Morice wrote his thesis *La Folle Pensée* which dealt with Lawrence's use of birds, beasts and flowers.

John **Noonan**, a New York poet and song writer, has since the 1980s lived in Paris, where he works at OECD. His poems appear in **Frank 10** in a dossier on New York writing. Noonan collaborates musically with James Wilson and Mike O'Niel.

Alice **Notley** has entitled her most recent book *The Descent of Alette* (Penguin 1996). Her autobiographical sequence, *Mysteries of Small Houses*, is also being published by Penguin. In Paris, she and her husband Douglas Oliver founded the journal *Pharos*.

Douglas **Oliver**, British poet-novelist, is a senior lecturer at the British Institute in Paris. He recently published *Selected Poems* (Talisman House) and (with Iain Sinclair and Denise Riley) *Penguin Modern Poets 10*.

Josh **Parker** is a fiction writer in Paris preparing a dissertation at the Université Denis Diderot on expatriate literature. Paris, he claims, is the perfect place to work.

Ralph **Petty** is an American"French" painter from Colorado living in Montreuil with his wife and two kids. In France for over 20 years, he teaches drawing classes at the American University of Paris, sings and plays sax in a local blues band, and exhibits his work internationally. An exhibition of his work can be found at www.paris-anglo.com/GAP.

Carol **Pratl**, native of Chicago, has lived in Paris since the age of 16. Artistic director of the Compagnie La Bacchanale/Isadora Duncan Center–France, she has performed in Paris, Moscow, Prague, London, and New York. She co-authored the book *Life into Art - Isadora Duncan and Her World* (Norton, 1993) and edited the woman's magazine *Sphinx* in the 1980s.

Leo **Romero's** fiction was recently published in *Under the Pomegranate Tree: The Best New Latino Erotica* (Washington Square Press).

Miriam **Sagan** is the editor, with Sharon Niederman, of *New Mexico Poetry Renaissance* (Red Crane, 1994). Her most recent book of poetry is *The Art of Love* (La Alameda Press, 1994).

Jim **Sagel** is the author of 14 books of bilingual poetry and prose. He is the winner of several international literary awards, including the *Premio Casa de las Américas* in Cuba (1981), the *Premio de la Revista Poesía* in Venezuela (1992), and the *Premio de Teatro de la Ciudad de San Sebastián* in Spain (1997).

Shari Leslie **Segall**, born in Philadelphia, is a public relations and marketing specialist who moved to Paris in 1985. The things that matter most to her include running and writing. She is currently seeking a publisher for her innovative first novel *Our Lady*, an erotic thriller fairy-tale.

Joël-Peter **Shapiro**, author of the multi-volumed *Gnomon's Land*, recently represented the United States at the first PAWA World Poetry Festival in Tunisia. He lives in Paris.

Anthony **Sheridan**, born in 1959, studied law, English, and French literature at the Universities of Sussex, East Anglia, and Paris/Sorbonne. He previously worked as an administrator for a film production company in London, while co-editing *Pix* (film journal) before moving to Paris in 1994.

Raya **Sorkine** is a leading contemporary artist, whose drawings are found in André Journo's *Nouveau Receuil de Pensees*.

Marcia **Southwick**, is the author of *The Night Won't Save Anyone* (University of Georgia Press) and *Why The River Disappears* (Carnegie Mellon University Press). She teaches at the University of New Mexico in Albuquerque.

Nicholas **Stedman**, English painter an scientist living and working in Paris, has multiple diplomas in science and art from Cambridge University, the University of Paris VI and the *Ecole Nationale des Arts Decoratifs*. Caught between art and science, he opted for art in 1985, exhibiting his paintings and winning awards throughout Europe. His most recent exhibition *"Le Corps en Danger"* is at the Le Monde des Arts, 33 rue Guénégaud, in Paris.

Gwen **Strauss**, poet and novelist, lives on a barge in Burgundy with her writer husband Jody Jenkins (**Frank 15**). Author of the poetry collection *A Trail of Stones* and the children's book *Night Shimmy* (Douglas & McIntyre, 1991), her work appeared in **Frank 14**.

Arthur **Sze** is a Chinese-American poet and teacher and recent recipient of a John Simon Guggenheim Memorial Foundation Fellowship. His books include *Dazzled* (Floating Island, 1982), River River Lost Roads, 1987), Archipelago Copper Canyon, 1995), and *The Redshifting Web: Poems 1970-1997*, forthcoming by Copper Canyon Press in 1998. He teaches at the Institute of American Indian Arts in Santa Fe. Arthur and his wife Carol Maldaw collected the New Mexican texts in **Frank**.

Andrej **Tisma** lives in Novi Sad, Yugoslavia. Artist, critic, and curator, Tisma since the early 1970s has carried the torch as international mail-artist and cultural networker. He is the founder of the Institute for the Spreading of Love (1991), Embargo Art campaign (1992) and a driving force in the on-line art project, "Chaos in Action." See: http://www.geocities.com/SoHo/Gallery/9855

YOU MET ANDREJ TISMA

Alexander **Trocchi**, founding editor of the 1950s expat journal in Paris, *Merlin*, was born in Glasgow in 1924 and died in London in 1984. His published work includes *Young Adam*, *Cain's Book*, and under various pen names (Francis Lengel, Oscar Mole, James Pidler and others) wrote some of the best literary erotica published by Maurice Girodias' Olympia Press. Titles included *Helen and Desire, The Carnal Days of Helen Seferis, School for Wives, Thongs, White Thighs* and the 5th volume of Frank Harris' *My Life and Loves*.

Erika **Wanenmacher**, born in 1955 in Ohio, has been an instructor at the Institute of American Indian Arts in Sante Fe since 1995. Her one-woman exhibitions have been held at the Linda Durham Contemporary Art in Galisteo, Braunstein/Quay Gallery and the Center for Contemporary Art in Santa Fe.

Kathleene **West** has published seven books of poetry and fiction, including *Water Witching* (Copper Canyon Press) and *The Farmer's Daughter* (Sandhills Press). Recent work has appeared or is forthcoming in *Notre Dame Review, Ploughshares, Prairie Schooner, Triquarterly, and The Alaska Review*. She teaches at New Mexico State University where she is Poetry Editor of *Puerto del Sol*.

Edmund **White**, writer, essayist, biographer, served as an editor and writer at Time/Life Books in the late 1960s. Since 1983 he has lived in Paris. He has taught literature and creative writing at Yale, John Hopkins, New York University and Columbia, was professor of English at Brown University, and recently accepted a teaching position at Princeton University. He has served as executive director of the New York Institute of the Humanities and was inducted into the American Academy of Arts and Letters in 1996.

Emmi **Whitehorse** lives and creates in New Mexico. Her works are not only consummate abstractions but also metaphysical representations highly informed by Navajo traditions.

ANDREJ TISMA - *stamp*

She has exhibited at the Jan Cicero Gallery in Chicago, the Bentley Gallery in Scottsdale, Arizona, and the Jan Maiden Fine Art Gallery in Columbus, Ohio.

C.K. **Williams** divides his time between Paris and the creative writing program at Princeton University. He is the recipient of the National Book Critics Circle Award, the Morton Dauwen Zabel Award of the American Academy and Institute of Arts and Letters and a Guggenheim fellowship, amongst others. He has published 12 books including his most recent volume of poetry, *The Vigil* (Farrar, Straus and Giroux, 1997).

Keith **Wilson**, a native third-generation New Mexican, has long written about *la gente de la tierra encantada*, the people of the enchanted land of New Mexico, in his 25 volumes of poetry and his short stories. He has received several awards for his writing, including the Governor of New Mexico's Excellence in the Arts Award and his work has appeared in over 35 anthologies, both national and international.

William S. **Yellow Robe** Jr. is one of America's leading Native playwrights. He was born and raised on the Fort Peck Indian agency, located in northeastern Montana and is a member of the Assiniboine Tribe. He is a member of the Dramatist's Guild, Inc., and the Drama League of America. With over twenty five works, Yellow Robe also directs, acts and teaches, and belongs to LIFEBLOOD, Native Writers in Our Homeland.

Cheryl **Yellowhawk**, painter and sculptor, lives in Santa Fe, New Mexico and is seeking a publisher for her book *Spiritual Healing: A Shamanic Experience*. A graduate of the Institute of American Indian Art (1987), Cheryl also holds a degree as a massage therapist from the Scherer Academy of Natural Healing.

Nina **Zinvancevic**, a poet born in Yugoslavia and raised in the United States, lives in Paris. She is the former assistant to Allen Ginsburg, and has published nine books of poetry and three books of fiction in the United States and Europe.

Michael **Zwerin**, an American from New York in Paris, has played the trombone with Miles Davis and Eric Dolphy and he is currently the Music Editor of the *International Herald Tribune*. As far back as 1976 Zwerin predicted that ethnic entities such as Scotland, Catalonia, Bosnia and Chechnia would take their freedom from the States that occupy them. The text published in **Frank** is adapted from "A Case for the Balkanization of Practically Everyone," first published in 1976 by Wildwood House in London.

ANDREJ TISMA - *stamp*

Achevé d'imprimer en mai 1998
sur les presses de la Nouvelle Imprimerie Laballery – 58500 Clamecy
Dépôt légal : mai 1998   Numéro d'impression : 804131

Imprimé en France